SOMETHING *of me*

MY LIFE DOWN HOME AND OTHER PLACES

Canada Council for the Arts · Conseil des Arts du Canada · Canada · Newfoundland Labrador

We gratefully acknowledge the financial support of the Canada Council for the Arts, the Government of Canada through the Canada Book Fund (CBF), and the Government of Newfoundland and Labrador through the Department of Tourism, Culture and Recreation for our publishing program.

Cover Design by Todd Manning • Layout by Joanne Snook-Hann
Front cover photo by Robert Young
Printed on acid-free paper

Published by
CREATIVE PUBLISHERS
an imprint of CREATIVE BOOK PUBLISHING
a Transcontinental Inc. associated company
P.O. Box 8660, Stn. A
St. John's, Newfoundland and Labrador A1B 3T7

Printed in Canada

Library and Archives Canada Cataloguing in Publication

O'Neill, Paul, 1928-, author
Something of me : my life downhome and other places / Paul O'Neill.

ISBN 978-1-77103-067-0 (paperback)

1. O'Neill, Paul, 1928-. 2. Historians--Newfoundland and Labrador--Biography. 3. Television producers and directors--Newfoundland and Labrador--Biography. 4. Authors, Canadian (English)--Newfoundland and Labrador--Biography. 5. Newfoundland and Labrador--Biography. I. Title.

MIX
Paper from responsible sources
FSC® C011825
FSC www.fsc.org

FC2175.1.O54A3 2015 971.8'04092 C2015-904704-8

SOMETHING *of me*

MY LIFE DOWN HOME AND OTHER PLACES

PAUL O'NEILL

FOREWORD BY EDWARD ROBERTS

CREATIVE PUBLISHERS

St. John's, Newfoundland and Labrador, 2015

For my father, my mother, my brother,
and all the O'Neills of Bay de Verde
who made me the hand-me-down I am.

TABLE OF CONTENTS

Foreword

Paul O'Neill was at the very center of Newfoundland's cultural life for more than sixty years, from his return home permanently late in 1952 until his death in August 2013. He was a remarkable man, and he made a memorable contribution to Newfoundland and Labrador (as the province is now known, although he never referred to it as such). His last written work is an entrancing account of his early years, from his birth in 1928 until he came home to stay. The story is that of an intelligent young man who grew up in a loving family and nourished an ambition to know the greater world beyond his island home. He tells it fully and honestly.

At the outset let me say that Paul was a long-time acquaintance who became a cherished friend for the last ten or fifteen years of his life. We shared a passionate interest in all things about Newfoundland and the history of our people, and each of us was fascinated by stories of our fellow Newfoundlanders, past and present. I admire his immense contribution to the development of arts and culture in Newfoundland over many years. He did me an immeasurable favour in helping me find the "lost" manuscript of the second volume of Peter Cashin's memoirs by responding to my tale of being unable to locate it with the simple statement "why, Michael [Cashin, Peter's son] has it."

Something of Me: My Life Down Home and Other Places is a memoir. It recounts, in detail, the first twenty-five years of Paul's life. His O'Neill forefathers came to Newfoundland from County Cork, in southwest Ireland, in 1824. Their decision to make their home in Bay de Verde was both brave and foolhardy. The community, nestled in the lee of the furthest part of Conception Bay's north shore, was then the largest settlement between Carbonear, to the south, and Bonavista, to the north. Its great attraction was that it was close to good inshore fishing grounds. Its merchants bought salted fish from the fishermen who in turn bought their supplies from them. Strong-minded, principled and upright, the O'Neills became pillars of their community as well as leading figures in the northern part of Conception Bay. They became well off, although not rich by even the standards of the age. Paul writes compellingly about the financial realities of outport merchants, particularly the familiar criticism that they oppressed the fishermen.

The Bay de Verde O'Neills were a large family; Paul had only one brother (his only sister died very young) but many cousins. His family's prosperity, he says, was hard-won. He writes about their trials and tribulations fondly but candidly. He recalls an "enchanted childhood" filled with affection. I know of no better account than Paul's of growing up in one of Newfoundland's fishing communities during the first decades of the twentieth century.

Young Paul O'Neill was not content to remain in Bay de Verde, and early developed ambitions to see the greater world. These were nourished by his years at St. Bonaventure's Academy in St. John's, the leading Roman Catholic school in what was then the Dominion of Newfoundland. He left Newfoundland in September 1948, a month before his twentieth birthday. He wanted to become an actor. His dreams and ambition took him to the National Academy of Theatre Arts, in Pleasantville, New York, a few miles north of New York City. The school was a well-regarded institution for young would-be actors.

A year later, his academic studies finished, the handsome young Newfoundlander eagerly accepted an offer to join the National Academy's touring theatre company. He and his comrades spent the next two years travelling back and forth across the United States, to small towns and large cities alike. Television was still in its infancy; theatrical troupes brought live productions to those who hungered for professional theatre but would never have a chance to see a production on Broadway. It was a grueling way to make one's living, but Paul enjoyed it. He recounts incident after incident, most of them humorous, and speaks fondly of his fellow thespians and the important and noteworthy actors he met from time to time. He sketches a glowing portrait of a world that can only be imagined by most of us.

The American sojourn was followed by two years in London, where he eked out a living playing minor parts in provincial theatres and made cameo appearances in largely-forgotten movies. He enjoyed his experiences, and treasured the friendship of those he met.

Paul came back to Newfoundland at the end of 1952 to spend Christmas with his family. His father's health was failing, and he remained in St. John's to help his mother to care for him. (Mr. O'Neill died in June 1953). He found work in the spring of 1953 with the Canadian Broadcasting Corporation, first in St. John's and then in Corner Brook. The memoir ends with an all-too brief account of his year-long sojourn with the CBC radio station in Corner Brook and his return to St. John's, where he lived for the rest of his life.

Paul talked often about the memoir because it was important to him. A year or so before he died, I asked him where it stood. He responded he had brought it up to the beginning of his years with the CBC, to the point where he had become Executive Producer of Schools and Youth for CBC's Newfoundland Region, and thus responsible for both the provincial school broadcasts and the region's radio and television programming for young people. I told him that I hoped he would finish it, because I thought his years at the CBC and those that followed upon his retirement from full-time employment had not only seen some of his best work, but were important in themselves.

Paul published twelve books and contributed chapters or essays to another nineteen. He was a gifted writer; his work embraced children's stories as well as poetry and an anthology of work by Newfoundland writers. But his greatest work was his history of St. John's. First published in two volumes as *The Oldest City: The Story of St. John's, Newfoundland* (1975) and *A Seaport Legacy: The Story of St. John's Newfoundland* (1976), the book is a classic. Based on exhaustive and impeccable research, *The Story of St. John's* stands alongside such works as Daniel Prowse's *History of Newfoundland* (1895) as one of the handful of books that belong in the library of anybody interested in Newfoundland's history. Paul rightly regarded it as his most important legacy.

He was a national treasure; I use "nation" to mean both his homeland of Newfoundland and the Canada of which he became – somewhat unwillingly, as he tells us in his memoir – a citizen. He treasured his appointments to the Order of Canada and to the Order of Newfoundland and Labrador, the two highest civic honours that can come to a Canadian. He was proud, too, of the other accolades that were showered upon him, including an Honorary Doctorate from Memorial University and an endowed scholarship awarded each year to an undergraduate at Memorial who has demonstrated "academic excellence, enthusiasm and interest in some area of Newfoundland studies" as part of his or her degree program. He became a cultural icon and a mentor to scores of young men and women.

Paul was determined to finish his memoir. He told me so several times. But the infirmities of age intervened. He did not live to write his recollections of the last sixty years of his life. Everybody who reads *Something of Me* will share my belief that that story would have been even more interesting and an even better one than the one he did leave us.

Paul cherished his friends, and was cherished by them. Those who never knew the joy of his friendship and his companionship will be able to glean from his memoir the measure of a Newfoundlander in whom we should all take pride, a man for whose time among us we should all be grateful.

Edward Roberts

Prologue

Autobiography is nothing more than an individual's own remembrances of an instant in the millenniums of an ancestral history, an almost insignificant blossom among the many hundreds of thousands on a family tree. Life began for me, as for every human, as one of millions of eggs implanted in my mother by nature when she was herself an unborn embryo. These tiny eggs die as a woman gets older, and by the time she reaches forty plus, they are all gone. On the other hand, the spermaceti, which develops in males with puberty, remains with them until death.

My father was forty-five years old in 1928, when he married my mother, who was twenty-nine years old, in front of the altar in the Presentation Convent, Cathedral Square. I was born on the afternoon of 26 October 1928, in the White House, where Dr. Cluny MacPherson, inventor of the first gas mask in World War I, spanked me into life. The White House in which I was born was the former mansion of a wealthy St. John's custom tailor, William H. Jackman, Liberal government member for Placentia in the 1920s. The building eventually became a hospital run by the Sisters of Mercy and known as St. Clare's Mercy Hospital. It was in the second floor front room, at the eastern corner, that I began my journey of days, months and decades. No one could have foretold then what would become of that adorable baby, but I can do so in hindsight, up to a point, and my doing so is the substance of this autobiography.

In order to hold, what A.E. has called, "the golden heresy of truth," against the sceptred myths which rule our lives, we must embark alone on a journey that takes us much further inward than it does outward. Therefore, if we are ever to truly understand the wellspring of our identity, it is necessary to know something of our ancestors, something of those of our blood in preceding generations. Such a search, or journey, is not an easy one, and along the way, as A.E. says, truth can often end up as a golden heresy. It is the human part of our nature for us to justify our failures, blind ourselves to the pain of our mortality, and insist on our own self-righteous beliefs. Each generation is born into prisons constructed by previous generations, but the prisons we die in are of our own making.

There is a Hindu proverb which says, "Seek no Paradise of the east, seek no Paradise of the west along the way you have come, all things are within you," even the kingdom of God, according to Jesus. This means that within me are also some of the demons that plagued my ancestors, as well as noble spirits that made them great. It was with a prodigious curiosity that I began the wonder of discovering my paternal and my maternal heritage.

Chapter 1

How Vast a Memory

In Act 1 of *The Importance of being Earnest*, the playwright Oscar Wilde has one of his characters say, "memory is the diary that we all carry about with us." If I were to leaf through the pages of my childhood, as recorded in that diary, it would be a recollection of love and being loved. I am sure my father, still a bachelor at forty-two years of age must have long before abandoned himself to the thought he would grow old alone in his father's big house at Bay de Verde, cared for by his devoted housekeeper. A shy, solitary man, who garnered great respect from humble fishermen and formidable St. John's merchants alike, he spent his days fishing with his sharemen, and doing the unending tasks required of a fishery and supply merchant in the years after World War I. Instead of boozing and carousing, when not in his office poring over his ledgers until midnight trying to balance the books, he spent his evenings alone at home with his newspapers, magazines and pipe.

To my knowledge there had been only one brief romance in my father's life to that point. Her name was Catherine FitzPatrick, a registered nurse from Placentia, who did home nursing in St. John's. The daughter of Captain Thomas FitzPatrick, her sister Molly (a lifelong friend of my mother) was married to a classmate and friend of Dad's, a prominent St. John's lawyer and Grand Knight of Columbus, Cyril Cahill. Their sister Blanche was married to a politician and a longtime friend of my father, Major Peter Cashin, a war hero and son of one-time Prime Minister Sir

Michael Cashin. A third FitzPatrick sister, Alicia, a multi-talented local actress, singer and painter, married Bernard Norris, the well known northern Newfoundland merchant and a partner in Rambler Mines. The youngest FitzPatrick sister, Petronella (Neila), married a Murphy and stayed in the community of Placentia until her death in the '50s.

Each spring my father would leave Bay de Verde on an annual trek of approximately 50 miles up the Trinity shore looking for sharemen. There being no transportation available, he would walk from Bay de Verde as far as Heart's Content, signing up sharemen for the coming season, and stopping overnight with friends. This 50-mile trek was almost the death of him in 1918 when he caught a cold walking through the icy winds and wet snows of March. He told me he was often drenched to the skin in freezing rain. By the time he reached Heart's Content, what he thought was a cold turned out to be the Spanish flu, one of the deadliest natural disasters in human history then raging throughout the world. Realizing the peril he was in, he crossed to Carbonear and caught the Conception Bay branch train home to Bay de Verde.

The influenza pandemic of 1918-1919 killed more people than the Great War, World War I. The tragic flu took the lives of somewhere between 20 million and 40 million people. It has been cited as the most devastating epidemic in recorded world history. More people died of influenza in that year than in four years of the Black Death, bubonic plague, from 1347 to 1351. Known as Spanish flu or La Grippe, the influenza of 1918-1919 was a global disaster.

In the fall of 1918, the Great War in Europe was winding down and peace was on the horizon. The Americans had joined in the fight, bringing the Allies closer to victory against the Germans. Deep within the trenches, these men lived through some of the most brutal conditions of life, which it seemed could not be any worse. Then, in pockets across the globe, something erupted that began as the benign common cold. The influenza of that season, however, was far more than a cold. In the two years in which this scourge ravaged the earth, a fifth of the world's population was infected. The flu was most deadly for people ages 20 to 40. This pattern of morbidity was unusual, for influenza generally kills the elderly and young children.

When he returned to the family home in Bay de Verde, my father had no one to help him, except an aged housekeeper from up the shore. With no doctor nearer than Old Perlican and feeling utterly miserable, he decided to take the train to St. John's and stay at his sister Nellie's house, 17 Patrick Street, where she arranged for him to be cared for by a full-time nurse whose job it was to try and pull him through the illness. This was how he met Catherine (Kit) FitzPatrick of Placentia, who eventually succeeded in getting him over the crisis. By the time he was on the road to recovery, a romance had blossomed between them and it was believed he proposed matrimony to Nurse FitzPatrick.

When Kit went home to Placentia and told her parents about her intended, a young merchant from Bay de Verde, her mother, the no-nonsense wife of the famous Captain Thomas FitzPatrick, put her foot down. There were to be no more merchants in the family. Blanche's husband, Peter Cashin of Cape Broyle (a merchant as well as politician), and Alicia's husband, Bernard Norris of Baie Verte, were two merchants too many. Having a third daughter marry a merchant, this time from Bay de Verde, was out of the question. In this day and age it seems incredible that such things happened, but according to what I was told by Kit's nephew, Michael Cashin, her mother broke up the romance by packing her off to Cape Breton, Nova Scotia, where she ended up marrying a sea captain. Ironically, today, Catherine's daughter and I are very good friends.

My father had been born 10 December 1883, at Bay de Verde, a fishing community located at the northernmost tip of the Avalon Peninsula a few miles from the island of Baccalieu. At the time of his birth the population of the community was probably around 500 people; mostly fishermen and their wives. My dad was the youngest of the five children of John and Ellen (Buckley) O'Neill. Ellen, his mother, was the daughter of a cooper, Thomas Buckley, a native of Cahir, Tipperary. Her father owned a large cooperage on the southeast corner of Factory Lane and Duckworth Street, and a cul-de-sac of houses that were known as Buckley's Range. There were four duplex houses in the Range which were rented as eight apartments. The rear of the present Sheraton Hotel Newfoundland now sits on the site of the Range.

In the late spring of 1872, my grandfather, John O'Neill, came to St. John's on board his schooner *Springbird,* to get supplies for his shop in Bay de Verde, such as large wooden casks in which merchants shipped salted, dried cod to city merchants and overseas. Having looked about, grandfather settled on Mr. Buckley's casks as being the best buy. He made a deal with the cooper, and was starting out the door, when Thomas Buckley called to him and asked if he was going any place special for dinner, as the mid-day meal was then called in Newfoundland. When he answered he was going back to his schooner, Mr. Buckley invited him to his nearby house, saying his wife had plenty for one more. That invitation was to affect a number of people yet unborn, me included. At the house, the 30-year-old outport merchant met the cooper's daughter, 28-year-old Ellen Buckley. In the autumn their engagement was announced. They married at St. John's, November 7th that same year, 1872. His brother James O'Neill, and Ellen's friend Bridget O'Donohue, were the witnesses. Five children followed: Thomas, Michael, Daniel, Ellen and James, my father. One of the housemaids dropped Thomas as an infant. He became a sickly hunchback who died at the age of seven, two years before my father was born. My dad never knew his oldest brother.

At the age of fifteen, my father, the apple of his mother's eye, was shipped to St. John's by her to get a good education as a boarding student at St. Bon's, so he could become a doctor or a lawyer or whatever else he wanted to be. At St. Bon's he developed lifelong friendships with such boys as James Foley, Cyril Cahill and Harry Howlett. I once asked Dad why neither he nor Uncle Mike spoke with outport accents, growing up in an out-harbour as they did. His answer was, "Our mother's thimble." That I did not understand. He explained that their mother was always sewing, with a metal thimble covering the tip of her right index finger. Every time they, or their sister, mispronounced a word as a child, she would knock the offender on the head with her thimble and would order the word be pronounced correctly.

His father, like his mother, was determined to keep him out of the fishery. In 1898 he passed with honours in the First Division Council of Higher Education, but stayed on at the school until Easter 1899, when he left to be Best Man at his brother Mike's wedding to Catherine (Kitty) Lynch in Harbour Grace. After the nuptials, his father, a friend and valued customer of Sir Edgar Bowring, took him to meet the head of the famous St. John's mercantile and insurance firm. Sir Edgar put him to work as a clerk in the dry goods department of his Water Street business where he was expected to learn all about trade and commerce. A fellow employee, who became a close friend, was Jimmy Lang, father of a friend and classmate of mine who later became Justice Gerald Lang of the Newfoundland Supreme Court.

On 9 March, 1904, after five years selling dry goods on Water Street while living with his sister Nellie Kennedy on Patrick Street, Dad had had it. He gave in his notice at Bowring's to return to his first love, the fishery. His father, shocked at the news, refused him financial help. That meant returning home to Bay de Verde was not an option. With his brother Daniel as partner, he went to Golden Bay at Cape St. Mary's, and started fishing there with a $500 loan from Bowring Brothers. He returned to the city to row for the firm in the Regatta, but the summers of 1904, 1905 and 1906 were spent in Golden Bay. I recall Dad saying the worst problem he and Dan had, in the cramped shack they occupied with a couple of hired hands, was lice. Always meticulously clean about his person, he discovered the problem could be solved by washing their clothes in salt water, and burying them in the sand until all the unwanted creatures crawled out and vanished. The clothes were then washed free of sand in a freshwater brook and dried on bushes.

Wanting desperately to return to the settlement he loved, Bay de Verde, my father paid off the debt he owed to Bowring's, and with his small savings entered into a partnership with two brothers named Riggs. The trio started fishing out of Bay de Verde in 1907. That same year he built and opened a general store in his home town, hiring a shop manager and several shop assistants. With a flake borrowed from his brother Dan and the use of a stage owned by the Riggs, he fished with them for several years. The partnership was dissolved in 1912, when grandfather, seeing the determination of his son James to take part in the fishery, retired from it himself and awarded a stage each to Mike, Dan and Jim, as well as his flakes and equal shares in his oil factory. When my grandfather died, 18 August 1919, the big house in Bay de Verde that was the family home was left to my father. He lived there as sole occupant with a housekeeper from Harbour Grace. My grandmother had passed away four years earlier on 14 July 1915.

In 1914 my father enlarged his waterfront property by building on a wharf, and the following year, a large fish storage shed at the back, with a twine loft, bunkhouse and kitchen on the second floor. A ship's bell, that could be heard all over the harbour, was installed outside the upstairs kitchen of the bunkhouse, to call the men to meals or a mug-up, and we felt a thrill each time Cookie let John or me ring it as young boys.

Not only had Dad to cope with his father's death in 1919, but with the Great War over, there was a downturn in the price of cod on European markets and the business was facing bankruptcy. After settling his accounts, he took what little money he had left, and in the early spring of 1920 he went to New York to visit his Uncle Jim O'Neill, after whom he was named, and his Aunt Bess. He was a diligent observer and raconteur, and dined out on his New York adventures for several years. In 1922, the brothers, Mike and Jim O'Neill, built a new cod liver oil factory in Bay de Verde. In 1925, again nearly bankrupt, he took his remaining cash and went on what was called the Grand Tour, which began with a spring voyage from St. John's to Alicante, Spain, with his chum, businessman Robert Coleman. Dad was a meticulous diarist and I still enjoy the account he kept of that journey.

Undaunted by the near collapse of his business in 1920 and 1925, my father resurrected and expanded it.

Profits from his and Mike's joint ownership for the fifteen- year period 1921-1935 were $9,060.20 each. In addition, by working incredibly long and hard hours, from 4 a.m., when he got up and went fishing with his men, until 10 at night, when he finished doing the books in the shop and came home exhausted, he caught only five hours' sleep before starting another day of like activity. In addition to his income from the oil factory, in the same fifteen-year period, my father made $21,517 as a result of his own fishery, $12,249.14 on the purchase and sale of dry codfish, and $3,992.15 from selling coal, for a total of $42,045.05, or $2,777 per year, less than I made per month at the CBC before my retirement in the mid-1980s, with not one-eighth the worry, responsibility, physical or mental demands. So much for Smallwood's infamous attack on the integrity of outport merchants, and the fortunes they made fleecing the fishermen. For every Bonavista Ryan who made millions, there were hundreds of merchants like my father and his brother Mike, who were the lifelines of their communities during hard times. I make no apology at being the son of an outport merchant. Rather, it is a matter of pride. The numerous things he did for individuals and families are legion, often with ingratitude as his reward. When he died in

1953, the accountant found $80,000 owing him from debts he had written off, a fortune in an out-harbour in those days.

In 1950, M.J. O'Neill & Son transferred its share of the oil factory to Uncle Dan in exchange for a piece of land he owned at the side of their fish store. My father, in turn, bought Uncle Dan's shares in the factory for $150, sealing the deal 14 February 1951 by cheque. He was now the sole owner. Most of these facts and figures are of little interest today as money values are so changed. However, there is one that should be noted. In 1923, when his nephew John, whom he loved deeply, was ordained a priest, Dad erected a large building in Bay de Verde, containing a Post Office and Court House, both of which were leased to the government. He gave the building to the young priest as an ordination gift, to assure him of a continuing income.

Uncle Mike and Aunt Kitty had four sons and a daughter. Only three sons lived to be adults. The youngest of them, John (b. 1903), joined the priesthood, eventually becoming Bishop of Harbour Grace in 1940. The largest town in his Diocese was Grand Falls. With the war in 1939, the demand for paper changed Grand Falls from a small mill town to a much larger community, partly due to an increase in the number of mill workers and others employed in the trade of paper making. While Grand Falls grew, the seat of the Diocese, Harbour Grace, declined in population. On 5 December 1953, the name of the Diocese was changed to Harbour Grace-Grand Falls, Immaculate Conception Church in Grand Falls being named a co-cathedral to the one in Harbour Grace. Ten years later in 1963, the seat of the Diocese was permanently moved from Harbour Grace to Grand Falls. In 1965, the Bishop, having taken up residence there two years earlier, dropped Harbour Grace from the name of the Diocese and it became simply the Diocese of Grand Falls. His newly-built cathedral was consecrated in Grand Falls that year. Bishop O'Neill retired in 1972 and died within a few years, on 2 March, 1974.

Brendan (b. 1898), the second of Uncle Mike's sons, who seemed always to have an interest in medicine, went to Queen's University at Kingston where he obtained his medical degree with high honours in 1939. He interned at Kitchener, Ontario, afterwards returning to Newfoundland where he served the Port au Port Peninsula area, being named resident doctor by the mining company in Aguathuna. He married Marjorie Abbott of nearby Port au Port, whose father was a leading businessman in the community. A monument was raised to Brendan on the Port au Port Peninsula by the people of the Diocese of Corner Brook and Labrador. According to a biography published in the *Adelphian* in 1948, "For the past seven years he served the people of the Aguathuna, Port au Port and the outlying settlements of that district, and it is they who knew and loved him, who will feel his loss most keenly. For his untiring devotion to duty under the most trying circumstances, at all hours, and in all kinds of weather, coupled with his sympathetic manner has enshrined him in their hearts for many years to come." Cyril (b. 1896), the oldest of the sons, worked with his father in Bay de Verde as a merchant in the fishery and supply business. A sign over the shop door read, M.J. O'Neill & Son.

Mary, only sister of the boys, born at Bay de Verde in 1901, was sent as a boarding student to Littledale College in St. John's when in her early teens. The story is told in the family how Mary woke up one morning feeling just awful and told the nun on duty in the dormitory she was too ill to go to class that day. The nun is said to have hauled the covers off the bed and ordered her to dress and go to class. She obeyed without hesitation, got dressed and went to class where she fainted. A doctor was sent for. After a brief examination he pronounced her to be suffering from pneumonia and ordered her back to bed. She died within three and a half days. The young girl's body was embalmed and sent by train to Bay de Verde where she was interred in the large O'Neill family plot. Her mother, Aunt Kitty, did not die until 1936, twenty years after Mary.

In 1939, to the delight of both my parents, my widowed Uncle Mike had a romance with an English nurse at the hospital in Old Perlican. She had come from England to be matron of the Perlican Cottage Hospital. My uncle and the nurse began a romance which got to be quite serious and it looked as if marriage was in the offing. My parents continued to be most approving as they often talked about how lonely it must be for Mike after Kitty died. More than once I heard Mother say to my father, "She'll make Mike a wonderful wife, it's been lonely for him all these years." Dad would look up from his newspaper, nod knowingly and say, "They'll work things out among themselves." However, because of family interference nothing got worked out and the marriage was not to be.

Meanwhile, my cousin Cyril was the one who got married. I recall him coming to my bedside on Cochrane Street in 1938, just before the war, and showing me a photo of his intended, a lovely young woman from Bell Island named Mary Billingsby, whose father operated a shoe store in the town of Wabana. To our surprise, Mary suddenly died, bringing their romance to an end. Cyril then later met and married a black-haired, Irish beauty from Carbonear, Ellen McCarthy, who moved with him into his father's house in Bay de Verde. She had been a school teacher in Turk's Cove. Nellie, as she was usually called, was to have an influence on my life and career and I came to love her very much.

Things deteriorated between father and sons, including the Bishop, to the point where Uncle Mike hired carpenters to divide up his rather large house. Apparently after a few years of disagreement and confrontation, Nellie wanted her father-in-law out of the house. Instead of going to live in the city, his hired carpenters partitioned the home, building a wall between the east and west sides, upstairs and down.

After the partition Uncle Mike and Nellie continued to have major disagreements. Uncle Mike decided to have his own quarters in one end where he lived with his housekeeper, Mary Noonan, who was once my mother's maid, while Cyril and Nellie occupied the rest of the divided residence with their children, John, Sheila, Catherine and Bernard. I found all this very strange, but was too young to fully understand the cause of the upset. It appeared, from what I heard my father and mother say, that his sons were afraid Uncle Mike would marry the English nurse whom they considered a money-grabber, anxious to gain control of his estate, which was something they did not want to have to consider. Mother kept up her friendship with the nurse and our whole family was invited several times to supper in her quarters at the hospital. She, in turn, would come from Old Perlican to visit us.

The arrangement came to an end in the fall of 1943 when Uncle Mike retired and tore down the partition. He turned the restored house over to Cyril and went to live with his son the Bishop in the Palace at Harbour Grace. A year or two later, I head my father say to Mother, "Mike is like a fish out of water, up there living with all those priests. He should have married that nurse, even over the Bishop's objections." Mother agreed. "They should never have interfered with their father's plans." I gathered John Michael (the Bishop) had something to do with the breakup of his father's romance with the nurse. I myself heard him say to Dad, on a visit to our house on Cochrane Street, that she was just a fortune hunter. My uncle was well to do, but he certainly had no fortune. With time, the affair faded from my memory, including the name of the nurse.

It was a time of strained relations within their family which took time to straighten out. After the end of Uncle Mike's romance, disputes were in the air, one being over property. I recall my parents arguing about attending Cyril's wedding. Mother went alone to Carbonear for the nuptials, while Dad sulked at home in Bay de Verde. I don't know what that had to do with his brother, my Uncle Dan, but he was somehow involved as well. By the time I got to my midteens everyone had come together again, thank God, with Uncle Mike spending half his year at the Bishop's residence in Harbour Grace and, in winter, as a guest at the Balsam Hotel in St. John's. He also made a few brief visits to Cyril and Nellie in Bay de Verde, so it would appear their differences were made up, or partly made up. My father was successful in his insistence that none of us become involved with our cousins' family differences.

Cyril carried on his father's business until finally selling the shop to a long-time employee, Paddy Murphy. He moved to Bell Island, where he bought the Wabana Shoe Store, once owned by the Billingsby family. That put my father in a state of depression, knowing it would be the end of the O'Neill family in Bay de Verde after five generations. Suffering from a lifetime of strenuous overwork, his health began to decline. I was working in England at the time, and John was finishing university at Boston College, with no likelihood of either of us returning to the family business. Mother said Dad's depression became unmanageable when Cyril sold out and moved to Bell Island. He went about the house weeping and moaning that the O'Neills were all gone from Bay de Verde after a century and a half. It got so bad Dr. Garrett Brownrigg sent him to Dr. Jerry O'Brien for psychiatric help. Dr. Jerry ordered him to undergo shock treatments at the Mental Hospital, afterwards called the Waterford Hospital. They did the trick, and in his last year or two he was fairly contented, although not entirely.

According to all three of his siblings, Uncle Dan had not just a few screws loose but several missing as well. A simple man, he was a visionary, writer of flowery prose, a stringer for the *Evening Telegram*, and an amateur photographer. He leased his share of his inheritance at Bay de Verde: boats, a stage, a house, meadows and one third of the oil factory profits, while he scoured the wilds of Northern Ontario in search of a mining fortune. An underachiever all his life, my beloved uncle ended up in a little confectionary shop in Holyrood, from where Dad brought him back to Bay de Verde in old age and placed him in the care of a cousin of my mother, Rose Moore, who had married Joe Keys. Rose always called him Daniel and was extremely kind to him until he died. He spent his days in the oil factory, sitting on a stool in a corner, and chatting with all who came and went.

Chapter 2

The April of Her Prime

My mother was born 26 April 1899, just before the end of the 19th century. Her father, John Flynn, was the son of Edward Flynn who came to Newfoundland from the Irish town of Cahir in County Tipperary. Edward Flynn, born in Cahir, in 1805, came to St. John's with his sweetheart, Ellen Hanigan, also from Cahir, where she was born in 1810. In time they were to become my great-grandparents. They married in the Roman Catholic Cathedral at St. John's, 3 November 1839, with William Landergan and Johanna Crotty as witnesses. With them came another couple from Cahir, John Buckley, born in 1810, with his fiancée, Alice Prendergast. They were also married at the Cathedral, now called the Basilica, and became my great-grandparents also.

Edward eventually worked for the Ordnance Department as the town's waterman, there being no fresh water available on the wharves in those days. That meant he and his helper were responsible for watering all the vessels that put into port, no mean task in those days. Along with Edward's job there came a hosecart for connecting the vessels to the water supply, a horse to pull the cart, and a barn to house the horse. This yard was at the back of Wood Street, at the foot of Ordnance Street, where the East End Fire Station afterwards stood. When Edward Flynn died, and St. John's was incorporated as a city, the job of waterman, which came under the municipal council, was given to my grandfather, John Flynn, with the new title of Superintendent of Watering Vessels.

When the yard was destroyed in the Great Fire of 1892, which levelled two thirds of St. John's, his house and barn were destroyed. In the aftermath, a fire hall was built where the Ordnance Yard had been. Council deeded my grandfather the land on which his house had stood, but he had to rebuild the place at his own expense. With the yard no longer there it had to face Wood Street, which had been at the back of the old house. While her husband went about the charred ruins of what had been the city, in a vain search for funds Mary Flynn and her children lived in military tents put up by the government on the shores of Quidi Vidi Lake, as well as in Bannerman Park, for 30,000 of the fire sufferers. As he worked for minimal pay, most of which he drank, grandfather had not the money to rebuild.

Before the fire, Canon William Pilot, an Anglican priest, came to Newfoundland from England in 1867 as Vice-Principal of Queens (theological) College, becoming Principal in 1878. He was also Superintendent of the Church of England schools. Pilot's Hill, opposite grandfather's house and stable, was named after the Canon. He lived in an imposing Victorian mansion at the foot of Ordnance Street, next to the yard, which he rebuilt in the aftermath of the 1892 inferno. He and grandfather were over-the-back-fence neighbours. When the Irish Catholic John Flynn told the Church of England Canon he hadn't the money to rebuild, the Canon offered him the loan of it interest-free. The house he built at 10 Wood Street, for little more than $1,000 at that time, sold in the year 2000 for $170,000.

Canon Pilot had a son, Edward, who married Barbara Merchant, the daughter of a wealthy Irish Catholic named Valentine Merchant. He owned several shops on Water Street known as Merchant's Block. The couple married in the Roman Catholic Cathedral. A few days after the wedding, when Grandfather spied the Canon digging in his garden, he went to the fence and asked him what he thought of his son being married in the Catholic Church. "I'll tell you, John," he replied, "they're just as well married as if I married them myself." Mother told me both he and Mrs. Pilot were wonderful people. Anytime she went over to the Pilots' house as a girl, Mrs. Pilot always had a slice of jam or molasses bread on hand. Young Edward and his wife, Barbara, who lived with his parents in their big house, gave birth to a boy she called Robert Pilot. A year older than my mother, they played together as children, and even sinned together, when they robbed apples from Hammond's apple tree next door.

When Robert was still a boy, his father died. In 1910 the young widow met and married a Newfoundland-born painter, who had been living in Canada but was home on a visit — Maurice Cullen. Mother and son went with Cullen to live in Montreal, where he became one of the great names in painting, and is the acknowledged father of the movement in Canadian art known as the Group of Seven. Cullen adopted Robert Pilot in all but name, and encouraged his stepson to paint, so that he, too, is now recognized as one of Canada's great artists, with paintings in the national galleries of France, Spain, Italy and the United States, as well as private collections such as that of Queen Elizabeth II and Winston Churchill. During the 1950s, Robert Pilot had an exhibition of his paintings in St. John's at the former USO building, which I took my mother to see.

While we were walking about, looking at the artworks, Pilot materialized in front of us, saying, "Don't tell me it's my old neighbour and dear little friend, Josie Flynn?" Mother assured him it was. They embraced after more than forty years, and spent some minutes reminiscing about their childhoods. She never understood how he recognized her after all those years, and decided Muriel Hunter, who lived across from us on Long Pond Road, or some other person at the exhibition, must have told him her name. He never knew her as Josephine O'Neill, only as Josie Flynn.

Grandfather once won a gold medal for playing championship bowling, which my grandmother never attended, as she did not think a bowling hall a proper place for a woman.

His passion was the music hall, especially when The Rossley Family, who frequently played St. John's, were in town. The Rossleys, mother, father and daughter Bonnie, were enormously popular and drew large crowds.

Curious to see what all the fuss was about, grandmother allowed herself to be talked into going to Ours, a theatre on the second floor of the Mechanics Hall, just west of the War Memorial, where the Rossleys were performing. When Bonnie, in a very brief, frilly costume, with bare shoulders, and long, gartered legs, came on stage, wiggling her nearly bare behind at the audience, and sat in the lap of a customer on stage singing, "Cuddle up a little closer, lovey mine...," the place went up. Grandfather told my mother that her mother's face turned to stone. When she got home she berated her husband, "John, you must never again take me to see anything as disgusting as that Bonnie Rossley." He looked her in the eye and smiled, and he said, "Well, Mary, I thought she was a damned fine girl."

He found employment with the St. John's Municipal Council as Superintendent of Watering Vessels. In those days, almost every ship in port was moored at the finger piers on the north side and had to be watered from horse-drawn carts. It was an important job that knew no hours. When Edward Flynn retired, his son, my grandfather John Flynn, followed his father into the position of Superintendent with the council. A quiet, sentimental and affectionate man, Grandfather met his future wife through a photograph and correspondence.

The relationships within my family were complicated because two sisters married two brothers. Mary Buckley, a sister of Ellen Buckley, my grandmother, married James Flynn, John Flynn's brother. When James died, still a young man, Mary married Edmond O'Neill, my grandfather O'Neill's brother. Uncle Ned, as he was called, and grandfather, had a sister Elizabeth who married Edmond Moore of Bay de Verde. Their daughter Mary, a slim, very pretty girl and first cousin of my father, was educated at the convent in Harbour Grace, where she had a photograph taken that was sent to her Uncle Ned and Aunt Mary. They displayed it on their mantle in St. John's where it was seen by her Aunt Mary's brother-in-law by her first marriage, John Flynn. Told the girl was Mary Moore, and that she was the daughter of Ned's sister, Flynn wrote to the young woman in Bay de Verde. Their letters quickly blossomed into a romance. Mary came to the city, met her correspondent, and married him, making them my maternal grandparents. Six children were born of that union, four girls and two boys. Their second child was my mother, baptized Mary Joseph, but called Josephine by all except a few girlhood friends who called her Jo. She should have been called Mary Jo. The house in which she was born is still standing at 10 Wood Street.

Mother's father was an inveterate moviegoer in the days of silent films, but grandmother looked upon motion pictures as the Devil's work. So my mother, a girl in her teens, would troop off to the Nickel Theatre in tow with her father, to see all the great stars — Mae Murray, John Gilbert, Mable Normand, and others — perform on screen in silence, while Professor D.J. McCarthy pounded out the score on the piano. She was especially impressed by the Swedish actress Anna Q. Nilsson, star of the long-running serial *Who's Guilty?* Nilsson, who came to the U.S. as a teenager, had worked her way up to stardom. Her career came to a stop in 1925 when she was seriously injured while horseback riding. Like Greta Garbo and Ingrid Bergman, fellow Swedish stars, she was a true beauty. In later years, when recalling her girlhood, mother often mentioned Anna Q. Nilsson to me.

Grandfather was usually found at the Army & Navy Tavern on the southeast corner of Duckworth and Cochrane streets. He was a lovable man, who enjoyed singing and telling stories. On Sundays, he would tackle his horse in the barn behind the house and walk it to Carnell's carriage factory opposite the Army & Navy Tavern. His friend, Andrew Carnell, the future Mayor of St. John's, would then have him hitch the horse to one of the carriages in the factory and take the family to the country for a picnic.

Mother's early life had not been easy. She was fifth among the six living children born to her parents. Four others died in infancy, the infant mortality rate among both rich and poor alike being exceptionally high at the time. They were Andrew, Nellie (probably Ellen), Mary and May (probably a second Ellen), just as my mother was a second Mary. When she was born 26 April 1899, her mother had her baptized Mary Joseph Flynn, Mary after her dead sister, while Joseph came from my grandmother's obsession with St. Joseph, to whom she constantly prayed, and attributed all sorts of favours, from a fine day to relief from asthma. When Mom Flynn, as we called her, died, she was buried in the brown habit of St. Joseph, which was a special gown with a monk's cowl, worn to the grave at the time by extremely devout Irish Roman Catholics. She bought the material at the Royal Stores and sewed it herself years before her death. It was kept neatly folded in tissue paper and placed in a drawer in her bedroom.

When she was ailing and had taken to her bed, she sometimes showed the habit to us on our endless visits to the sick room after school. We gaped at it with much fascination. I never did get to see her wearing it in her coffin as I was in bed with a bad chest cold at the time of her death. Although she was a humourless woman, I was very attached to Mom Flynn, and always felt she loved me in a very special way. I wept copious tears into my pillow when word of her death was brought to me.

Not wanting to have her dead child's name in everyday use, grandmother added the letters "ine" to the new baby's middle name so that she became Josephine. In time everyone assumed it was her name. She was Jose or Jo to family and friends, except to her cousin, my father, who was sixteen at the time of her birth. He called her Joey, which he had probably done from her cradle. Few knew her name was actually Mary, including herself. Some fifty years after her baptism, when mother went to get a Newfoundland passport, she was astonished to discover her name was Mary, not Josephine, and she was disgusted with her mother for what she called "robbing me of my beautiful name, Mary." But grandmother was in Mount Carmel Cemetery by then, in a grave next to my grandfather near a cross at the top of Kenna's Hill.

Forced by family finances to leave school after completing Grade Six, Mother found employment in a place on Duckworth Street where bottles were washed for recycling. It was a kind of Dickensian hole, dark and dreary, with a proprietor who might well have doubled as the abominable Mr. Bumble. Although she was only fourteen, Mother had to deal with some very difficult situations in this job. Her own mother refused to intervene so her father was never told and she had to cope with the situation as best she could by herself. That experience, and grandmother's reaction, taught my mother to be fearless when standing up for herself, and although she was often in frail health and ailing, she was a fighter to the end of her days, taking on business tycoons, lawyers, accountants, Income Tax inspectors, clergy, and even the Irish Christian Brothers.

Alfred MacNamara was a watchmaker and jeweler with a shop on Water Street almost opposite Williams Lane. He opened for business 1 November 1899. His daughter, Jose Mack, was a classmate of Mother's and perhaps her closest friend. Jose had a sister Dorothy, afterwards married to the architect Grahame Rennie, but Jose remained an unmarried woman all her life. In 1916, at the age of seventeen, Mother went to see Mr. Mack about a job as salesgirl in his shop and was immediately hired. He was a kind and affable man who always looked after her interests. For instance, when the Duleys, brothers of the Newfoundland novelist Margaret Duley, who were notorious ladies men, came into the shop and began flirting with her, Alfred MacNamara would call her aside, saying in a loud voice something like, "You're needed in the back room, Miss Flynn, I'll look after these gentlemen." Her biggest sale was a huge silver service to Major Peter Cashin, bought as a gift for his mother, Lady Cashin, from whom he was afterwards estranged over the terms of his father's will. He even took his mother to court, but lost. The silver service was left by Lady Cashin to her grandson, my friend Michael. Years later I saw it on display in his New York apartment.

While working for Alfred MacNamara, Mother and his daughter Jose, who also loved music and especially dancing, decided to try out for the chorus of one of Charles Hutton's musicals, he being one of the truly great Newfoundland musicians. After auditioning for his local stage production *The Prince of Pilsen,* Mr. Hutton said to her, "Josephine, you'll never be a star but you'll be great as a chorus girl." And so she was in Mr. Hutton's musical success. *The Prince of Pilsen* was a story about an American beer manufacturer traveling through Europe who is mistaken for a prince. The real prince arrives with friends and poses as a commoner. What follows is an extremely popular, turn-of-the century musical comedy beloved in its day by audiences everywhere.

As a teenager, Mother had two serious romances. Her first, which ended in tragedy, was with the brother of her close friend Gertrude Chown. She first met Frank Chown on the Furness Whitty pier where she and Gertie had gone to see off to war another of her friend's brothers, a volunteer with the Newfoundland Regiment, who left for the battlefields in France with the second contingent to sail overseas. Although Frank was only sixteen at the time, and she seventeen, they were immediately attracted to each other and a romance ensued. In the full flush of youth, and sharing a love for parties and dancing, which were the rage during the Great War, they began courting whenever possible. What fun they had together came to an abrupt end on the stormy night of 23 February 1919, when Frank Chown was among the 95 passengers and crew who drowned on board Bowring's vessel *S.S. Florizel,* after she was wrecked off Cappahayden on her way from St. John's to New York.

Mother was the quintessential wartime young woman. When she had time off from Mr. Mack's jewelry store, and on weekends, she helped wherever help was needed, at Government House rolling bandages, or wrapping Red Cross parcels for the men overseas. A very pretty, slim and outgoing young woman, she was extremely popular. Her popularity upset her older sister Margaret, who was a bit of a wallflower. The two never really got on together. I was told by one of Mother's admirers, when he found out I was Josie Flynn's boy, "Your mother was a beaut. We all gathered about her like flies around the molasses jar ... and dance, she could dance 'till dawn with never a feather out of her." In retrospect I think these must have been among the happiest days of her life. She told me she and another of her close friends, Leonore Lily from nearby Hill O'Chips, were invited to the Armistice Ball after the men began coming home from France. The girls hadn't any formal dresses to wear, so Mrs. Lily rummaged about and found two different, old window drapes from which she made each of the girls a ball gown. Mother said, when she stepped out on the dance floor, at the Mechanics Hall on Water Street, "I wouldn't call the Queen my aunt," an expression of self-pride at the time. It wasn't until I took her to the re-release of *Gone With The Wind* at the Paramount Theatre, and she watched as Scarlett O'Hara made a ball gown out of a window drape, that I heard the story.

My mother's next serious romance began soon after the death of Frank Chown. It was with a returned war hero, Captain Gerald Whitty, who had asked for a dance at one of the many post-war parties then on the go. After several dates Gerald invited her to the Armistice Dance, where she again wore the window drape. Leonore was with Leo (Jack) O'Dea, a step-brother of Lieutenant Governor Fabian O'Dea, who had been seriously wounded in the war. He later married Leonore's sister, Dorothy, while she married the Canadian manager of a bank in St. John's, Hugh Van Buskirk, and moved to Toronto. By 1920 mother and Gerald were talking marriage, but made no public announcement as there were details to be worked out. One evening, Gerald and three former officers from the war went out to Donovan's to enjoy a small reunion. Donovan's was a popular dance hall and tavern on Topsail Road where the four companions went for an evening of fun and reminiscing about the horrors they had somehow managed to survive in the trenches. On the way home, the car they were travelling in was involved in a head-on collision. All four were killed.

When she recovered from the sudden, tragic death of Captain Whitty, mother had a third affair of the heart. This one was with a handsome man named Frank Buckingham, one of a trio of brothers who were ship's engineers with the Newfoundland Railway. Both Frank and Ambrose later worked for the Bowater paper mill in Corner Brook, while the third brother, Edward, married mother's younger sister, Ann, and served for years with the Newfoundland Railway, and afterwards with Canadian National, as chief engineer of such coastal boats as the S.S. *Burgeo*, S.S. *Northern Ranger* and the S.S. *Baccalieu.* John and I were enormously fond of Uncle Eddy and Aunt Annie, as we called them, and loved them dearly. Aunt Margaret gave me her theory as to why her sister ended her Buckingham romance, but mother would never discuss it, saying "That's all in the past now and is best left alone."

With two failed romances behind her, Mother decided to follow her sister Margaret and her brother Phil to New York. Having turned part of her pay from Mr. MacNamara over to her mother each month, she put aside as much of the rest as she could save in a bank account for her passage to America. Shortly after breaking up with Frank in 1923, Mother sailed for New York from Harvey's pier on board the Red Cross liner S.S. *Rosalind*, one of Bowring's Shakespeare fleet, ships named for characters in the Bard's plays.

In Manhattan she lived for a while with her sister Margaret, while looking for employment. Her brother Phil was there working as a harbour pilot. Years later he became the chief pilot for the port. A stint at Macy's as a salesgirl did not satisfy my mother. She tried several other jobs until at last she was hired by a Jewish dentist and his wife as a nursemaid, or a governess, for their little girl. This really suited her. Mrs. Hoffman was a nice lady, but the doctor was domineering of the mother, the child, and Nanny. The parents were endlessly quarreling and shouting which made the girl opinionated and obstinate. After a year, in which her charge learned to become respectful and manageable, Mother decided she'd had enough and decided to seek employment elsewhere as a governess. She departed armed with an exceptionally good reference from Mrs. Hoffman, who understood why she was leaving.

The job she landed was with one of the wealthy American families, the Spaldings, a branch of the sports suppliers. There were two boys, Jesse, her favourite, and one a year or two older, whose name I've forgotten. She could not believe her good fortune. Within a few years of arriving in New York from St. John's, with little formal education, and not much more than a suitcase full of belongings — having always had to scrimp and save — she was now provided with her own small apartment. It was next to the boys' playroom and bedroom, in a very fashionable brownstone on Fifth Avenue, with maids to serve her meals with the boys in the playroom, and a chauffeur at her disposal any time she wanted to take the boys to the Bronx Zoo, a Broadway show, the Metropolitan Museum of Art, or wherever. She was not allowed to mix with "the help," although she developed a friendship with Annie, the Irish-born cook. It was a time when Irish help was looked down upon, and Annie had a song she often sang, "No Irish Need Apply." Also looked down upon was the poor old washerwoman who scrubbed the floors of the Spalding mansion, Mrs. Lopez. Her son, Vincent Lopez, was then at the height of his fame as the leader of one of America's top dance bands. Mother could never hear his signature tune, "Nola," without thinking of his mother on her knees scrubbing floors.

It was while working for Mrs. Spalding that Mother bought the one thing that was a joy to John and me when we were growing boys in Bay de Verde, a wind-up gramophone. I still have the gramophone and many of the 78 rpm wax records she bought. They are scratchy and almost worn out from having been played so often on wet or stormy days by two small boys in a remote outport. There we were introduced to such songs as "Living in the Sunlight, Loving in The Moonlight," on a Brunswick black label by the great Ben Bernie and his orchestra. "Dancing With Tears in my Eyes," on another Brunswick black label with the Regent Orchestra, "Moonlight and Roses," a Victor black label with Fred Waring's Pennsylvanians, backed by "Let Me Call you Sweetheart." And so they went on. To this day I recall the words of each song, although I have difficulty remembering the names of friends. There was even a Brunswick recording of Charles Hutton's setting to Governor Sir Charles Cavendish Boyle's "Ode To Newfoundland" by the Grand Male Quartet with orchestra, and several more recently acquired recordings of nursery rhymes such as "Mary Had a Little Lamb" and "Hickory Dickory Dok."

Among the trove of records Mother brought back with her from New York were a number of classical recordings. The first opera air I ever became aware of was one we played over and over on that wind-up, portable gramophone, in our playroom in Bay de Verde, "Song of India," from Rimsky-Korsakov's *Sadko* on Brunswick gold, and "Petrushka," a concert song, with the vocal by Arthur Fields, on Harmony Red. I learned the name Fritz Kreisler from an RCA Red of Rudolfh Friml's "Indian Love Call" before I learned the name of Water Street. I knew the song anyway, from hearing Mother sing it so often. She learned it after seeing Mary Ellis warble her way through *Rose-Marie,* on a Broadway mountain top, yearning for her Mountie, Dennis King.

The Spaldings also had a summer home at East Hampton on Long Island that was occupied by a caretaker staff all year. Whenever Mother wanted to get away from New

York with Jesse and his brother, she had only to tell her employer, who would arrange rail tickets to the Hamptons and have her man there meet them at the station. It was a charmed existence that came to a sudden end when Mr. Spalding had an accident that left him in need of constant care. The family moved away from New York and my mother sought another position as governess. She hit the jackpot again when she was hired by a Mrs. Houbt as a governess for her little girl, Peggy, in a mansion overlooking Central Park. The grandmother, who had over one $100 million, denied Mother nothing she requested for Peggy.

From a window of her bedroom that overlooked Central Park, Peggy Houbt, a typical poor little rich girl, would watch the children playing in the park sunshine and say wistfully, "Miss Flynn, I wish I could go over there and play with other boys and girls." The reason she was not allowed to do so was out of fear she might be kidnapped for ransom. That did not stop Mother from taking her across the street anyway, and letting her run, jump, play hopscotch and skip rope with the other children, while keeping her keenly in sight. Forbidden to tell her mother where she had been, Peggy loved her afternoons in the park, and the withdrawn child began to open up like a blossom. It was so much more fun than being driven to snooty society teas with her governess.

On her afternoons and evenings off, Mother and one of her several boyfriends went dancing. Her favourite partner was an old friend from Newfoundland, Frank Hogan, who visited Bay de Verde as a boy and knew the O'Neill family quite well. He had been living in New York and was a good friend of Mother's sister, Margaret, and brother, Phil Flynn. The couple's favourite place of entertainment was Roseland, a world famous dance hall on Broadway that came to epitomize the era of the '20s. There, dressed in the latest flapper fashions, Jo developed into an experienced votary of Terpsichore, especially when it came to the waltz, the fox trot, the Black Bottom and the rage of the time, the

Charleston. She was still dancing in a pink dress, yellow hat and corsage of yellow roses, at the wedding reception of her grandson James, who married Karen Binkewicz, in Norwood, Massachusetts, in 1982. At the age of eighty-three, she and Jimmy's Best Man put the other dancers to shame. I often told her if she had gone to Hollywood, instead of New York in the 1920s, she could have given Halifax's Ruby Keeler a run for her money.

Mother's incredible life in New York came to an unforeseen end in 1926 when her father had an eye poked out by a woman adjusting a long hat pin at the Nickel Theatre. Her mother wrote her to say the eye had turned cancerous and was removed, but the cancer had begun to spread to his brain. He asked if she would come home and help care for him as her sisters, Liz and Ann, who were living in St. John's, had husbands and families to care for. Despite all his faults, she loved her father dearly and agreed to come home. Her employer in New York, Mrs. Houbt, and her mother-in-law, hated to see her go, as she had done so much for Peggy. The chauffeur drove her to the East Side pier where she boarded the old, familiar S.S. *Rosalind* for the return journey. Having lived such a wonderful life since landing in Manhattan four years earlier, she must have been overcome with sadness at saying goodbye to all that as the ship sailed past the Statue of Liberty on Bedloe's Island and out to sea.

Chapter 3

The Land Was Ours

My mother, having just arrived home from New York, answered a ring of the doorbell in her family's house on Wood Street to find her mother's cousin, Jim O'Neill from Bay de Verde, standing on the doorstep. He was in town fixing up his accounts and purchasing supplies for the 1926 season about to begin and had called to tell his first cousin, Mary Flynn, Josephine's mother, about the trip he took to Europe the previous year. Amazed to see the beautiful, elegant woman in the doorway that his skinny, freckle-faced cousin had grown into, he was, to use a cliché, swept off his feet. Next day he took her to dinner at Cochrane House, afterwards the Cochrane Hotel, where he was staying. On other nights they went to the Sterling Restaurant, and to Ginnou's on Water Street, and out to the Bella Vista for dancing. Unfortunately, like me, he had two left feet. By the time he left to return home to Bay de Verde on the coastal steamer, they were in love, in spite of a difference of sixteen years in their ages. Soon afterwards he made another visit to St. John's and they became engaged. Because of the consanguinity — she was his first cousin once removed — they were forbidden by church law to marry without a dispensation.

Having known Archbishop Edward Patrick Roche from girlhood, Mother made her way to the Palace, his residence next to the Roman Catholic Cathedral, and into his presence, where she explained her predicament. He asked her the man's name. When she said "Jim O'Neill," His Grace sighed. "What Jim O'Neill?" Mother answered, "The merchant from Bay de Verde. Do you know him?" "I do," His Grace replied. "You couldn't find a finer man. Go on girl."

They were married on Candlemas Day, 2 February 1928 in the small chapel at the Presentation Convent in St. John's, where she had gone to school years before. The Maid of Honour was mother's friend, Nan Phelan of King's Road, and the Best Man, Jimmy Lang, a colleague of my father at Bowring's.

One day before the wedding, Dad arrived in St. John's from Bay de Verde. Mother, who had not seen him for a few months, was getting nervous at the delay. Both he and his brother, Mike, usually spent much of their time in St. John's during the winter months, but that year Dad had a problem in finding a new manager for his business while he was away. A lifelong bachelor, who'd had loved and lost only one girlfriend, my father wasted no time in getting down to business after the wedding. The bride was soon pregnant, and Dr. William H. Newhook, who operated a surgery in Old Perlican, predicted my arrival the first week of November. I think that was one of the happiest times of their lives. Skipper Mike's wife, "Mrs. Kitty," as she was known, warmly welcomed "Mrs. Jose," Skipper Jim's wife, as my mother came to be called, and they soon became bosom companions.

I arrived in this world 26 October 1928, as a seven-pound little darling at a time of day my mother couldn't even remember when I asked her, but she thought it was afternoon. When I arrived in the delivery room at St. Clare's, a week or so before I was due, Mother's physician was unperturbed. Fortunately for Dr. Cluny Macpherson, she had come to town early and was staying with her mother on Wood Street. When my arrival appeared to be imminent, my grandfather rushed her to St. Clare's. My father, who hoped to be in the city with her for the appearance of his first-born, was still attending to business, and closing accounts for the year in Bay de Verde, over 100 miles away. He was advised of my birth by telegraph, and next day took the train to St. John's. At forty-five he had never expected to marry and be the father of a child, which accounts for his incomparable delight and hasty train trip to the city followed by a dash up Patrick Street to the hospital, where he experienced the thrill of holding his newborn son in his arms for the first time.

Within days of Dr. Macpherson delivering me into the arms of my mother, I was taken to the small chapel of the Sisters of Mercy in the hospital for baptism by Father Harold Summers, along with my teenaged cousins as sponsors: Mary Cronan, the daughter of my Aunt Liz, and Brendan O'Neill, of Bay de Verde, my Uncle Mike's son, who with his brother Cyril was, at the time, a boarder at St. Bon's. I was christened Paul James O'Neill. My mother once told me she always wanted a son called Paul, even when she was a teenager. Dad would not hear of her calling me by his name, as he said another James in the house would only lead to confusion.

My physical incarnation on that October day in 1928 was not the beginning of my story, nor was it to be the end. While the mother and the father bring differing genes to the child, all that I could have been, all that I was, and all that I have become, had been preordained by the gene pools of many ancestors over millenniums of time in Ireland, long ages before my actual birth. My mother's grandmother, Elizabeth O'Neill, was the sister of my grandfather, John O'Neill. My mother's mother, Mary Moore Flynn, was my grandmother in addition to being my father's first cousin.

After my birth and baptism at St. Clare's, my soul no longer in jeopardy of Limbo, my father returned to his business, while Mother quickly recovered and we moved from the hospital back to stay with my grandparents on Wood Street. Mother booked passage on the train for us and within a few days we were on our way back to Bay de Verde. I would have to face a train journey of many hours before I would arrive home. Bassinets were unknown in those primitive times, so I made the journey tucked in a laundry basket, purchased for mother by her sister, Aunt Liz, at the Martin Royal Stores a few days earlier. Elizabeth Cronan, who had known great sorrow in her life, was the favourite aunt of all her nieces and nephews.

Although the train left the city at 8:00 in the morning, on its journey of a little over 100 miles, it did not arrive in Bay de Verde until supper time. On that interminable ride, like Mistress Mary, I became quite contrary. The only thing that kept me from screeching my tiny lungs out, to the complete annoyance of other passengers, was conductor Paddy Lee's signal lantern. Poor Mr. Lee, and my dear mother, took turns swinging it in my infant face until their arms ached and my eyelids drooped shut. I was often reawakened by a jolt of the train, and would begin to howl again. I am told each time I opened my small eyes, and the lantern started swinging, I stopped my banshee's wail.

We chugged along the narrow-gauge railway, making endless stops at every community and crossing until at last we reached the station in Carbonear where everyone disembarked, there being no dining cars on the train. Passengers and crew made their way to Aunt Polly McCarthy's Hotel for dinner, which was then eaten at midday. Aunt Polly, so called by everyone, was not a relative of anyone, but a courtesy aunt. Almost every older person in every Newfoundland community in those days was a courtesy aunt or uncle. I remember going to eat at Aunt Polly's as a child. It was a typical Victorian hotel, with spittoons in the lounge, and tall, potted plants in the dining room. McCarthy's Hotel stood on the northwest corner of Water and Bannerman streets until it burned down.

As the train ambled down the north shore around Flamborough Head, that November day in 1928, I lay in the wicker basket both restless and hungry. Mother told me years later, we reached Bay de Verde about 7 o'clock that evening. At the railway station, my father met the train with his precious son and heir on board. The station was located on the barrens, high above the community. That November night, he did not greet us in a motor car but with the O'Neill family's horse and carriage. It was a cold night but I lay snug in my laundry basket which Mr. Lee handed to my excited father. Safe in the carriage, I was driven down Cherry Hill, around the steep turn of the lower hill, in front of Mary Frances Flynn's house, and under the flakes to our family home. I was the first of the third generation of O'Neill's to live there. Eighteen months later, my brother would become the last. I was to retrace the journey to and from St. John's many times, and in many ways, as the years passed, by train, by Ol Blundon's large skiff, by schooner, by the railway steamers, in our own car, and in the hired taxis of Levi Wheeler and Alan Morris.

After 18 months at the centre of my mother's life, and as my adoring father's only son and heir, I was growing into a chubby chatterbox when mother suddenly kissed me goodbye at home and disappeared on the train for St. John's. I suppose I never understood why she deserted us for a visit to the city. I was left in the care of Emily Pryor, my nursemaid, or what the English called a nanny. Mary Ann Noonan was our housemaid and I remember loving both Emily and Mary Ann long years after they left my mother's service. Each time I went to Bay de Verde and met them in later life, I was greeted with a warm hug. Em married Arch Pryor, the mailman, who, after the railway tracks from Carbonear to Bay de Verde were taken up, brought the mail overland from Carbonear on his horse and cart twice a week. Mary Ann married Jim Sullivan, whose father was the only Boer War veteran in Bay de Verde. When Mary Ann left, Mother replaced her with another girl, Nellie Durdle, who like Em was from Victoria, Carbonear. Emily's place as nursemaid had already been taken over by Paula Moore, the daughter of Mother's first cousin Mary, the wife of Andy Moore. I must have been aware my mother would be gone a long time, but I don't think I was too distressed, as she promised to bring me back a baby boy or girl so I would no longer have to play alone in the house. I am told I was over the moon at the thought of having a sibling and waited impatiently for the infant's arrival.

My Grandmother Flynn's house was full at the time, so when mother got in the Waldegrave Taxi outside the railway station in St. John's, and asked the driver where she might find a nice boarding house for a few weeks, he recommended his own place. The man's name was Frank Wheeler and his house where he took her was at 47 Prince of Wales Street. The Wheelers proved to be very friendly and wonderfully hospitable people. A week or so later, suitcase in hand, Mr. Wheeler drove Mother to St. Clare's Hospital, the former White House, where on 29 June 1930, she delivered a healthy, howling boy into the waiting hands of Dr. Cluny Macpherson. He was baptized John Flynn O'Neill after his two grandfathers, John O'Neill and John Flynn, in the small chapel at St. Clare's. His Godparents were my mother's sister, Aunt Liz Cronan, and a relative, Linus Hennebury, a popular porter with the Newfoundland Railway.

In early July of that year, Dad got a telegram from Mother in St. John's, telling him she and the child would be arriving on the train the next evening. When I was told the news I insisted Em take me up to Aunt Kitty's house where I gave her the news that "Mom's baby" would be coming home next day. As I have no memory of these events, except hearsay years later, I expect he came on the train as I did, in a basket. Meanwhile, not knowing anything about him, I was going about the roads of Bay de Verde, so I was told, clutching Em's hand, and telling one and all about the infant Mother was bringing from St. John's. They tell me I referred to him for the first year or so of his life as "Mom's baby." It took me awhile to connect him with the name John.

I know Dad and I met the train at the station in Bay de Verde. Having no car yet, my father took mother and her infant by horse and carriage down two steep hills to our house near Emberley's Point in Bay de Verde. I was intensely curious about "Mom's baby," kissing it, hugging and almost smothering the little creature until I had to be banished from the side of the crib, lest I do him unintentional injury. I could hardly wait for him to become human and start playing with me.

Around 1929, at the insistence of his son Cyril, my Uncle Mike bought his first car, a Dodge. Other car owners sprang up in the area about the same time to fill the muddy roads with their cars. Josiah Blundon bought one for his son, Cecil, John Lockyer got one for his son, Johnny, and in 1932 my father followed their lead when he went to St. John's and bought his first car, a second-hand Oldsmobile. We often went on picnics or trouting in those two cars — Dad's and Uncle Mike's — as summers, autumns, winters, and springs came and went.

John learned to toddle and then to walk beside me wherever I went. Although we grew into very different personalities, and our paths diverged over the years, we walked beside each other for the rest of his life. Together we spent our boyhoods exploring the wondrous freedom of outport life. The only disturbing factor was that Mother was often ill and suffered terribly from headaches which I now know were migraines. The cause of her health problems is my first real memory of childhood. It dates back to the spring of 1933 when I was 4 1/2 years old and Mother lay close to dying in the bedroom over the kitchen. John was too young to share the memory. It was many years afterwards before she told me what happened.

Finding herself pregnant, she had made arrangements to go to St. John's again to have her baby at St. Clare's. However, for some unknown reason, the birth came on prematurely. The nearest physician was Dr. Newhook, who operated a surgery in Old Perlican, seven miles away. There was only one trained nurse in Bay de Verde, Augusta Barter. Gus, as she was known, was sent for while frantic calls were made to Dr. Newhook on the one telephone I knew of in the community at John Lockyer's house.

In 1991 I was invited back home to Bay de Verde by Rev. Don Nicholle, to give the after-dinner speech at a banquet marking the 100th anniversary of the opening of St. Barnabas's Anglican Church. For me it was a very great honour to be invited, nearly 200 years after my Great-great-grandmother, Anne Duffit, was baptized there in the Church of England. At the event in 1991, I met Gus, who had remained a dear friend all her life, and we talked about the time Mother almost died from a miscarriage. She said when she arrived at our house, she found John and me standing beside Mother's bed. It was already too late for her experience as a nurse to be of much help. I told her I remembered being lifted up by my father to kiss Mother goodbye as everyone wept. I seemed to know she was going to see Holy God, but John was very puzzled by what was going on, as he was not yet three. We recalled that the parish priest, Father John Mackey, who, poor man, was an alcoholic, arrived at the house the same time as Gus. He anointed the half-conscious woman.

Mother told me years, later shortly before her death, that the priest's breath reeked of booze, and during the anointing he passed out and fell on top of her. She said she got such a fright that the baby who had been giving the midwife such trouble was suddenly born. Gus told me the tiny girl, who was in the midwife's hands, was already dead and Mother was hemorrhaging badly. She had all she could do to save her life. Whether the baby was born alive or dead Mother had no idea. By the time Dr. Newhook arrived from Old Perlican, Mother was unconscious. There being no hospital in Old Perlican in those days, she remained at home in the care of Gus, with frequent visits from the doctor, until she finally began to recover. As soon as she was well enough to travel, my father took her to the nearest hospital, in St. John's.

Since the priest had been incapable of baptizing the infant at birth, my tiny sister was quietly buried in an unmarked grave in our family plot in the Roman Catholic Cemetery at Bay de Verde. Not having been baptized, she was not supposed to be buried in consecrated ground. Her interment was, therefore, in defiance of church law, but she was buried with the co-operation of a repentant Father Mackey. It is impossible for anyone today to fathom some of the inhumane church decrees by which people lived their lives in those days. Even a married couple of different religions could not be buried side by side but were each buried in a cemetery of their own religion.

The doctors who examined my mother when she arrived at the General Hospital in St. John's recommended she go to Montreal for a hysterectomy. Although several had been done in St. John's since the late 1920s, the operation was uncommon there. My father began to arrange the journey to Montreal for her. She had to go from Bay de Verde to St. John's by coastal boat and on to Port aux Basques by train. The trip from there to North Sydney, Nova Scotia, was by ferry, and from North Sydney to Montreal by train. Her doctor had booked her into the Royal Victoria Hospital for surgery.

When the time came for her to depart for Canada, Mother left Bay de Verde by the coastal steamer *S.S. Home*, which moored just outside the harbour mouth. I suppose John and I cried as we stood with others on the public wharf waving goodbye to our loved ones who were being taken out to the steamer. I have a flash of memory in which we are clinging to each of Dad's arms, watching Mother in a cloche hat and sealskin coat being helped on board the rodney in which she was rowed out to the *Home*. As happened when John was born, there was again no question of Dad going with her. It was the beginning of the fishing season and he needed to be with his crews in Bay de Verde. Mary Ann Noonan was more than capable of looking after the three of us. Women in those days were made of stern stuff. Looking back, I believe Mother was a woman of remarkable courage to undergo such an operation alone in a foreign country and afterwards to return home by the same route with no one to accompany her. Within a few years, the operation for which she had to travel to Montreal became quite common in St. John's.

As it turned out, our mother was gone nearly six weeks. I was eagerly anticipating her return because of the surprise gifts she promised to bring us, including bananas, plums and pears, rare items indeed in a Newfoundland outport in the early '30s. The only fresh fruits available in our shop were the barrels of apples from Nova Scotia in the fall and the crates of Sunkist oranges, each one wrapped in orange-coloured tissue paper. We also sold dried apples, pears, apricots and prunes. They were usually handed out when filling the dole notes of the poor. A few years ago, my friend Michael Cashin and I were walking along a street in New York when we chanced upon a popular health food store. There on display were dried apples, pears, apricots and prunes, like those we ate in the outports in the old days. They had become the latest health food craze. Michael said, "Who would have believed even poor people were eating health foods in Newfoundland during the Depression?" We both laughed.

Mother came home from Montreal to St. John's and then traveled to Bay de Verde by Alan Morris's taxi. Alan lived in Old Perlican and drove the first around-the-bay taxi to and from the city. After you left Topsail, the journey took five or six hours on unpaved roads. When King George V and Queen Elizabeth visited Newfoundland in 1938, they landed from a British destroyer in Holyrood and motored to the city on a newly paved road. In the direction of Conception Bay, from Holyrood to Bay de Verde, it was nothing but dust and pot holes.

When a tall, thin woman walked into our kitchen I rushed over, threw my arms about her, gave her a big kiss and demanded the fruit and gifts she said she would bring me, while John, having no clue as to who she was, stood shyly in a corner, his thumb in his mouth, his look furtive. She walked over to him and mischievously asked, "What's your name, my son?" With downcast eyes he answered,

"Johnny O'Neill." As she swept him up into her arms he began to cry. It was the only time I ever heard him call himself Johnny in his life. Mother had always insisted he be called John. Within hours we were a family once again.

Chapter 4

Backward, Turn Backward

In early November 1928, I first peeped through infant's eye at the community of Bay de Verde. After having learned to crawl, I began to walk along the lanes and paths of the place, disguised to everyone who saw me as a small, blue-eyed boy with freckles, wearing short knee pants, well scuffed sneakers with worn heels, and black lisle stockings rolled below the knees on elastic garters. Since those days, sunrises and sunsets beyond number have cast their long magenta shadows among the towering cliffs, while uncountable periods of light and darkness have marked the passing years in my own life, as well as that of my beloved outport, a place wrapped in decaying leaves of memory where the seasons of my journey began. For me, each time I go back there, my visit down the winding road before me is always an essay in nostalgia.

Bay de Verde, where the graves of my ancestors scar the rocky soil, is a place to which I must return from time to time, in order to know fully who I am. Among what is left of twisted lanes and old houses, among what is left of rotting flakes and tumbling stages, among the wooden bones of upturned skiffs in abandoned meadows, are the ghosts of things that are mine alone, and will be mine forever. Ghosts of things irretrievable, abandoned long ago, surrendered when I left to stumble on my own discoveries, to find my own viewpoints, to make choices, to create the person I helplessly remain to the end of my days. Love it or hate it, only in Bay de Verde, the place I call "down home," can I ever hope to find that long discarded first blueprint of "me."

The years are both many and long since I put away my toys, like Little Boy Blue, and left Bay de Verde for the last time. On a forgotten day in an autumn long ago, I went up Cherry Hill, to places I had never been, to do things I had never done, and to discover life is, as one writer said, "a carousel on which we ride the painted ponies of our dreams." And yet, curiously, although I have been long gone from the place, I am still there, in my familiar home above the stages and the flakes, peering through rain-soaked windows in my father's house, my freckled face flattened against the panes, trying to imagine the world of clear blue sky that lay beyond the misty shores where breakers tumbled endlessly among the rocks and kelp.

Around every corner of my memory, Bay de Verde lies in wait. Not a month of my life goes by when I am not trapped into some blurred vision of those years of boyhood recollections of my father, my mother, and especially my brother — all gone from my life forever, but not in the least forgotten, because we never forget love. Down home is where I shared my first secrets, where I played with my first friends, where I dreamed my first dreams. It is where I learned to chew frankum, seeping from the wounds of tree trunks, and tar that solidified as it dripped from the roofs of sheds.

Down home I learned to love, and what love is, as I set out, hand in hand with my little brother, two boys discovering the world together in twine lofts, fish stores, stages, punts, dirt roadways, fields of new mown hay. As we grew more adventurous we hiked up over Walsh's Hill with our friends to the Frenchman's hole, or grave, where we puffed our first cigarettes, ill-gotten packs of Flags snitched from a shelf in our father's store when nobody was looking. We also snitched such chocolate delights as banner caramels, union squares, chocolate mice and all-day suckers. When we got old enough to confess these thefts to Father Mackey, as we knelt at his knee in the sacristy of the chapel on Saturday evenings, we were admonished to tell our father what we had done. Somehow we always forgot to mention these transgressions to Dad until the next confession, when we raked up the same old sins of taking "stuff" from the shop, meaning cigarettes and candy. To give bulk to what we had to confess we would drop the snitching between admissions of lesser offenses, such as disobeying our father and mother, or missing our morning or night prayers, although we rarely did. I am sure most of what the long-suffering priest had to listen to went in one ear and out the other.

I can remember eavesdropping on the things grownups talked about and the magic their knowledge brought into my life. I heard my mother and father, my Aunt Kitty and Uncle Mike, laugh at Joe Penner's jokes on our big, two-piece, Atwater Kent radio. My first bit of acting was imitating Penner's famous line, "Do you wanna buy a duck?" We followed the involvement of Amos and Andy with Kingfish, and a lady called Most Precious Jewel (of the Stars in the Crown). To give you some idea of its popularity, the 10,000th broadcast was heard locally on VOWR in 1952. We appraised the talent heard on *Major Bowes' Amateur Hour*, many of whom became stars. We also tuned in to hear the *Grand Ole Opry*, a weekly country and western radio show on WWV in Wheeling, West Virginia, probably the most powerful radio station in America.

As the 1930s drew to a close and the Second World War began in September 1939, I was fascinated to hear my father discuss the grim war news with the men lounging about in his fish store or shop, or in Bill Broderick's forge, while my brother and I pulled the bellows to stir up the fire pit in which Mr. Broderick fashioned horseshoes for Prince and other nags. He was the grandfather of entertainer D'Arcy Broderick, of Bay de Verde, whose father Kevin, a few years older than me, was often given the chore of babysitting me as a child. Mother called him my "minder." D'Arcy is considered as one of the best fiddle players in Newfoundland

and Labrador and is especially one of the finest ballad singers in the province.

I recall once listening as my Uncle Mike and Cousin Cyril argued the merits and demerits of a Dodge car Cyril wanted his father to buy. They eventually bought it, and John and I often went fishing in the car with our uncle, who, unlike our father, would take time off from work around sunset for a jaunt to the ponds on the barrens with a can of worms dug by John and me. I remember my mother complaining to Dad, "It's a queer thing, Mike can take time to go trouting with your sons, and you can't." A workaholic, Dad would reply, "Mike has Cyril." I think Mother envied Aunt Kitty because Uncle Mike would leave the shop or the stage to go trouting with her, berrypicking or just to take an afternoon drive over the barrens in his Dodge car while our Oldsmobile sat in the garage, unmoved, sometimes for weeks. In my mind's eye, the odd time Dad took us in his car, Mother would sit on a rock beside a pond, her hat shading her eyes and reading a book, while we fought off mosquitoes (called nippers) and fished for trout.

In Bay de Verde I ate fruit from the tree of knowledge, and learned a water dog wasn't a pup that liked to swim but a blister on a fisherman's wrist, a puffin pig wasn't a hog but a porpoise, a water doctor wasn't a physician on a ship but a spider, and a collar chain wasn't something you attached to your dog but something you attached to your skiff when you moored it at the end of day. I learned ochre wasn't quite the same thing as ochy, a gommil was a half fool, the first snow came in a scad, and times were scattered. I absorbed such old wives tales that claimed jellyfish gave you warts, eating dandelion flowers, called by us *piss-a-beds,* would cause you to do just that, and if you crossed your eyes and the wind changed, they would stay that way forever — little bits of lore that have stayed with me all my life.

Wind rustled in the light of morning, and the shade of evening. In the end, all the things I saw, like time itself, passed away and will never come back. Community is about the lives of generations of people who lived in a certain place at a certain time. I seemed to know by heart each blade of grass in our garden, each castor plant and black-eyed Susan my mother coaxed into bloom, each spruce and fir my father planted with a determination that proved hopeless in the end. Every spring, for as long as I can remember, Dad always gave me two packs of seed from the shop, sweet peas and marigolds, which I planted in my own corner of our potato garden behind the house. I fertilized them with Prince's manure from the stable floor and tended them daily with my little watering can. I was thrilled when the first blooms appeared. I still enjoy planting flowers in spring.

When I go "down home" these days, I go as a pilgrim, wandering amidst shadows and knowing that life among them is too unattainable ever to reclaim. Time passes with a swiftness that has no sound, like a leaf turning or a flower fading. The years flow unhindered, distances lending them loneliness. Thomas Wolfe, summed up the experience in these words: "Time passing as men pass who will never come back again and leaving us,... knowing that this earth, this time, this life, are stranger than a dream.

To turn backward and be a child again is impossible but what is possible is to recall many of the things of childhood. Bay de Verde was the place in which my immigrant great-grandfather planted family roots, after coming out from Ireland, in the early 1800s. Three generations of my kin have lived and died among the two steep hillsides which enclose the settlement, linking me forever, by blood and by sentiment, to a place that afterwards took pride in being considered the largest fishing settlement in Conception Bay, with more fishermen, more fishing boats, more fish and more fish flakes for drying and storing the salted cod than anywhere else in Newfoundland.

The talk of our fishing crews, the sharemen who ate and slept all summer in our bunkhouses, puzzled me because much of what it had to say concerned the charms of the women and girls in the harbour whom they were dating.

Whenever the cook let us join them for a meal in the cookhouse, it was a big deal, and we thought his cooking was sometimes far superior to what we would have had to eat at home. Often when he rang the cookhouse bell, which hung outside the kitchen over the stage in order to call the crews to their mid-morning or mid-afternoon mug-up, John and I joined the men whenever Cookie served them molasses cookies. Uncle Mike had a bunkhouse attached to the back of Dad's, but we seldom went there as the cook was not nearly so welcoming.

My family roots in the settlement go back more than two centuries. The earliest record I have been able to find of anyone in my family being resident in Bay de Verde is 1786, only ten years after the beginning of the American Revolution. George Washington had yet to be elected first president of the United States. According to Church of England baptismal records in which I found a son, Thomas, was born that year, on August 5th, to a Thomas and Anne Duffit. In 1799 Thomas Duffit's sister, Anne, was born in Bay de Verde. Like her brother she was baptized in the Church of England. Anne Duffit, who was named for her mother, eventually married an Irish immigrant, Edmund Moore, who made his way to Bay de Verde from Kilmaganny, County Kilkenny, Ireland, where he was born in 1800. These two were to become my maternal great- great-grandparents.

One of the children of Edmund and Anne (Duffit) Moore, Andrew, married Elizabeth O'Neill, the oldest of my grandfather O'Neill's sisters and brothers. By this marriage, my great-aunt became my great-grandmother, when her daughter Mary Moore, born in Bay de Verde, married John Flynn, who came from Ireland by way of St. John's. Their daughter, Mary Joseph, was my mother. Some years ago, my cousin, Margaret Buckingham, whose mother, Ann Flynn, was my mother's sister, went with me to Bay de Verde, where we hunted through the tall grass, matted yarrow and Queen Anne's lace, and found among the weeds the gravestone of our great-great-grandparents Edmund and Anne (Duffit)

Moore. Evidently she must have turned Catholic after marrying him or she would not have been buried in the Catholic cemetery.

Elizabeth Duffit, Anne's sister-in law, was a thorn in the side of the first Church of England clergyman to take up residence in Bay de Verde, Rev. Oliver Rouse, born 1820 in Northlew, Devon. Rouse, whose very informative diary has been edited and privately published by his great-grandson, John C. Street, was appointed by Bishop Edward Feild. He left St. John's on the evening of Monday, 16 September 1847 in an open boat owned by one of the Blundons, and, accompanied by his wife Maria, his two children Bridget and Mary Ann, a goat and some hens, arrived at Bay de Verde at 5:00 a.m. the following morning. Only the girls' mother was seasick on the 7 1/2 hour voyage. Friday, 9 February 1849, Rev. Rouse noted Mrs. Duffit was not on good terms with the Church of England school teacher, Mr. Norris. Rouse notes in his diary, "Spoke to Mrs. Duffit about sending her children to the Roman Catholic School. She said, they did not get on at Norris's. However, the real cause appears to be a pique between the two families. I told her that she acted very wrong in exposing her children to temptation."

The previous year, Rouse reported having a scene on a Sunday with my great-great-grandfather Edmund Moore, husband of Anne Duffit. He wrote on Sunday, 16 July 1848, "Seeing Ellen Blake (a Protestant) on the flakes spreading fish, I went to ask her the cause. She replied that the fish would spoil if not spread. After some further talk with her, during which she was several times told to go on with her work, she said she was obliged to do it. I then went up to Mr. Moore, who was near, and asked how it was he compelled a Protestant servant to work on the Lord's Day. He answered me in this manner: Go along! Be off, etc. I however again repeated the question; when he became more civil. He endeavoured to justify his conduct: but I told him, he as a Romanist might act as he pleased: but that he had no right to compel a Protestant. I also exhorted Ellen B. to listen to God rather than man." One wonders what the Parson thought of Anne Duffit having been lured into the Roman Catholic faith.

As for my father's side of the family, in 1824 my great-grandfather, Thomas O'Neill, came almost penniless from Ireland to Harbour Grace at the age of twenty-five, having found employment as a bookkeeper in the counting house of the prosperous Ulster merchant Thomas Ridley in that place. Ridley's stone building, in which he laboured over the firm's bookkeeping, still stands on the beach at Harbour Grace where it is a registered Historic Site. As Ridley's agent on the North Shore of Conception Bay, Thomas O'Neill often visited Bay de Verde where he met and married Ellen Noonan, who was then seventeen or eighteen years old. Looking at both of them in humorless, grim-faced, no-nonsense poses, on faded tintype photographs in my possession, I would say falling in love, in the modern sense, was an alien emotion to them. But you can never be sure with Victorians. Beneath those prim exteriors, who knows what consuming fires of passion may have raged within the flesh. In any case, whatever the attraction, they married and evidently found connubial bliss. In those days, you took what God sent you without complaint, and in their case He sent them twelve children, all of whom lived into adulthood.

In 1841, Thomas O'Neill borrowed money from Ridley, using the equivalent of $140 of it to purchase the property of Thomas Phelan, at Seal Cove Point, in Bonny, near Bay de Verde. It consisted of a plantation, house, cellar and fishing room. I possess the deeds to that property. Six years later, in the settlement of Bay de Verde itself, O'Neill acquired the estate of the late Dominick Flynn, which had been known as White's Room, and built a two-storey, salt box style house for his growing family. I have been able to trace Samuel White's claim to his Room in Bay de Verde back to the late 1600s through the Governor's letterbooks when a survey of the property was ordered to settle a dispute over a right-of-way.

According to my father's sister, Nellie Kennedy, she was the last O'Neill child born in the old family house in 1881, and my father was the first as well as last child born in the new house in 1883. She concluded, it must therefore have been 1882 when her father, my grandfather, John O'Neill, had the builder Southcott come down from Heart's Content, where he was constructing houses for the cable company, and build a substantial second empire, three-storey house, with a Mansard roof, for his family and ailing parents. It was erected opposite his domain of fish flakes, and across the roadway from his shop. For nearly 100 years that house stood gazing majestically towards the Bight. With my brother at university in Boston, and me working in London, England, my father, finding the disused residence too much of a burden, sold it, furnished, to our neighbour Joe Broderick. It was eventually occupied by Joe's brother Kevin and family.

The Brodericks first removed the verandah along the front and then the Mansard roofed upper floor, turning the place into a square box. Eventually much of the remaining house was torn down and rebuilt as a modern bungalow. I have always deeply regretted my father's action in selling the home of my childhood, with the eight bedrooms and many fireplaces. Over the years, I have often longed to have it in my possession. But, as with many things in my life as I grow older, they are no more. And yet, I still see the place very clearly, in my mind's eye. There is not a nook or cranny of it I do not remember and treasure, because to me, like Bay de Verde itself, it was a place called home.

I am bound to the community by ancestors whose dust lies mingled forever in the grit stone graves of the old and newer Catholic cemeteries, where lie my great-grandparents, grandparents, great-uncles, great-aunts, uncles, aunts, first cousins — O'Neills, Noonans, Moores — and in the old and newer Church of England cemeteries where my great-great-grandparents, great-uncles, great-aunts, and other Duffit relatives lie buried. And so the story goes, in my home town, a community where people have lived and worked and died, have laughed and wept, have unspooled generations of their lives over centuries of time. That is what makes any place home, whether it be a collection of igloos in the Arctic, thatched huts in the jungle, or clapboard houses in a fishing town on the shores of Newfoundland.

My mother Josephine came to live in Bay de Verde in 1927. The community was the birthplace of her mother, Mary Moore, whose mother was Elizabeth O'Neill, the oldest of my Grandfather O'Neill's numerous brothers and sisters. John and I often went, with our mother and alone, to visit her Uncle Tom Moore and his wife, Aunt Missy (North), who lived in the harbour. Elizabeth O'Neill, the mother of my maternal grandmother Mary Moore, who married Andrew Moore, was the sister of my grandfather, John O'Neill. I always heard my father spoken of by almost everyone as Skipper Jim, just as my uncle was always referred to as Skipper Mike. Skipper Jim and his bride moved into the old house built by my grandfather, which he had occupied with a housekeeper for the many years of his bachelorhood.

The house to which my mother came as a bride had many advantages, but no electricity and no running water. These two things were installed in 1929, a year after my birth. There was also not yet a hospital in Old Perlican, and she, a townie, was what was called "delicate."

They say what the eye sees, the mind records and never forgets. To this day I see every room of that house to which I was taken as an infant, and I still hear its distinctive sounds: the click of the latch leading to the pantry, when I was sneaking in to steal a finger full of fresh, clotted cream, or the special noise the back door made when it was banged endlessly on summer days by two small boys running constantly in and out, while their harassed mother called to them not to let the flies in. A house develops a personality of its own from the generations who live in it, ours no less than any other.

My father told me the parlour was always kept locked when he was a boy, except on Sundays or when there was a wake or wedding reception. A prime minister of Newfoundland, Sir Robert Bond, once came to tea with my grandparents when he visited Bay de Verde while campaigning for election. On the floors of that house I learned to crawl and then to walk, to gurgle and then to talk. Once I learned to do the latter, I'm told I never stopped, and still haven't. In a letter dated 5 July 1930 from my father, written in Bay de Verde to my mother, who was then in St. John's awaiting the birth of her second child, he wrote, "Paul is the limit. He does not shut his mouth at all, always talking and trying to say things." Trying to say things was undoubtedly the beginning of my becoming a writer as I have been trying to say things ever since.

When my mother returned from St. John's a few weeks after that letter was written, she brought with her to the rooms of the old house in Bay de Verde what my father referred to in his letter as "the new gent," wrapped in a bundle. That infant was to alter the pattern of my life forever. John and I, like most brothers, had some monumental rows as we grew into boyhood and manhood, but by the time of his early death, he was the dearest person in the world to me. My heart still bears the scarred wound of this loss. As time goes on I miss him more and more, not less and less, because together we knew things we did not have to put into words, things I can never share with anyone else ever again.

John Flynn O'Neill proved to be a feisty little kid, whom I loved deeply from the moment he was brought into our home in Bay de Verde until the day of his death and beyond. I have not in my life loved anyone more than I loved my brother, and I mourn his passing with tears, even to this day. In spite of warnings and punishments for disobeying, he spent much of his early wanderings hanging out in our father's bunkhouse, hearing the language of the sharemen, so that by the age of four he could swear with the best of them. Once when I was subjecting him to some torture or other, such as the Chinese burn, just so he would remember who was boss, my mother overheard him repeatedly bellow the name of the man from Nazareth, the one at which every knee should bend. Realizing he heard such language from the hired men in the stages or on the flakes, Mother, remembering her book of parental advice, *Talks to Mothers* by Angelo Patri, tried to make the best of a bad situation by calling him in from play.

I have a memory, ravaged by time, of a winter evening long ago, before there were such things as furnaces or electric heat, at least in Bay de Verde. After supper in the evenings we were dressed in pajamas, bathrobes and slippers, and allowed to sit on the stairs in the glowing warmth of the big round hall stove that heated the house, and listen while our nursemaid, Paula Moore, read from the stories of Thornton W. Burgess which appeared daily in the pink pages of the St. John's *Evening Telegram*, which came in the mail twice a week. I recall, on the evening of which I speak, the hall stove was banked with coal and sizzling hot. I sat quietly near the foot of the stairs listening intently to the latest doings of Reddy Fox and the rabbits in Mr. McGregor's Garden. John sat a step or two above me, with his head in Paula's lap. As she read on, he evidently lost interest in Mr. McGregor's problems and formed a mischievous intent. Stretching out a small foot, he kicked me in the small of the back. As I fell forward I put out my hands to stop my headlong plunge into the red hot sides of the hall stove and burned the skin from off my fingers and palms.

You never heard a howl like the blood-curdling screech that brought my mother running. Pardon the expression, but all hell broke loose. It seemed to me there was an unbelievable cacophony of howling, screeching, scolding and weeping. Paula rushed up to Dad's shop to get my father who was at work in his office. I am unable to say what punishment my dear little brother was given, because within minutes I was in Dad's car, moaning and awash in tears, being rushed to Dr. Newhook's surgery in his yellow house in Old Perlican, at the end of the road to Bay de Verde. As I remember it, the doctor encased my scorched and blistered palms in a mixture of powered chalk and olive oil. I returned home with my hands swathed in bandages, like a creature from a mummy's tomb. The best part came later when the scars healed and the bandages were removed. I used to delight my friends by letting them watch as I used a straight pin to prick the huge blisters at the ends of my fingers and palms so that water squirted out.

I seem to have been a fairly consistent patient of Dr. Newhook, and later his replacement, Dr. Short. There was a stone wall at the back of our house I had often been warned not to climb. One day I climbed it, fell off, knocked myself out, and split my lip so that I carry the scar to this day. I badly damaged both knees, in which I now have diabetic neuropathy. Another time I was scaling a post to the roof of the verandah which ran along the front of our house, also something I was forbidden to do, when halfway up I slipped and fell. When I grabbed the post, a hook on it dug into my hand and I hung there suspended like a slab of meat on a butcher's hook. Arthur Emberley, the father of my friends Virtue, Arch and Dulcie, was passing below and heard me howl in pain. He came up from the road and lifted me down. Dr. Short stitched up the wound, but I still bear the jagged scar on my right hand. Other scars I bear are from the time I broke a lamp chimney in the shop, gouging out a chunk of finger, and the time I fell on an anchor in a boat, splitting my kneecap to the bone. It is boyhood misadventures like these, as well as happy times, that play a very integral role in making Bay de Verde home to me.

O'Neill home in Bay de Verde.

1934.

Bay de Verde.

Bay de Verde.

1937 storm in Bay de Verde.

Bay de Verde.

My first car, a 1953 Meteor.

Chapter 5

Childhood is the Firey Furnace

Life as a child "out our way" wasn't all violence and tears. One of the happiest things about it was our endless parade of pets. Always, when I think of my life in Bay de Verde, I think of the animals we had. My first love was a big black dog, Prince, a kind of mongrel Newfoundland, who came in the mail one Saturday evening, packed in a wooden crate. When he bounced out on the kitchen floor, John, who was just a toddler, was so scared of the active bundle of black fur that he scrambled up on the kitchen table. He sat there for days, cross-legged, and only came down for meals and bed.

To our sorrow, some years later dear Prince had to be shot for attacking my sibling one especially hot summers day, by biting his face and drawing blood. My mother said the attack was probably not unprovoked. She did not realize how close she was to the truth. I had been playing with Prince on the grass in the side garden of our house when John came toddling in through the gate carrying an old stick. He began to poke the dog in the ribs and face. An overheated Prince responded by biting him in the face, a thing he would never have done had he been left alone. My shrieks brought Mother running with the maid. Dad was nowhere around, unfortunately, but Kevin Broderick who lived across the lane ran down to the oil factory where he had been last seen, found him, and they rushed back to the garden. Within minutes my father took his car out of the garage and loaded Mother, John and me on board. We were quickly off to see the doctor in Old Perlican who gave my little brother several stitches around the eye and warned him to be careful when playing with the dog.

After Prince came an endless parade of dogs, like Pal and Towser, cats like Topsy and Eva, a cow named Belle, rabbits, turtles, small sea birds (brought to us by the Ryan brothers from Baccalieu, and kept in the garden under netting), and another fondly remembered Prince, a dear old brown work horse from up Trinity Bay. He became a beloved pal to my brother and me for years. Those adored dogs are still there on their haunches in memory. Their heads are cocked gravely to one side, waiting patiently for my brother and me to come home, so they can frisk with us in meadows of new mown hay, or in fresh drifts of powdery snow. Our dearly loved cats are also still on their haunches, meticulously paw-washing placid faces in the kitchen window, among red clay pots of Mother's geraniums and roses.

Of all the pets we ever owned, neither John nor I ever loved any of them, before or since, as dearly as we loved our cat named Topsy. She came to epitomize our teenage years. A black and white kitten that we saw straying around Bond Street on our way to school one day, she was still there when we came home at 4:30. We picked her up and brought her to the house where Mother also fell in love with her and allowed her to stay for the next sixteen years. While Topsy, in her turn, was totally loving of us, she had two peculiarities. We never heard her purr in the whole of her life and, as a mother, she was an utter failure. Few of the two or three kittens Topsy gave birth to about once a year were ever delivered alive. If they did survive their delivery, she would invariably lie on them in the night, smothering one or two of the litter. Little Eva was among the fortunate to survive. Our dearly loved Topsy and Eva shared our lives until an American serviceman, renting the house next door, told Mother, "I hate cats," and fed them poison.

Speaking of our pets reminds me that my first association with death came as a child in Bay de Verde. You will see why pets remind me of that in a moment. I recall some poor old gentleman died. Like hearers of the bush telegraph in Africa, the boys and girls of the settlement seemed to know instantly when a coffin was being hammered together. My brother and I hurried with our friends to a carpenter's shed, located between Aunt Martha Norris's house and Aunt Mary Ann Moore's little shop. The latter place I remember as being always more famous for its roses and geraniums in tin cans, wrapped in colorful wallpaper, than the goods she had for sale. We crowded into that shed with other curious children to gawk at the carpenter as he constructed the coffin. He was a fast worker, because that afternoon we all trotted off to the wake, held at a house in Backside, located somewhere near the community well. I can see us in my mind's eye, a ragtag regiment of kids, standing on tiptoes, gaping, goggle-eyed at the corpse in the long box. Things like that always live on in memory.

My father told me his Uncle Mike, my grandfather O'Neill's brother, reputed to be the tallest man in Newfoundland at nearly seven feet, died when he was only thirty-six years old. His body lay on a bed awaiting a coffin which had to be made to order. On the day of his funeral, when the extended coffin was nailed shut in the parlour, there was a problem getting it around the doors of their house, without tipping it up. To solve the problem, the parlour window frames were removed and the tallest of the O'Neills was passed out, feet first, through the window in his extra long pine box. It was then lashed to a longcart for the funeral procession to the church and up the hill to the graveyard. Both the Catholic and Anglican cemeteries in Bay de Verde were up several steep hills. Mr. William James Emberly, who was our neighbour and the father of Paul Emberly, the postmaster, wrote a song about our cemeteries called "Hard, Hard, Times," which became quite popular and remains a Newfoundland favourite. In one verse he says;

> The best thing for to do is to work with a will,
> For when she's all finished you're hauled up the hill;

You're hauled up the hill and put down in the cold,
And when she's all done, you're still in the hole
And it's hard, hard times.

He knew the Bay de Verde cemeteries, all right.

John and I had a pet rabbit that died. We decided, with the help of our playmates, all Emberlys — Billy, Viola, Arch, Dulcie, Mervyn, Phyllis and Johnny (who had serious mental problems)— to give the deceased rabbit a proper wake and funeral, just like we had seen with the old man in the coffin shortly before, so no makeshift cardboard box would do. We wanted the works for our dear rabbit, a wooden coffin and all. I took the quest for a proper box to our beloved Maggie Noonan, who worked as a shop assistant in my father's store for nearly eight years, before leaving us bereft to become Sister Mary Alphonsus of the Order of Our Lady of Mercy, in St. John's. Years afterwards, Sister Alphonsus and my brother were to die within months of each other and, sadly, I read the scripture lessons at both their funeral masses. In the meantime, while my brother and the Emberly boys dug a grave in our garden and began hammering together a cross for a grave marker, Viola, Dulcie and Phyllis gathered buttercups, clover, daisies, and dandelion flowers, and set to work making wreaths. I continued to act the part of the preacher.

Maggie had emptied out a box of black pepper, which in those days was sold loose by the ounce, and gave me the oblong, wooden crate into which the rabbit's corpse just fitted. I carried the pepper box coffin to where everyone waited in my father's fish store, along with some material for a lining, which I snitched from the pound goods bin in the shop when Maggie wasn't looking. Because the box had "Black Pepper" printed on it in bold letters, we decided to call the deceased rabbit by that name, and painted the words "Black Pepper" on the cross John and his friends made to mark the grave.

My mother, who was always wonderfully tolerant of the imaginations of her children, allowed Black Pepper to be waked in style in the parlour, with the Venetian shades drawn and candles burning. By funeral time that afternoon, over a dozen mourners had gathered from all parts of the harbour, none above the age of twelve. Besides O'Neills and Emberleys, there were kids with names like Riggs, Murphy, Doyle, Moore and Blundon. I don't recall if Mother's tolerance extended to reading prayers over the departed — probably not — but we did anyway. With me as a pretend clergyman, everyone said the rosary, Protestants and Catholics. I then sprinkled real holy water on the corpse, while a three-foot-tall, plaster statue of St. Theresa the Little Flower, once the object of my grandmother's devotion, looked on from above the coffin. I even passed out Necco candy wafers from a silver patten, taken from a Last Rites outfit we had, which also belonged to my grandmother. When the coffin was finally closed, the pallbearers carried it out of the house and placed it in our truckly-muck, a little four-wheeled cart used by us children for pulling small things around. The cortege of mourners then wound its way out Emberley's Point, past Aunt Dinah's, as far as Aunt Amelia's house, where Viola lived, and back to the gravesite in our garden. As I recall it, the internment had a rather festive atmosphere, everyone thoroughly enjoying the funeral. The cross bearing the name Black Pepper has long since disappeared.

In Bay de Verde my boyish energy, blended with the melancholy of marshlands, was woven in the texture of peat bogs and mingled like the special joy of familiar sounds with the awesome silence of rock-strewn hillsides reaching up from granite cliffs that rose out of a sea of lapis lazuli. Human attachments to places, as to persons, are sealed by hate, as well as by love. I know there was poverty in my community and there was hunger, too. There was anger and there were feuds. Sometimes, sad to say, these were because someone had married into, or abandoned, this religion or that religion for another. Such things time and understanding have made meaningless. There were houses in which there was little food and no coal. As a boy I often helped in my father's shop when they were filling the pitiful six-cents-a-day dole notes of the poor. Our parents never let us forget the children in the place who went to bed hungry. But such thoughts are difficult for someone young, who is not hungry, to comprehend. When we turned up our noses at some vegetable or fish we didn't like, Dad would say, "we're not interested in your likes and dislikes. There are children in this harbour going to bed hungry tonight. You boys live very fortunate lives. Eat whatever is on your plate." The result of that lesson is that today, when I'm invited out and asked what I like or dislike, I always answer, thanks to my father, whatever you put in front of me I'll eat (except sweet potatoes).

When I was six years old and John four and a half, Mother decided the time had come for us to undergo what was a ritual for almost every boy or girl in those days – having your tonsils out. One rarely hears of it being performed today, but in my boyhood I don't believe I knew a young person whose tonsils were not removed, male or female. Mother arranged for us to travel from Bay de Verde to St. John's by way of Allan Morris's taxi. A shared outport taxi was the way most people around the island travelled to St. John's in those days, the train service having been taken up and no bus service supplement provided. We had two taxis in Bay de Verde that both came from Old Perlican and went to St. John's in one day and returned the next. Over the years, while living in St. John's without transport, my father having gotten rid of his car, we used Allan Morris and Levi Wheeler at least twice a year to get us down home and back to the city. When we grew older and Quinlan's took over the mail delivery, John and I would ride down home in the back of the truck among the mail bags from Carbonear station where the train tracks ended.

On arriving in the city there was no room at my grandmother's house so we were dropped off at the Wheelers'. Mother immediately contacted the hospital to make sure all was in readiness for us. We were then taken to St. Clare's and registered. I recall we were put in a room with two beds. Next morning a nurse appeared with two men pushing gurneys. John was placed on one with me being put on the other and we were wheeled away to the operating room. A nun, Sister Mary Alacoque McDonald, was bustling about setting up things for the operations. John was taken first from the gurney to the operating table while I lay quietly on my gurney against the wall taking in all that was going on.

Sister Alacoque took charge, giving orders to the nurses and orderlies. Her first duty seemed to be to put John to sleep. She approached him with a container of what I afterwards found out was an anesthetic known as chloroform, which the Sister poured on a mask for the doctor. It had a sickening odour which John managed to get a whiff of as it was about to be put over his face and he began to yell the Holy Name at the top of his little voice, "Dee-sus!... Dee-sus!... Dee-sus!" I caught a look of horror on Sister Alacoque's face. The quick-thinking nun said, "What a nice little boy to say your prayers." To add to the Sister's horror, he screeched in answer, "Dem's not prayers, dem's curses!" whereupon the doctor immediately clamped the mask over his face and he was rendered unconscious by the chloroform. When I afterwards became a tattletale and told this story to Mother, she sighed. "He must get that kind of talk down around the stages with the fishermen. He certainly doesn't hear it in his home."

I often went to bed tired as a boy, but never troubled; that is, until a weekend when my childhood came to an abrupt end. I was told I would be starting school on Monday morning. The forbidding, two-storey gray building that housed St. Joseph's School on the upper floor was almost opposite my father's shop. In the carefree days, when I was a small child, I often saw the older boys and girls going and coming from the school, but gave the place no thought. Now I was suddenly being fitted out with a satchel, slate, slate pencils, a small bottle of water and a rag for wiping the slate. Without ceremony I had left childhood and entered into boyhood. From that weekend onwards, I could only look back with yearning to those fun filled and unorganized days that had gone before.

I would no longer be free to ride my tricycle up and down the lanes or under the flakes, to poke in the earth or ditches for worms, wander about the hills looking for blooms of mountain laurel, Labrador tea, cotton sedge and the pitcher plant to bring home to my mother, not free to go out in one of Dad's skiffs, to watch the men haul his traps in Baccalieu Tickle and the Bight, or play all morning with the rabbits in the hutch, from which they seemed to be forever escaping, not free to run with my dog in Uncle Dan's meadow, or paddle barefoot in the tiny brook near the barking kettle at the back of our carriage house, to make a visit to the chapel where everything was silence, incense and mystery, or to do any of the noisy, wild and wonderful things that had been childhood.

On the appointed Monday, holding tightly to my mother's hand, I remember being tugged up the steep staircase into an unknown future, where I was to get something called "an education." The room to which I was assigned took up half the upper floor space of the building, and was known as the Low End. The other half was called the High End. A charming child of six, or so I believed myself, I was abandoned by my mother into the welcoming hands of Master Noonan. Will John Noonan was not all that terrifying to me because his sister, Mary Ann (who afterwards married Jim Sullivan), had practically raised me from infancy, and I loved her very much. Although I must confess my first love was Emily Pryor, who came to work for my mother from Victoria village. I like to think I was one of Em's loves, too, at least until she met Arch Pryor, and left us to marry him. That was when Mary Ann entered my life. After Mary Ann there was Nellie Durdle from New Melbourne. I attended dear Nellie's funeral in St. John's in 1991. She was followed by more Noonans, Lucy and Alice, all of whom entered my life and my heart. Nellie did not stay long, but left to work for many years with my Uncle Mike and Aunt Kitty. Lucy, on the other hand, was with us for seven or eight years and was the longest serving housemaid we ever had.

On that fateful September morning, I found myself in a schoolroom surrounded by other boys and girls, all eager to become scholars. The place had windows on both sides and a blackboard along the front wall. There was a door in that wall leading to the mysterious High End, where senior pupils would disappear, a territory none of us tots in the Low End was ever bold enough to invade, but we did sometimes take a peek. Confronted by unfamiliar voices of children I didn't know, some in garments that were handed down and didn't properly fit their wearers, I looked into the stares of their blank, non-committal faces.

Most of my closest friends, being Protestant Emberlys, were in St. Barnabas's Church of England School across from the playground. My first day of school I hobbled, self-conscious in my tightly laced boots, to the desk Master Noonan assigned me. It was a long wooden space with four other beginners crowded on the bench. We small sufferers reached into our satchels, took out slates, and attempted to draw our ABCs, while the older classes were spelled, parsed, and led in chanting arithmetic tables, like members of a religious cult mumbling mindless prayers, "Twice one is two, twice two is four, twice four is eight..." The boy who answered seven, with a knowing smirk, was smartly boxed about the ears and his smirk dissolved in tears. That experience taught me our gentle Master Noonan would tolerate no frivolity. I gaped at the huge maps and posters on the walls, stared incomprehensibly at words and sums chalked on the blackboard, and looked down at the wooden desk in front of me, a desk on which generations of scholars had carved their names with penknives, including, I was afterwards to discover, my own father.

My gaze often floated out the open window to where the sun played ever so invitingly on the grassy hillside above

St. Barnabas's school, and I would hear the voices of children singing through the open windows. Hearing horse hooves and cart wheels pass by on the roadway, I wondered if it was our shoreman, Steve Barrett, going somewhere with Prince tackled to the long cart, or the boxcar for coals, and I wasn't with him anymore. A dog barked at the horse. That set my Aunt Kitty's hens squawking in her garden next to the school. I wouldn't be helping her gather the eggs that morning, as I often did in earlier days. Nor would I go running helter-skelter down the hill like I used to, to tell my mother the latest news Aunt Kitty heard on Uncle Mike's crystal set regarding the kidnapping of aviator Charles Lindbergh's baby. Although I was only a young boy, living in the isolation of Bay de Verde at the time, I knew from overhearing my parents talk of him who Charles Lindbergh was.

In the den, we had a tall RCA Victorola that took up a corner of the room, and the small portable gramophone which my mother had bought in New York City. One of the favourite recordings John and I played on the gramophone, after winding it, was called "Lucky Lindy," which told how "Lucky Lindy flew all alone / in a little plane of his own." On the flip side was "The Eagle of the USA," a song which suggested "Others may take this trip across the sea//Upon some future day//But take your hats off to plucky, lucky Lindy//The Eagle of the USA." Even when she was an old lady, Mother liked to recall the day I came running down the hill from Aunt Kitty's and rushed excitedly into the house, shouting the news, "Mom, Mom, Lindbergh's baby is found!"

About the only plus I could see to this school business was that I would no longer have to perform the hated daily chore of "going for the milk." That had meant interrupting play every day, in mid-morning, so I could take a large jug over to Mrs. Sutton's house and bring back fresh cow's milk, which was immediately scalded to kill any germs it might have. In future, "going for the milk "would be the chore of that free spirit, my little brother.

The evening of my first day at school, when my father asked how it had gone, I complained I did not get the present. He wanted to know what present I was talking about. I said, the one Master Noonan promised he would give me. Dad was very puzzled, and wanted to know when the Master had promised to give me a present. I said, "When he sat me down at the desk and told me to sit there for the present." I sat there all day but never got the present.

School days! Were they ever golden rule days? Do you remember learning to accept your fate, to shout and yell when turned loose, to pull and punch with the best of them in the playground? Our school playground was a very old cemetery with tilted headstones, down which we would slide during recess, the names of most of those buried beneath long since erased by time and the elements. Sometimes we played hide and seek among them.

It didn't take me long to find out I could get a few minute's respite from the scratch of nibs in copying books and the scrape of pencils on slates as we wrote endless declensions of verbs or the monotonous chanting of arithmetic tables if I raised my hand and asked to leave the room. No explanation was ever asked for since there was only one place to go, the two-door outhouse with HIS on one side and HERS on the other which stood among the gravestones in the school yard. You had to go downstairs and leave the school building to reach it. Sometimes, when you got outside the door for a breath of fresh air, you met up with an older boy, a senior scholar from the High End, using his few minutes of freedom to lean boldly against the outhouse wall, pull a pack of Bugler tobacco from his pocket, and nonchalantly roll it into a cigarette. You watched hypnotically as he lit and puffed right in front of your wondering eyes. You had to admire the bravado of these lads. Such was the stuff of heroes. It was many years before we learned cancer wasn't just a Tropic, like Capricorn, but a deadly disease caused by smoking. I recall sometimes, two or three of us would sneak unnoticed into the boys' side of the privy. There we would wait quietly until we heard some girls enter on their side, twittering among themselves. After a minute or two we would suddenly shriek loudly, while pounding on the partition with our fists. This would put the girls to flight, and send them fluttering back to school, squealing in dismay, like a flock of alarmed seagulls.

Since schoolwork was proving more than I could cope with, I decided to fall back on the time honoured escape of the schoolboy and "mooch," or what is today called "playing hooky." I recall it was a lovely, sunny morning in late September, no day to be indoors in a stuffy two-room schoolhouse. With cunning foresight I hid my three-wheel cycle under our verandah and marched off up the lane, my satchel on my back. When I was hidden from view by Mr. Broderick's house, I sidled into our shop meadow through a loose picket and doubled back to where my tricycle lay concealed by steps. Without a care in the world I hid my books and set off hurriedly under the flakes, across the harbour, to make some morning calls, as I used to do in earlier times. In those days, every elderly woman in the community was Aunt Somebody-or-other, and her husband Uncle Whoever. We children entered houses after knocking on the door, sat in silence on a wooden settle by the cast iron wood-and-coal stove, and spoke only when spoken to. If a slice of molasses bread, or a figgy bun, was not soon forthcoming, we took our leave, saying, "We must be off," while Aunt So-and-So, without looking up from her chores, invariably said "Time enough," as we headed for the door.

On the first morning I decided to mooch from school, I rode off on my tricycle, under the flakes as the roadway was called, past Eliza Moore's house, to call on Aunt Missy, the widow of my mother's uncle, Tom Moore, my grandmother Flynn's brother. Aunt Missy expressed her surprise when she saw me standing in her kitchen so early in the day. She wondered why I wasn't in school. I informed her we had a holiday, barely knowing what the word meant. She thought it strange since she saw many children go by her kitchen window with their satchels. She leaned over and whispered something into the ear of Bride North, a young relative who lived with her. Bride, who was later to live in our house in Bay de Verde as the wife of Joe Broderick, left the kitchen. I was in high hopes she had been told to fetch me a slice of homemade bread from the pantry and spread it with jam or molasses.

I paid no heed when I saw Bride go past the window and head up the hill instead of taking the much shorter route under the flakes. If I thought it strange, I probably figured she was out of molasses and was going to my father's shop to have more drained from the huge wooden puncheon kept in the back store. A born talker I prattled on, giving Aunt Missy what news I had collected. Because I was keeping up my endless line of chatter, I failed to notice Bride returning until she entered the kitchen. When I looked up, my jaw fell. Behind her the unmistakable shape of my father loomed in the doorway. I was in shock, betrayed by Aunt Missy.

It never crossed my mind that my dear old great-aunt was capable of such an action. Crestfallen and humbled, I was chastised by my father who took me by the scruff of my neck and hurried me out the door. I was frog-marched across the harbour and up to the schoolhouse. When told of my crime, all Master Noonan did was close the door behind my father, tut-tut to himself and usher me to my seat. Perhaps he felt my freckled face, a blushing mask of shame, was punishment enough. It was several days before I found the courage to return to Aunt Missy's after school and retrieve my tricycle. I was determined not to forgive her for her act of betrayal, but when she smiled warmly, and gave me a couple of raisin buns, hot from the oven, I just had to forgive her, although I said nothing. I have no recollection of my parents taking any action. They undoubtedly knew my rebellion against schooling had been nipped in the bud. I did mooch again, several times, but by then I was older and living in St. John's, as well as a more sophisticated player of the game. My ill-starred act of truancy in Bay de Verde was not without one dividend. It seemed to go down well with my schoolmates, and brought me several new friends among the boys and girls. Because I was painfully shy, and found great difficulty in making new friends, I'm sure they previously thought me stuck-up. The word snob was not yet in our vocabulary. I imagine my defiance of the system, by mooching, showed me in a different light. One they understood.

Although I learned my ABCs from my mother and nursemaid Paula Moore, at home, and how to read the time on the face of a clock from my father, I was to prove a disappointing scholar over the years. In time I was able to memorize such chants as,"twelve inches — one foot, three feet — one yard" and "two pints — one quart, four quarts — one gallon," to say nothing of bushels, pecks, roods, furlongs and perches, but I hated anything to do with arithmetic, although my father was a whiz at it, and afterwards my brother was also. As for those cursed times-tables on the back of our exercise books, I developed an aversion to adding, subtracting, multiplying and dividing that has stayed with me all my life. Later, in my C.H.E. (Council of Higher Education) examinations, I was to earn the lowest marks ever given in Newfoundland for Algebra and Geometry – Zero! It's too bad there wasn't a booby prize.

While I was able to idle away my first year in school, drawing, making things out of paper, learning hymns and other songs, all that soon changed. In my second year at St. Joseph's my little brother John joined me as a pupil. My parents could now threaten, "If you don't shape up, he'll catch up," which he did in time, as I never really did "shape up." Whenever I tried to bully him a little in the school yard, just so he'd know who was still boss, it wasn't long before he learned to use a threat of his own, "Lay off, or I'll tell Master Noonan." Once, when I wanted the chore of pouring ink from the big bottle into the inkwells on the desks, John beat me to it. I poked him angrily in the side with my elbow. He told me to lay off or he would tell the teacher. I called his bluff with another poke. It was an unfortunate miscalculation. Master Noonan sent me to sit on a high stool, facing the wall in a corner of the classroom, where I was left for half an hour to contemplate the folly of my aggression. I finally had to accept what my parents often told me at home: the world was not my oyster but one I would have to share with others.

During that second year of school in Bay de Verde I did something that was to forever change my life, and decide my future career. A concert was staged in the parish hall, on the ground floor of our schoolhouse building, by adults and children. My cousin Cyril, who was in the High End, took part in the show. Uncle Mike and Aunt Kitty were in the audience, but had no idea what Cyril would be doing. He appeared on stage wearing his mother's long evening dress, a false bosom, and hat with long feathers, singing in falsetto, "I'm Only a Bird in a Guilded Cage." As they say, he brought down the house, but I remember Mother turning to Dad as we were leaving the auditorium and saying, "Kitty will murder him when she gets him home tonight."

The thing about that evening's concert, which so affected my life afterwards, was that I was making my first theatrical appearance. The rolled canvas curtain on the stage was pulled up, and there I stood, all alone. Feeling full of self-confidence, instead of the nervousness of a debut, I recited a poem by Edgar A. Guest, "A Boy and His Dog." From the moment I bowed low afterwards, and heard that first exhilarating applause wash over me from the audience, acting was in my blood, and eventually theatre, in one form or another, became my life's work.

Life as a boy or girl in Bay de Verde in the '30s was never dull or routine. As growing boys, my brother and I found every day was packed with new adventure. When we were small we would often ramble off over the hills on summer afternoons with Aunt Fanny Cotter, and the Brodericks' dear old dog, Frisk, hoping to catch a glimpse of the elfin fairies as they sat on their toadstools and danced in the glen. Aunt Fanny always waved and called to them. There were trips out to the collar when skiffs were being moored, tom cods to be caught on trout hooks from stage heads, with fish hearts for bait, and hay to be jumped in each fall as soon as the men scythed the grass in Uncle Dan's field or the shop meadow and pulled it into hayricks. After it was carted to the stable, and pitch-forked up into the loft, we would get the key on wet days, sneak into the stable when Prince was out in the fields, and jump from the hay loft down into the manger. Eventually, my father would enter his fish store, which was next door, hear our shrieks of joy, and come to drive us out, muttering about the horse having to eat the hay after we were finished thrashing about in it with dirty boots and sneakers.

On fine days we would sometimes slip into a rodney tied to a stage, let go of the painter (a tow rope up front) and scull about the harbour, until we spied our frantic mother on the edge of the flake in front of our house, waving and calling for us to come in, because we couldn't swim. Other times, when we saw a schooner's sails coming around the point, we would race to the public wharf to see if any apples, oranges or lemonade were being unloaded from the hold of Josiah Blundon's schooner *Dorothy B*, or Oliver Blundon's *Josie F.* Some sunny days we would ride our bikes to Middle Ridge where nearly all the boys and some of the men skinny-dipped. The pond was a sort of community swimming pool where none existed. On other days we would tackle Prince to the old carriage and go to Island Pond where we sailed John's sailboat.

Some evenings, before or after supper, we drove with Uncle Mike in his car, or Dad in his, to Rocky Pond for an hour or two of trouting before dark, using worms we dug up for bait, and bamboo trouting poles. Other evenings, for want of something better to do, we would amble down the steep hill to my father's cod liver oil factory and watch Steve

Barrett reduce the bubbling vats of smelly livers to oil. It would nearly turn John's and my stomachs inside out when Steve would dip up some fresh oil and taste it to see if it was ready for processing. Nearby were huge puncheons of stinking blubber left over from decomposing cod livers which were hung in canvas bags above the open puncheons. Among the dripping oil we sometimes played hide and seek. That almost came to disaster in later years when my little cousin, Cyril's son John, fell through the lid of one of the puncheons, up to his neck in thick blubber, and nearly drowned. His mother Nellie stripped off his clothes in their garden where they were burned, and she had to thoroughly scrub his skin to get rid of the stench before she could let him in the house.

By the time I was in Grade Three we wintered in various rented quarters in St. John's, returning home to Bay de Verde each spring until 1936 when Dad bought a house in town for our use in winter. How I looked forward to coming back to my own bedroom in the old house when school let out at the end of June, because in the city I had to share a bedroom with my brother. As I grew into my teens I was especially fond of wandering out on my father's flakes, opposite our house in Bay de Verde at sunset. I would sit alone on one of the faggots, which was the name given to piles of salt fish that had been spread out to dry on a flake. I would gaze out over the harbour watching the schooners, skiffs and rodneys tug at their moorings as they rode the evening swell. There I could think what one poet called "the long, long thoughts of youth," interrupted sometimes by the put-put cough of one-lung engines, as punts came back late in the day from hauling the trap or squid jigging in the Bight. At times a chapel bell would sound in the distance, signalling women in the harbour to come with buckets and brushes to scrub the floor of one or other of the two churches, Assumption Catholic or St. Barnabas Church of England.

In my bedroom, sitting on my father's flakes or rambling the barrens alone on my bike, in the long, lustrous, summer afternoons of youth, I would read book-of-the-month club selections, borrowed from Nellie, Cyril's wife, write poems and stories, and invent the person I became. Later in life, when I embraced other places such as New York and London, Bay de Verde was forever printed indelibly on that corner of my mind where the truth of childhood lies. While I did not realize it at the time, I was beginning to emerge as a writer.

Black people in the United States have a saying, "Man get older – sin get bolder," and as we got older it proved true. The temptations that led us to blot our religious copy books were such chocolate delights as sugary union squares, snowballs, dolly delights and chocolate men. I remember those chocolate men, all gooey and filled with a pink creamy substance. At the end of the main counter in my father's shop there was a glassed-in candy case, full of tempting candies and chocolate bars. It was strictly off limits to my brother and me on pain of more than just sin. If we were caught falling prey to temptation, which often happened, our stealing could mean bed without supper. Sometimes when the shop assistants, Maggie Noonan or her sister Rose, were distracted by a customer, and the store manager Jimmy Jacobs wasn't perched on his accounting stool, peeping into the shop through a hidden window beside his desk, it was possible to slip a banner caramel or a chocolate mouse into your mouth and be out the door before anyone knew what you were up to. However, for most chocolate delights we depended on another beloved friend, Gus Barter, who saved my mother's life when she had the miscarriage. My memories of Gus Barter go back to when she was Augusta Blundon.

I recall one specific red February dawn, in the winter of 1934, a blustery morning, when my father loaded Mother, John and me, into Oliver Blundon's trap skiff for a trip across Conception Bay to St. John's. Both Oliver's sisters, Gus and Eva, were on board. He used a canvas to rig up a shelter from the wind for us in the bow of the skiff. To keep us warm, he erected a small coal stove, known as a "bogie" inside the shelter, with a funnel to carry off the smoke. As we made our way across the bay, a winter gale blew in from the Atlantic and the sea became quite loppy. Mother had the foresight to bring along an empty Chase & Sanborn coffee can for John and me to throw up our insides in when we got seasick, which was often that day. Even now, when I think of how seasick I was, I get green at the gills.

Gus, being an angel of mercy, used to wash out the can each time we used it until a wave tore it out of her hand. From then on we had to throw up over the gunwales. The rising wind tore the canvas awning away and sent it flying across Conception Bay. A huge wave broke over the bow and knocked down the funnel, dousing the fire in the stove. That evening, when three deathly pale and totally disheveled travellers appeared at the door of Grandmother's house on Wood Street, the startled old lady made the sign of the cross on herself. "Sacred Heart, Jose!" she exclaimed. "You must be cracked to cross the bay in an open boat on a day like this in the dead of winter with those two small boys!"

Gus set aside a little room in her house near the Catholic Church as a shop. Among the things she sold were assorted sweets and chocolate bars. In those days, a fish was as good as money. My brother and I had a miniature, child-size hand-barrow Dad had made for us. A hand-barrow was a flat wooden frame with handles at each end for two men to carry codfish or anything else. With my cousin Margaret Buckingham, who came out from St. John's to spend several summers with us, we would take that barrow and wander about under our flakes looking for fish that had fallen through. We sometimes encouraged their passage through the longers by prodding them from beneath. When we had a yaffle we would take them to Gus and swap them for candy and bars. After all these years I must cleanse my soul by confessing we were sometimes aided and abetted in these petty thefts by an adult accomplice. My father's brother, our dear, ne'er-do-well Uncle Dan, would send us under the flakes and drop a few nicely cured cod from my father's flake or fish store down to us on condition we tell no one. He probably got more fun out of seeing us scurry off across the harbour to Gus's shop, where the pilfered fish became jawbreakers, licorice sticks, Jumbo Bars, Turkish Delights, Butterfingers or Graham Sandwiches. I don't know if Gus ever realized she was fencing stolen property.

If I mention my boyhood, in what was for me a place of enchantment, it is because, I hope you, with your own memories, will be able to look back in wonder at what was lost with innocence. Growing older we found our Newfoundland is at best a turbulent Eden, a place where one must forever cope with the onslaughts of nature and its daunting effect on those who live there. Its heritage is largely rural. For centuries our people spent much of their lives fishing its spectacular coastline. Perhaps because survival was such an elemental battle, "going home," revisiting familiar points of reference etched forever on our lives, is always one of the most moving experiences a Newfoundlander or Labradorian can have.

Bay de Verde was certainly no place for romantic empathy. It has gotten some very bad press from its many critics over the years. My father had an uncle who used to say the place was habitable only under duress. Rev. Oliver Rouse, who was Church of England parson there for twenty-three years, from 1846 until his death in 1869, wrote in his journal, that when he told the St. John's merchant Robert Prowse that Bishop Feild was posting him to Bay de Verde, Prowse exclaimed; "Oh, but you must not go there. It is a perfect hell upon earth." The parson's daughter, Jane Rouse, who grew up there, certainly exaggerated when she wrote a friend that Bay de Verde (Portuguese for Green Bay) "was surely wrongly named, for there is not a blade of grass in the place." My great-grandfather, in the year of his death, 1883, was visited by a nephew from New Jersey. I have in my possession a letter that nephew, a Dr. O'Neill, wrote his uncle from New York. The doctor said of Bay de Verde, "Uncle

Tom, how could you settle in such a God-forsaken place?"

But in the end, does it matter how lonesome this little serrated valley of rock, how foreboding the cliffs, how wild the seas? The truth is, none of us can ever completely walk away from the past we have accumulated in the place we called "home" as the very word is remarkable for the intensity of its images. It is in the burning emotions of "home" that we find a part of ourselves. The thing we have lost is childhood, that irretrievable time before we were tussled and twisted into what we helplessly remain for the rest of our lives. I think most of us have lived long enough to realize all that we have accomplished, as well as all that we have failed to accomplish — our outward triumphs and our inner turmoil — were shaped as children between these hills. If any of us should ever hope to make sense of the disorientation we call life, we will do so only by identifying ourselves with "home," that special place where the roots go deep.

To say the two churches in Bay de Verde are over 100 years old is merely to state a fact. But to say St. Barnabas and Assumption churches have been at the core of family life in the community for 100 years is to say they have molded the lives of people so deeply their influence can never be undone. Life in this world may be only a great dream, but the quality of that dream depends on how we learn to absorb the shocks of living, and the lessons of faith, the substance of things hoped for, the acceptance of things not seen.

When my brother and I were growing up, almost all our friends were Church of England, Emberley friends and neighbours from the Point: Arch, Johnny, Mervyn, Dulcie, Myrthis, Virtue, Viola, also Billy and Phyllis, whose father, Bob Emberley, was the Church of England sexton, as well as manager of my Uncle Mike's shop. We were hardly even aware we attended different churches on Sunday, which is as it should be in a community where people of differing faiths must live together. My father often told me that, as a boy, two of his closest friends were Church of England, Arthur Emberley and Moses Blundon. Until a few years ago

I had in my possession a beautiful bookcase-desk made in Bay de Verde for my father by Rev. Max Way, who served St. Barnabas as rector from 1925 to 1928. He was a master craftsman when it came to furniture making and the desk he turned out for my father is today a valuable item among collectors of Newfoundland-made furniture. I did not want it to go out of the family so I gave it to my nephew, James.

I am ashamed to say it, but until Vatican II, Roman Catholics had to ask their priest's permission to attend a religious service in a church of another faith. My father, however, always attended the weddings and funerals of Church of England friends in Bay de Verde without ever asking permission. I recall him one time saying, "The Almighty has more important things on His mind than spying on me to see what church I enter." When his own time came to die, he left in his will a sum of money to Rev. William Gill and the Church of England parishioners to be distributed each year at Christmas among the needy of St. Barnabas parish. A similar gift was made to the incumbent of Assumption Church until it, too, ran out. Like George Santayana, he believed all his life, and taught my brother and me to believe, "What religion a man shall have is a historic accident, quite as much as what language he shall speak."

Time passes with a swiftness that has no sound, like a leaf turning or a flower fading. The years flow unhindered, distance lending them loneliness until little is remembered of the distant past but the place called home. Like children sitting in darkness on a staircase, watching a little pool of light spill beneath the door, we hear the voices and the laughter on the other side, but know we can never cross the threshold.

The American writer, Thomas Wolfe, in his great novel *You Can't Go Home Again*, sums up the experience of attempting to do so in these words: "Time passing as men pass who will never come back again ... and leaving us, Great God, with only this ... knowing that this earth, this time, this life, are stranger than a dream."

Chapter 6

Knocking at the Door

My father often said, when he was sent to St. Bonaventure's College in St. John's in the late 1890s as a boarding student, the day-pupils had a poem they used to shout at him: "Bay boy! Bay boy! Come to your supper / Two cods heads and a lump of butter." When we moved to St. John's for the school year, education became a bit more complicated. John and I entered St. Bon's, an all-grade school taught by the Irish Christian Brothers, as day students. We were living in a house my father bought on Cochrane Street facing Colonial Street. My brother went into Grade One while I went into Grade Three having done grades one and two in Bay de Verde and even a winter in kindergarten at Our Lady of Mercy Academy in St. John's with Miss Eleanor Coady whose maternal family, the O'Keefes of Harbour Grace, were O'Neill first and second cousins.

My teacher in Grade Three at St. Bon's was Brother Strapp, one of the Strapp's Drugstore people from Harbour Grace, longtime friends of the O'Neill family. I remember on certain Sundays when we were living in Bay de Verde, we would be invited up to the Strapps' for supper. Outport families often visited each other on the Lord's Day. I had no inkling then that the Strapp who had become a Christian Brother would turn on me one day in class when I was talking to my desk partner. A hand suddenly came out of nowhere, struck me in the side of the head and sent me flying into the wall. I was stunned for a few seconds before realizing I had outraged Brother Strapp, who I didn't know was standing behind my desk when I broke his commandment not to talk. It was the only time I felt brutalized at St. Bon's by a Brother.

I went home and told my mother what happened and that I was afraid to go back to school. She said, "You go back to school tomorrow morning and I'll be up to see Brother Strapp." Needless to say I was on edge all morning, especially when a knock came on the door. The boy sitting in the front desk opposite the door went out, came back and said, "Brother, there's a woman out there wants to see you." Strapp looked puzzled and commanded us to keep on doing what we were doing as he went to the door. We heard the voices of a man and woman in argument. Then to my horror the door opened, the Brother appeared, and with his right index finger signalled for me to come towards him. When I went out, the door closed and I faced Brother Strapp and my mother in a small hallway.

He opened the conversation by saying, "I have never struck a boy in my life, Mrs. O'Neill, and I am sure Paul will not say I struck him." Mother answered, "I didn't come here to argue with you, Brother, but to tell you if you strike my son again, I am going straight to the Archbishop and tell him why I want you transferred out of this school." Without hesitation she left Brother Strapp agog and took me with her to lunch. That was the only teacher problem I was ever to have at St. Bon's. Some of the Brothers who taught me became lifelong friends, such as Brothers Kane, Darcy, English and Murphy.

Brother Kane taught English literature and it is to his inordinate knowledge of the subject that I owe much of my interest and career in writing. In our literature anthology there was a short story by Victor Hugo, "Jean Valjean and the Bishop," from *Les Miserables*, which inspired me to become a writer in my own high school years. Some years later, when I was living and working in London, a new musical opened in the West End. The story was based on Hugo's *Les Mis*. I went to see it with some friends and we were all totally amazed at what we saw on stage. To this day, it stands out in my memory as the greatest stage musical I ever saw. Watching it took me back to school days when I sat spellbound as a boy while Brother Kane read us "Jean Valjean and the Bishop."

I recall frequent suppers at Mr. and Mrs. Green's in Heart's Content, the Marchs' in Northern Bay, the Moores' in Carbonear, the Hopkins' in Old Perlican, the Quinlans' in Red Head Cove, and Dr. Short's in Hant's Harbour. The Moores' house in Carbonear had a beautiful stair railing which I remember my brother John, Frank Moores' sister Meghan and I used to get a great kick out of sliding down. Meghan always insisted on being the first to slide down the banister. Another group we enjoyed meeting with in Harbour Grace was the Olsen family. In turn, most of these people came as guests for a meal at our house in Bay de Verde and afterwards in St. John's.

I remember one evening, when we were living all year in Bay de Verde, probably in the mid-'30s, I was awakened in the middle of the night to the sound of ferocious winds and excited chatter. When I got up out of bed I put on my dressing gown and headed downstairs to see what all the action was about. There were strange men standing around in the hallway, the kitchen and the parlour (the word living room had yet to come into fashion). It turned out they were the captain and some of the crew of a schooner that had run ashore in the Bight, a bend in the coast which formed a small bay from which there was no exit. It appeared the captain had mistaken the Bight for the passageway between Bay de Verde and Baccalieu Island. My father was busy arranging places for the crew to stay overnight while attempts were being made to refloat the schooner. The captain stayed in the spare room at our house. I have no memory of him or his crew departing but I do know that when I got up the next day, all were gone. It's too bad my mother didn't man the cookhouse bell that night as she had done once before during a storm.

One night in the early to mid-1930s, Mother awoke to find a terrible storm raging. She got up and looked out the window. In the harbour, she saw hurricane winds washing boats off their collars and onto the rocks. After she shook my father awake, she dressed quickly, ran down to the cook-house in the middle of the night and vigorously rang the bell, awakening the sleeping townspeople, who rushed to save their boats and stages. Next day, Dad took pictures of schooners in distress, one with a broken spar, being swept ashore. Mother liked to claim, in after years, had it not been for her, the damage to property would have been much greater.

As I advanced in age and experience I continued to live the kind of enchanted life I always imagined myself living. I used to think how fortunate I was, living the exciting life of a bay boy in summer and a city slicker the rest of the year. Many of my most enjoyable holiday experiences in Bay de Verde did not take place in the community at all but on the sandy beach in Northern Bay, the Northern Bay Sands as they are known. I remember going to the Sands years later with some friends one summer's day to find the beach a mess of papers and bottles from end to end and rock and roll music being played loud enough to deafen you. I was so angered at seeing this beautiful place, where I spent many happy hours from childhood, in such disarray. When I came back to St. John's, I wrote Premier Joseph Smallwood a letter suggesting the beach and surroundings at Northern Bay be turned into a provincial park so that a stop could be put to the destruction of such a wonderful space. I received a letter from the Premier, which I still have, dated 25 August 1964, stating, "I would like to thank you for the interest you have taken in behalf of Northern Bay Sands. I am having your suggestion that the sands be made into a provincial park looked into by the officials concerned as I think it has great merit. Yours sincerely." There followed the sprawling signature of J.R. Smallwood. When I met him sometime later at a government function, he told me he had turned over my letter to Cabinet Minister William Keough and he would see that Northern Bay Sands was soon declared a provincial park by the Lieutenant-Governor in Council. I am glad to say he was true to his word.

One of the things I liked to do down home in summer was lie in the hammock on our verandah and read from my father's collection of books. At the end of my Grade Seven and the beginning of my Grade Eight year, I began to develop a serious interest in reading. I was twelve or thirteen years old at the time. Those long days of summer lead me to begin a hunt for adult reading matter. I soon found an 1890 novel, *The Bondman,* by Sir Hall Caine, who had been knighted because of his fame as a writer. The book was purchased by my father in London for the price of 12/6 during his 1925 visit to Europe. It was a literary masterpiece, although today Caine's novels are considered outdated by devotees of English literature, and despite his immense popularity during his life, he is now virtually unknown as well as unremembered. In his time he was exceedingly popular, and at the peak of his success his novels outsold those of most of his contemporaries. *The Bondman* was the first adult novel that ever really interested me, especially because Iceland was an unusual setting for a love story. Having read the novel, I was inspired by Caine's work to try writing a book myself. What I produced were four exercise books with four short novels. I have kept my father's copy of *The Bondman* with me down through many years as it has become dear to my heart.

When we were in our teens, the '40s was the big band era in popular music. In those days, band leaders such as the brothers Dorsey, Tommy and Jimmy, Harry James, Glen Miller, etc. were often better known than their singers. One leader who brought his band to St. John's after the war, to the excitement of almost every young person in the city, was Louis Armstrong. He gave a concert at the old Memorial Stadium on the shores of Quidi Vidi Lake. The first headliner or major star to come to St. John's, in my lifetime, and appear at the USO for the amusement of American Armed Forces, was Joan Blondell. At the time she was married to the popular singer and Hollywood star Dick Powell. Miss Blondell became involved in a big local controversy when she went back to Hollywood and appeared on the popular weekly radio show for American Armed Forces, "Command Performance." She sang a song she learned while in St. John's called "The Newfoundland Express," about a man who decides to commit suicide and ties himself to the railway tracks so the train can run over him. He waits so long for the train that he starves to death. When Blondell sang it in a broadcast over the American Forces stations around the world, there were a number of Newfoundlanders who failed to see the humour in the song. They deluged Joan Blondell with letters claiming outrage, so much so that she wrote a letter to the *Evening Telegram* stating she was sorry and had no intention of offending people by singing the song, which she found very humourous. I was one of those who wrote telling her not to be upset and asking if she would kindly send me an autographed photo. Some weeks later I received a 5x7 envelope in the mail which contained a photograph of her and Dick Powell. Both had signed their names but she added, "To the O'Neill boy with my warmest wishes." I treasured that photo for many years but it has long since disappeared.

The biggest name among celebrities to come to St. John's in the war years was Frank Sinatra, the world's top male singing star. He visited the city in 1945 on a USO tour. At the time I was a member of the British Frank Sinatra Fan Club. It published a quarterly magazine in which I wrote a column about goings on in Hollywood. Later that year Sinatra arranged a USO tour to American troops in Europe, accompanied by tour mates Phil Silvers, who had just married Jo-Carroll Dennisson, a former Miss America 1942; Fay McKenzie, a star of B pictures who was married briefly to Steve Cochran, the Warner Brothers tough-guy actor who mysteriously died at sea in 1965; the pianist Saul Chaplin (later a great name in American film music); and a female contortionist, Betty Yeaton, an acrobatic dancer who could twist her body into all sorts of shapes. After rehearsing in New Jersey, the tour left to visit American bases overseas. Its first stop was in Newfoundland where a concert was given by the troupe in the USO Building on Merrymeeting Road. With my brother and several friends, we tried to gain admission to the show in the USO building's auditorium but, without servicemen escorts, we were turned away at the door.

Never known to take no for an answer, our small gang went around to the side of the building looking for an open door. Instead we found an open window, about twenty feet from the stage and fifteen feet above ground. We used a stepladder to pile some empty wooden crates against the wall, climbed on them, and from our "box seats" watched the entire performance. Afterwards, I wrote one of my fan letters to Sinatra, spilling out my ecstasy at having seen him perform in the flesh, or what little there was of it in those days. To my amazement I received a personally signed 5x7 photograph and a note from his secretary saying how much he had enjoyed his visit to Newfoundland. I wrote back to his secretary, Marjorie Divan, who assisted me in establishing a Fans of Sinatra Pen Club. Over the next three or four years, Marge put me in touch with a number of pen friends. Through her club I developed three close female friends, Beverly, Irma and Ellen, in New York, and one close male friend, Brian, who lived in New Jersey. After going to New York myself in order to attend drama school, I met all four of them, but only Ellen and Brian became a part of my life for some years to come.

Speaking of being a part of my life, nothing I did in childhood has become as much a part of me as the songs we sang. The first popular song I remember hearing was at my Uncle Mike's house. One sunny afternoon his son Bren, my first cousin thirty years my senior, took me into their house and had me sit beside him on the piano stool while he played songs he had learned at the University of Kingston, where he had obtained his medical degree. The song I especially remember him playing on Aunt Kitty's piano one summer's day in 1936 was "Red Sails in the Sunset." Published in 1935, it was made famous that year on a recording by Bing Crosby with Guy Lombardo's orchestra. Lyricist Jimmy Kennedy, known as the Irish troubadour, came from Ireland's causeway coast where his home was Portstewart. It would in later years be the inspiration behind some of his most famous songs. "Red Sails in the Sunset" harks back to the days of his childhood. The listener is invited to share in Kennedy's memory of a blissful summer's day when he watched a small yacht lazily wend its way westward towards the setting sun. I did, indeed, share the memory of a blissful summer's day in Bay de Verde where Bren not only played but sang "Red Sails in the Sunset," trying to teach me the words. My favourite song at the time was the hit "Three Little Fishies." It was enormously popular way back when. We loved to sing the chorus:

> Down in the meadow in a little bitty pool
> Swam three little fishies and a mama fishie too.
> "Swim" said the mama fishie, "Swim if you can"
> And they swam and they swam all over the dam.

Having been born in 1883, my father was a teenager during the second Boer War and 19 years old when it ended. He loved to sing many of the songs of that war and taught some of them to my brother and me, especially the two biggest hits, a military tune, "Marching to Pretoria "and a sentimental ballad, "Good-bye Dolly Gray." Although "Dolly Gray" gained widespread world fame during the Boer War, it had earlier been sung in the Spanish-American War of 1898 and returned once more to popularity with the onset of the First World War in 1914. Mother, too, had her favourite songs from the war of 1914-1918 when she was a teenager, and they included such immortal melodies as "Till

We Meet Again," and one she always loved to sing, "Roses of Picardy."

Not only did our parents give us a background in music, but as I have indicated they led us into the world of the printed word, books and magazines. It was about that time, pen in hand, I began what was to become a life-long involvement with writing. My first literary endeavour was to create a character in the mode of Nancy Drew and the Hardy Boys, two series of books almost every teenager read from cover to cover in those days. The Hardy Boys appeared first, in 1927, followed by Nancy Drew in 1930, but both were equally popular. In fact, John and I collected full sets of Hardy Boys and Nancy Drew books. I decided to base the first of my books on a teenaged female detective named Sadie Young, because I felt at the time a girl would have more popularity in print than a boy. These novels, each one written to fill a school exercise book, were illustrated with photos cut out of my parent's magazines. I read them to a few selected schoolmates in my home when we were on our way back from school in the afternoons. I would invite the boys into my house and read what I had written the night before. Between the spring of 1942 and autumn of 1944, I wrote four novels entitled "Sadie Young in the Tourist Cabin Mystery," "Sadie Young and the Professor's Secret," "Sadie Young and the Seagull Cliffs Mystery," and Sadie Young and the Missing Fortune." A fifth book, "Sadie Young in the Silver Creek Mystery," must forever remain unfinished. By the time I started work on it I had grown a couple of years older and was fast losing interest in Miss Young's adventures.

In any case, I had developed a new preoccupation that was quite demanding. I was beginning to spend weekends and evenings after completing my homework running my movie house. It was a cardboard box with two eye-holes in the back above the entrance and a screen at the front of the box with a large slit on either side. The movies were all handdrawn on rolled up paper and pulled through the screen from left to right allowing time for a pen-and-ink "audience" seated inside the box with their backs to the peepholes, while supposedly watching and reading the screen, while someone on the outside looking in did likewise. This may sound like a very primitive form of movie-making and showing, but it led me to an acting career in America and England which I have always treasured. To help advertise the films, I created a handwritten movie magazine with various columns as in a regular adult movie magazine from a drug store. None of these milestones from my youth would be available to me today were it not for my mother, who saved all my junk, including my Sadie Young books, my hand-drawn films, my movie house box and my self-written screen magazines.

My brother John was a sports enthusiast in our school days, but I was not. I enjoyed a football game or a hockey game as a spectator, but my real interest was in art and music. John had a beautiful baritone voice and in his days at Boston College, which were to come, he sang with the Boston College Glee Club. I made it into the St. Bonaventure's College Glee Club but our distinguished director, Ignatius Rumboldt, indicated to me I should only mouth the words of some of the more difficult music which I was unable to sing. That pleased me and I thoroughly enjoyed my years with the Glee Club. We could not have found a finer director than Mr. Rumboldt.

Ignatius Rumboldt was born in Curling, now part of Corner Brook, in 1916 and was sent as an orphan to Mount Cashel in St. John's at an early age, where some years later he became an organist and choir master. In the 1940s he took over that role at the Cathedral of St. John the Baptist, later to become the Basilica. "Nish" held a series of annual sacred and secular concerts and performed on VONF Radio (afterwards to become CBC) for many years and organized the Memorial University Glee Club. He was the organizer of the St. John's Extension Choir and Orchestra, touring his choral and orchestral group throughout the province as well as organizing the CJON Glee Club.

We found him a joy to work with and love to this day the songs he had us sing, such as "Old Man River," "Oh Shenandoah," "Land of Hope & Glory," and "Men of Harlech," the best known marshal air of Wales, played and sung throughout world. I can still hear the voices of our glee club gathered in the school's assembly hall, the Aula Maxima, singing; "With your valour you shall show men / How to vanquish Saxon foe-men …Cambria, God, and Right." In addition to marching tunes we sang many popular airs going back from our day to the turn of the century. Those of us who sang with Nish learned a love of music that has lasted all our lives.

I had the added pleasure of studying piano under Nish Rumboldt for about five years. I would leave school at 4 o'-clock when we all got out and make my way to his studio in the Imperial Optical Building on Duckworth Street just west of Church Hill. When I began taking lessons we did not have a piano at home so I would go to my grandmother's on Wood Street every day to practice. Later Mother bought a very nice piano at a house sale and I started in earnest to learn to play the instrument. A particular favourite of hers, which she asked me to play at least once a week when I was in the midst of my practice, was "Smoke Gets In Your Eyes," a hit from the 1935 Jerome Kern operetta *Roberta.* She heard it on the recording released two years later by Irene Dunne, a star she warmly supported. When I went to Hollywood in 1949, I attended a reception for out of work actors at Irene Dunne's home on Christmas Eve and had a long talk with her adopted daughter until Irene and her husband, Dr. Francis Griffin, came and joined us.

Around the time I was seven or eight years old, a poet was brought into my life by my mother, who truly loved the man's work. He was not really a poet in the modern sense of the word but a rhymester. On a visit to Montreal in the mid-'30s, she had purchased a book before coming home called *Rhymes of Childhood* by Edgar A. Guest. These rhymes became a part of my life and John's, as Mother read the poems every time she found an opportunity. I was in Grade Two when John and I were learning to recite these poems by heart.

St. Joseph's School, Bay de Verde was having a concert in the autumn of my sixth year. Our teacher, Master Noonan, asked John and me if we would each recite a poem from the stage. We were delighted and made our choices from Mother's book of Edgar Guest's rhymes. As I expected, John recited, "When the Soap Gets in Your Eye" which begins with the words "My father says that I ought to be / A man when anything happens to me," and four verses later ends with "But you got to yell till your face gets dry / Whenever the soap gets into your eye." My choice, of course, was "A Boy and His Dog." When the curtain opened on me for the very first time in my life, I was standing alone on stage in knee-pants with my little dog, Pal, sitting on the floor beside me. I began the poem: "A boy and his dog make a glorious pair / No better friendship is found anywhere..." and ended with the words "He sees the great soul which the body conceals / And it's great to be young with a dog at your heels." As the applause swept over me, I bowed my head and enjoyed those moments so much I think of them as the beginning of my theatrical career.

While I was in school, with John only one grade behind me, we became aware the *Evening Telegram* was publishing an Edgar A. Guest poem in its pages each day. My mother was in seventh heaven and I must confess John and I also enjoyed reading Guest's humorous verses. By then he was considered to be one of the best poets in America. Until his death in 1959, Guest penned some 11,000 poems which were syndicated in 300 newspapers and collected in more than 20 books, including my mother's *Rhymes of Childhood*. On the dedication page in the front of that book, the author had printed these words, "To the Little Mother who still watches through the window to see me come, this book is affectionately dedicated." In Mother's copy of the book, and only in her copy, the quotation is illustrated underneath by a crude pencil drawing of a woman looking out through a window exclaiming, "Edgar," while a man with a pointed beard and hat stands in front of a door adjoining the window, saying, "Mom." The artwork is primitive by any standard. When you read the signature of the artist you will understand why it states simply – PAUL. I must plead guilty to such boyhood nonsense. So much for Guest, a man who, in his time, was regarded as one of the finest American poets of his day. He is now all but forgotten. It seems fame, like time, quickly flies.

My parents, like many Catholic parents of the day, were what I would call quite religious. Besides having to say morning and night prayers which almost every child did, we also had to say the rosary as a family, the housemaid included, each night of our lives after supper. I must confess both John and I found this after-supper rosary a chore and often skittered and laughed to ourselves. In those days, everyone who could had dinner in the middle of the day. We were let out of school from 12:30 until 2 p.m. As soon as we moved to the city for the school terms, we were both enrolled as altar boys at the R.C. Cathedral and remained in that capacity until graduation.

A religious exercise in which the whole school took part was called the First Friday. It was reported that a 17th century nun, St. Margaret Mary Alacoque, had a vision in which Christ promised the nun that those who attended mass and took communion on the First Friday of nine consecutive months in an unbroken row would be instantly transported to Heaven after death instead of having to face judgment, and possibly even hell. It seemed a simple thing to do until you started and caught the flu, were out of town, or missed a First Friday for whatever reason, which meant you had to start all over again. I believe it took me three or four years before I was able to get to mass and communion on nine successive First Fridays. What a chore!

In 1941 St. John's was a city that was known for its fires, having suffered through three Great Fires in the previous century. St. John's was learning how to defend itself against incendiary fires begun by Nazi bombs, not that any German planes actually flew over St. John's, but it was a threat the people soon learned to live with as we were the first city anyone came to in North America after flying across the Atlantic from Europe. The tragedy of war was brought into our homes 12 December 1942. It was Saturday evening when everyone listened to a favourite local radio program called "Uncle Tim's Barn Dance," which came to listeners live on station VOCM, from the Knights of Columbus Military Hostel on Harvey Road. As the evening drew on, John and I were sent upstairs to bed. I chanced to look out through the Venetian blinds on the bathroom window when getting into my pajamas and saw a brilliant red sky near the top of Long's Hill. When I called for the maid, Alice Noonan, to come see it, she immediately identified the glow. "That's a fire somewhere near the cathedral. My God, I hope it's not the K. of C. Hostel. They're having a big dance up there tonight and a friend of mine from Bay de Verde is going." Sad to say, when the flames died out and the ashes were sifted through next morning, ninety-nine people were found to have died in the inferno, including the friend of Alice, Nellie Noonan, the twenty-one-year-old daughter of William Noonan and Margaret (Woodrow) of Bay de Verde where her remains were interred four days later.

I did not know Nellie Noonan but I had a close friend who also died in the K. of C. fire. Harry Walsh, a classmate of mine at St. Bon's, was in the Boy Scouts and volunteered most weekends to work in the cloakroom of the Knights of Columbus Hostel, taking and hanging up the belongings of soldiers, sailors, airmen, their wives and/or girlfriends who went there for the weekly dance. In the rush to escape from the burning building, Harry got caught in the cloakroom where he was overcome by smoke and smothered to death. In those days most wakes for the dead were held in people's homes, there being no funeral parlours as such in the city. After school the next afternoon, most of us trooped down to where Harry lived on Allandale Road. It was sad a day or two later to be walking behind our classmate's coffin to the church and cemetery for his burial. The K. of C. fire is remembered to this day as the greatest tragedy to take place in St. John's.

One of the most looked forward to events of my teen years were the community concerts, when some of the world's leading singers and instrumentalists would come to St. John's two or three times a year to perform on stage at St. Patrick's Hall Auditorium on Bonaventure Avenue. They included such highliners of the concert hall as Dorothy Maynor, Arthur Kent, Jennie Tourel and William Primrose. A community concert tour group, known as The Bel Canto Trio, was performing in Halifax and bound for St. John's when some sort of dissention broke out within the group that included the popular Metropolitan Opera soprano Frances Yeend, tenor Mario Lanza and baritone George London. After the Halifax concert, Lanza had a falling out with the Community Concert Association and his stage partners. Their relationship ended in Halifax with Lanza refusing to come to St. John's. He returned instead to New York while Yeend and London came to fulfill their Newfoundland engagement. They gave St. John's a standing-room-only concert. Within a year or two, Lanza was to begin a long period of international stardom in Hollywood, while Frances Yeend undertook extensive recital tours and operatic performances at the Met in New York. George London became known as one of the world's greatest operatic baritones.

A truly enjoyable pastime in my late teens was playing with a recording machine loaned me by my first cousin, Herb Buckingham, who was sadly to die in a car crash on a highway in Quebec. He and his wife had gone to the Canadian mainland on a summer holiday which included visiting their grown children out West. In 2011, when a friend and I were searching among the recordings I purchased in my teen years, and noting the many names of record companies there were in those days, we came across half a dozen homemade recordings. Most of the hit records were produced by Decca, London, Columbia, Capital and Bluebird. My collection also contained records from RCA Victor, Coral, Apex, Classics, Harmony, Victrola, Brunswick, Quality, Cameo, Starr, Parlophone and V Disc. My pride and joy, however, were the discs I made on the machine Herb loaned me. They are called audio discs and contain me at the age of 16 acting alone and with young friends in scenes from such works as *How Green was My Valley*, *I Remember Mama*, Hamlet's "Speak the Speech I Pray You," *The Grapes of Wrath* and a play in which I won the 1957 Best Actor Award in the Newfoundland Regional Drama Festival, *The Hasty Heart*.

My first appearance as an actor, as opposed to doing school recitations, had been on the stage of the Aula Maxima, St. Bonaventure's school hall. My St. John's theatrical début took place when I was chosen by the Christian Brother who directed me to play a part in one of the world's most famous plays. I believe I was in Grade Eight and our director was Brother Hearn when several classes got together to present *A Christmas Carol* by Charles Dickens, a classic novel about a Victorian-era miser taken on a journey of self-redemption, courtesy of three mysterious spirits, those of Christmas Past, Present and Future.

My friend Gilbert Higgins played the role of the miser, Ebenezer Scrooge. Gilbert was the son of Jack Higgins, barrister and solicitor and prominent 1909 Rhodes Scholar, as well as president of the Great War Veteran's Association. I was the Spirit of Christmas Past in a white wig that fell over my shoulders and a shimmering pale green evening gown belonging to my mother. I felt a thrill when I stood on the stage of the Aula Maxima playing my first theatrical role opposite Gilbert. After meeting with the ghost of his partner, Jacob Marley, Scrooge asked me, "Are you a Spirit, sir, whose coming was just foretold to me?" I replied, "I am." Scrooge looked at me and demanded, "Who, and what are you?" I answered him in a soft and gentle voice, "I am the Ghost of Christmas Past." "Whose past?" he bellowed at me. I replied,

"Your past, Ebenezer Scrooge." And with those few words began what would lead to a profession that has lasted for over 70 years so far.

The time came when I had to reveal my secret desire for a lifetime profession to my parents who seemed to me to be always asking what I wanted to study after graduation from high school, an event that was drawing ever closer. Knowing Mother would be a bit more understanding, I told her first. When the time came to tell my father, I wanted to have her back me up. Unlike today, the 1940s were times when even the suggestion of being an actor, singer, painter or whatever in the arts was looked upon by parents and others as an abnormality. My father was no different. He told me the majority of actors were starving to death and suggested I investigate law, medicine, teaching or some other more secure form of livelihood. It was not that he opposed me, he said, but only that he wished the best for me. I persisted for a year or so until I finally wore him down.

The late 1940s, while I was trying to decide on a career, were a time of endless political debate in Newfoundland. Joseph Smallwood, a politician and former radio personality, then a farmer in Gander, was leading a drive for the British government, which ruled Newfoundland with the assistance of six appointed Commissioners, to spearhead a proposal for a referendum that would lead Britain's oldest colony into a confederation with Canada where it would become the youngest province. As students in Grades 10, 11 and 12, our last years of high school, many of us became quite involved in the political process then taking place in which Smallwood was trying every trick he could to get our people to become the first citizens of a country in the 20th century to vote their nation and nationality out of existence. A National Convention on the subject was announced and members voted on in an election.

Most afternoons, following the end of school for the day, some of us would make our way to the Colonial Building to hear the great debate being waged there in the

National Convention by elected pro and con speakers. Smallwood headed up the pro-Confederation candidates while Peter Cashin led the Responsible Government movement, which he had been doing years before the convention was even thought of. Every Saturday night in the mid-1940s, families would gather around their radios to hear Major Cashin's pro-Responsible Government talks on Station VONF and its satellite VOWR.

The federal government had given in to Smallwood's demand for a referendum that would have three possible outcomes: (1) a continuation of government as it was, (2) Confederation with Canada, or (3) self-government as an independent nation within the British Empire. On the whole, people in Newfoundland and Labrador were divided into confederates and anti-confederates. When the vote was taken, the anti-confederates won. There were many who imagined we would then have to stand on our own feet and truly become a nation. However, it was not to be. The authorities decided there were mistakes made in the first referendum and another would have to be held. After much shouting and argument in the House of Assembly, a bill was passed calling for a second vote.

My parents and the parents of all my friends were deeply committed to seeing Newfoundland again become a nation. The pro and anti-confederate sides in the convention warred endlessly at meetings all over the island. The ones we most often attended were held by the Responsible Government league in and around the city, especially Bannerman Park.

My brother and I, as well as our parents, were staunch supporters of the Responsible Government League. Major Cashin, as he was often called, was one of my dad's good friends since school days at St. Bon's in the late 1800s, where they were both boarders. His wife, Blanche FitzPatrick of Placentia, was a lifelong friend of my mother. The Cashins had a daughter, Mary, who married a man named Waller, and a son Michael who, after a broadcasting career in

Newfoundland, lived most of his life in New York City. My brother John and I were also friends for a lifetime with Michael.

In this second referendum, approximately 2,000 more Newfoundlanders voted for Confederation than voted for a return of self-government. After the referendum it was arranged for Newfoundland to become the 10th province of Canada on 1 April 1949 until it was discovered the ceremony would take place on April Fool's Day. With people not wanting to be called fools, the date was protested and the federal government, in answer to their plea, announced the union would now take place a day earlier, March 31. By moving the event to the last day of March it became quite meaningful to me. On that night of the day we Newfoundlanders became Canadians, I made my professional acting début with a theatre company from New York on the stage of an auditorium in Oak Ridge, Tennessee, birthplace of the atomic bomb. Needless to say, when the curtain rose on *Toby Tyler*, a play in which I replaced an actor who had left the company, the elation I felt at finally becoming a professional actor was muted by my sorrow at the loss of my nation and nationality. I had visited Canada only once in my life, and that for less than an hour while the S.S. *Fort Townshend* unloaded part of her cargo in Halifax when I was on my way to study at a drama school, the National Academy of Theatre Arts, in New York.

Dad finally agreed to support me in whatever profession I chose. I felt it was time to reveal my secret ambition to him, that of becoming an actor, and I confessed to having written to a number of drama schools in the United States and England. I told him that after reading their brochures, I had chosen the Royal Academy of Dramatic Art (RADA) in London as the place I wished to attend. He answered by saying something to the effect that England was just recovering from the worst World War in history and people were still living on rations there. He felt I would be more employable if I chose an American school. I also told him I had chosen a backup school in New York, the American Academy of Dramatic Arts, which had graduated many famous American stage and screen performers. He listened with interest and promised to talk about it again in a few days' time.

When those few days were up, I told my dad I had changed my mind about the American Academy of Dramatic Arts and preferred a school in the up-state New York town of Pleasantville, the National Academy of Theatre Arts, about thirty minutes by train from the city, and home of the Reader's Digest. As it turned out, the Reader's Digest was published in a building next to the school. The academy was under the direction of an elderly woman from England, Clare Tree Major. A few days later my father seemed ready to make a final decision on my career, one that I would have to live with for a lifetime. For nights on end, Mother, he and I discussed the pros and cons of my wish to become an actor. No one they knew had ever taken on such a profession, although John Murray Anderson, son of Murray Anderson, a St. John's merchant and friend of my father, had become the biggest review producer on Broadway after Florenz Ziegfield. Another St. John's-born performer, Donald Brian, had enormous success when he appeared on Broadway as Prince Danilo, the leading role in *The Merry Widow*, which became one of the New York theatre's greatest hits. When born he was named Dennis O'Brien after his father, a butcher on Cockpit Road. An amateur dancer and actor in St. John's, he moved to Boston and New York with his widowed mother and was soon dancing and singing in clubs and bistros.

By the time Brian became an in-demand performer in Broadway musicals, he had already changed his name from Dennis O'Brien to Donald Brian. As he grew into his teens in the Boston area, he appeared in several plays as well as danced in Boston saloons. George M. Cohan was about to start rehearsals for a Broadway musical, *On The Wabash*. Having heard Brian sing and seen him dance in the Boston watering holes, Cohan offered him a contract to appear in the musical. His mother was thrilled to have her son on the stage. Donald Brian soon became well known to New York theatre-goers for his tap dancing and performance in *On The Wabash.* During the run of the show, a meeting with the Queen of Broadway, Lillian Russell, led to his becoming a musical star.

Eventually after several discussions with my parents, it was agreed I should apply for admission to the National Academy of Theatre Arts in Pleasantville. I wrote to Clare Tree Major, asking if there was an opening in the drama class that would be starting in September 1948. She assured me there was and if I were interested in joining it, she would get me a boarding house in Pleasantville near the school, the home of a woman named Mrs. Guion.

Chapter 7

Little Old New York

When I left home for what I imagined would be forever, on a foggy Saturday morning, the 18th September 1948, I was nineteen years old, and had no thought of loss, but only of the gain that lay ahead. The die had long been cast. Like a leaf, held captive in the currents of a stream, everything I imagined and did in my young life had borne me relentlessly towards that day of departure for America, on board the S.S. *Fort Townshend.* The watery boundaries of my beloved island home could not tether my ambition. I had no thought then or understanding of the invisible fibres that bind us to people we love and places in the heart, fibres that, in the end, sometimes make it impossible for our fantasies to become reality.

Leaning over the rail of the ship on that grey day of departure, I was so absorbed with my symbolic voyage of discovery that I gave little thought to the sorrow my parents must have felt in their hearts at the loss of their eldest child. John, who was with them, was also feeling very morose. When it came time for visitors to go ashore, I hugged my brother, "Mom's baby," who like me was by then in tears. Four hearts were breaking as I also hugged and kissed my father and my mother. Dad was too choked up to talk when we said goodbye. He muttered, "Always be true to yourself, my son." Mother wiped her eyes with a handkerchief and I saw they were red. "Live as your father and I have taught you to live, my son," she said, "and you will have no regrets." My own feelings were in tumult as I began to realize just how much emotion was involved in taking this leap into the unknown.

At 11 a.m. we cast off the hawsers and moved out from Harvey's pier. There was a change in the wind and the fog disappeared. The sun blazed in a blue sky as the S.S. *Fort Townshend* moved into the stream and headed for the Narrows. I stood at the rail awash in tears, while those I loved most in all the world vanished in the distance when the ship slipped through the Narrows and into the open sea. Once the harbour pilot went ashore, the captain set our course to the south. Alone, and in silence, I watched the familiar spires of the Roman Catholic Cathedral recede with my city until all I could make out was Cabot Tower, forlorn on the distant headland. I stood on that deck as if I were riding backwards on a train, seeing the life I lived vanishing from sight behind the ship. I knew I would return again to St. John's, but as a visitor; home for the holidays, someone who belonged to other places. I was leaving the awkwardness of boyhood behind so that I could be transformed into a mature man in the America of my dreams, a land I would eventually come to find out was as ethereal as Spenser's Faerie Queene. Once the sadness of my farewells had passed, I began to feel exhilarated by the deluding thought that I was free at last of all talons. From then on, I would be in control of my life and experiences and in my own way.

The fact that I believed I would never be coming home, except as a visitor, did not mean I loved my native land any less. Like children who grow up in a poor family, it never occurred to me that I lived on what other people saw as a bleak, backward, impoverished island, populated by naive colonists who failed utterly in making their homeland a viable country. As I grew older I developed a better understanding of why Newfoundland ancestors' failed ambitions, shaped in a grotesque imitation of England's, had fostered a lack of patriotism that would soon engender a deprived nation. My people had recently voted their country out of existence, and in six months' time it would become a province of Canada, a place I knew little of and cared less about, a place few of us had ever even visited. No matter where I went, or what I did, I would always belong to my father's outlandish vision of patriotism. I would eventually come to realize Newfoundland was as much a part of me as my skin and my bones. Yet on that September day, as the expanse of ocean grew ever wider, wiping the last hint of coastline from the horizon, I heaved a loud sigh but it was not the time then for cataloguing memories.

Walking the deck of the S.S. *Fort Townshend,* I was already beginning to breathe without pause. The future had become all that mattered. I was James Bruce, beginning my search for the source of the Blue Nile; Heinrich Harrer taking my first steps on the trek to Lahasa; Hiram Bingham starting my climb up the mountain precipices to Machu Picchu. I felt I was trading the oblivion of what I knew was attainable in order to confront the bravado of something I never for a moment felt might prove unattainable. It must be confessed, I was also as naive as a child awaiting the coming of Santa or a visit from the Tooth Fairy. I believed in, and found, an America far different from today's ugly reality. It was a place I had come to know and love through the eyes of Robert Nathan, Marjorie Kinnan Rawlings, Thomas Wolfe, Eudora Welty, John Steinbeck, Edna Ferber and a host of the other great American writers who caused me to haunt the public library in my teens. Now, after years of reading, reality lay just ahead, and like millions of immigrants to America before me, in a matter of days the first of these dreams would be mine. Once ashore, I felt certain my talents would lift me from the pavements to the seventh heaven, where I would not only see the stars, but would become one of them.

We hardly put out to sea when the toss and pitch of the S.S. *Fort Townshend* began to take its toll on my constitution. A bad sailor all my life, I was suddenly very seasick. To add to the discomfort of that awful malady, my lodgings in stateroom 44 adjoined the engine room in the aft section of the ship. The cabin not only vibrated ceaselessly whenever I went down to lie on my bunk, but it also smelled heavily of engine room fumes. I began to throw up so often that I slept topside most nights, bundled in rugs on a deck chair, tucked out of the wind by the funnel. The occasional puff of smoke didn't bother me nearly so much as those engine room odours, nor did the cold bother me so much as the awful feeling I got when I went below decks. Such visits were usually for what meals I could manage to eat. I also had to go below to accommodate personal needs in what on board ships is called "the head."

Among the diners at my table, and a far better sailor than I, was Nora Hogan, manager of both the Capitol and Paramount Theatres in St. John's. Miss Hogan was off to Halifax to confer with her employers, Famous Players, on the movie distribution business. She lived across the street from us in the Cochrane Hotel with her mother, who I often used to visit with my own mother when I was a small boy. When patrons were entering the huge Paramount Theatre, Miss Hogan would stand in the lobby, outside the door to her office, as motionless as a statue. To borrow a phrase from Shakespeare, she stood "like patience on a monument smiling at grief." Another traveller at my table was a French girl from St. John's, Denise Bonnave, who was my age and whom I already knew. Her father was the Consul for France in Newfoundland. Denise was on her way to Mexico City where she was to spend the winter in study at some finishing school. There was also a charming American lady at our table, a Mrs. Wilson, from Hastings-on-Hudson.

Having been so very seasick all day Sunday, it was with great delight that I staggered ashore in Halifax when the vessel docked there at 8 o'clock on Monday morning. So delighted was I with terra firma, I didn't even return to the ship for lunch. In the afternoon, after visiting the Citadel and other sights, I took in a double-bill at the movies, *Scarface* with Paul Muni, and *Sky Devils* with Spencer Tracy. In the evening I chanced upon my first beauty queen when I came to a downtown square where the mayor of Halifax was welcoming Miss Canada 1948 to the city. It was my first visit to her country, which, through no fault of my own, would soon be mine.

Darkness had fallen by the time I got back to the ship. I went to sleep in my bunk for a change, only to be awakened in the early hours of Tuesday morning by the cabin dizzily lurching about. My queasy stomach told me we were back at sea. I stayed in the cabin, being seasick, but come morning I made my way to my favourite deck chair, near the funnel, where I slept that night for the last time. Thursday the ocean seemed calmer and we spent the day passing numerous islands. Just after dark, the captain announced the lights of Long Island could be seen dead ahead. Denise and I took a look at the sparkling horizon and decided we would arise before dawn to see us slip past Miss Liberty, as she welcomed the "homeless masses yearning to breathe free." I was delighted we were in the lee of the land so that I could spend my last night on board the S.S. *Fort Townshend* sleeping peacefully in my bunk for a change.

September 23rd, as requested, the steward got me up at 5 o'clock. I met Denise on deck and we went to the rail and strained our eyes in the direction of New York. The dawning light of day was beginning to spread its faint line across the sky. Waves lapped the plunging prow as the funnel and spars caught the first glint of sunrise. The pilot came on board and we entered Lower Bay between Rockaway Point and Sandy Hook. After passing through The Narrows, (the same name as our harbour entrance at home), which separated Staten Island from Brooklyn, we were in Upper Bay. Like shadows emerging from a mist, the towers and spires of Manhattan began to separate themselves from a tangle of shapes that lay huddled on shore.

Quite suddenly, the "Lady" who had caused us to crawl from our bunks at such an early hour began to materialize atop a building on Bedloe's Island. Denise, a French citizen, looked at Miss Liberty lifting her lamp beside the golden door, and saw it as a gift from her country to a young United

States. For me, with a permanent residence visa in my passport, courtesy of my Aunt Margaret's husband Uncle Fred, the lady meant something very different. We stood side by side at the rail, hugging each other with the excitement one always felt in those days when travelling to America by ship. It would be weeks, even years, before that excitement began to diminish and eventually fade to black. If, as Percy Shelly said of Pisa, "Within the surface of the fleeting river/The wrinkled image of the city lay," it did not seem that way to me. There was no wrinkled image in the Hudson River. Surface ripples could not blemish New York in my eyes, and in memory it remains one of the two most congenial places I ever lived, the other being London. It was the cache of all my dreams, the place where life would complete its first sketch of me as an adult.

A tug came alongside nudging us into a Manhattan dock that seemed to jut out from the lower West Side Expressway. My Uncle Phil, Mother's brother, who was a New York harbour pilot, came on board. He introduced himself to me and with my trunk in a taxi we made our way to the Langwell Hotel, where I had booked myself a room by mail. I could tell by the look on my uncle's face he did not approve of my choice and he advised me to move to a better class hotel the next day, this in spite of the presence of many cheerful, scantily clad ladies who greeted us with smiles from open doorways as we walked along the corridors. Once in the room, to my shock, he pronounced the place "a whorehouse." Flushed as I was with a healthy innocence, the revelation was a bit startling. However, I was not unaware of the existence of such fallen angels as these. The war years had changed the old home town of St. John's quite a bit, and as schoolboys, we sometimes saw ladies of the evening, such as Babe Basset (who had been through two World Wars), Moo King and Mary Allan walking the streets in search of hanky panky.

After dinner that evening Uncle Phil took me to the Roxy Theatre, the last great movie palace in Manhattan.

Radio City is not the same thing. I knew of the Roxy, but never dreamed a movie house could reflect such magnificence and ornate splendor. It was truly a palace. The movie was a mediocre comedy, *The Luck of the Irish* with Tyrone Power, but it was the stage show that made the evening memorable for me. The name of the host, Ed Sullivan, meant nothing at the time, as we had no television in Newfoundland, but I knew all about the star of the show, Joseph E. Howard, one of the great songwriters and vaudeville entertainers of the Gay '90s. His name may not mean much to an audience today but in the years of vaudeville he was quite a famous entertainer and songwriter. The year before I went to New York, I saw Mark Stevens play Joe Howard in a movie based on his life. The wonderful evening at the Roxy ended with everyone joining in the singing of his greatest hit, "I Wonder Who's Kissing Her Now." My first evening in America could not have been more memorable. When the curtain fell and Joe Howard stepped forward for his curtain call, it was the first time I ever helped bring down the house.

My second day in New York, I set out to find a better class hotel. I looked about and picked the Hotel Paramount, because it housed Billy Rose's Diamond Horseshoe, the world-famous nightclub where John Murray Anderson, the great Broadway showman, also a native of St. John's, produced the cabaret for many years. It was obvious, from a quick glance at the prim and proper faces of the ladies sitting about the lobby, the Paramount's female clientele was decidedly less friendly than the ladies at the Langwell. Having secured Room 519, I headed up Broadway to see a woman who had become a good friend of mine through years of correspondence. She worked in an office near Columbus Circle.

Marjorie Divan was Frank Sinatra's New York secretary and had been since his early years of stardom. When "The Voice," as he was known in those days, appeared at the USO in St. John's in May 1945, it had the same impact on most of us as the resurrection of Elvis Presley would have on his fans today. We believed we were at the edge of the known universe, and it was beyond belief that a deity such as Sinatra, whom we considered to be *ne plus ultra* of the age, would step down from the shadows of the silver screen, or off those spinning 78 rpm wax discs, and walk among us mortals on a tour of U.S. military bases.

In a sky-high office that overlooked the Circle and the entrance to Central Park, I met Marge Divan face-to-face for the first time. While I sat chatting with her, a man stopped by the office. She introduced him to me as George Evans, which I recognized as a legendary name among Sinatra fans, since he was Frank's manager. Like Brian Epstein later with the Beatles, he had guided the skinny Jersey kid to fame and fortune. I couldn't believe that on my first full day in America I was sitting above Columbus Circle chatting with George Evans over mugs of coffee. It was my first introduction to that particular American phenomenon, mugs of coffee. When George left, Marge and I went out to lunch, cementing what had been a friendship on paper, in a manner of speaking, into an active one. Whenever I was in the city after that I would generally telephone Marge, or drop in on her.

When I got down from the New York train at Pleasantville station, having spent a few days with my Uncle Phil in the Big City, I had a taxi take me to my boarding house. Mrs. Guion proved to be a very charming woman who seemed always to have a smile on her face. The room she showed me was at the front of the house with its own bathroom. I was delighted with it until she told me I would have to share with another student as that was the way she had always rented it. A bit unsure of how such an arrangement would work out, I paid my rent and settled in. Next day, our first day of school at the Academy, I met a delightful and apparently amiable young man from Kentucky who was just out of the U.S. Navy, Doug Lynch, ready to begin his student days. Becoming a roommate with Doug turned out to be the best thing I could have done. I had always shared a twin-bedded room with my brother John, so sharing with Doug presented no difficulties.

Like brothers we did almost everything together, such as going to New York City many weekends to see a play or musical on Broadway, or to attend movies at the Roxy or other movie theatres where a stage show accompanied the film, such as Radio City Music Hall with its famous chorus line. Among the plays I saw in New York were some memorable works starring the very best actors and actresses in America and even the world. Besides going to theatres, I also took in the sights such as the wonderful Central Park Zoo (Connecting People to Wild Nature) and many other places to be talked about in letters home.

If Marge Divan wasn't too busy when I dropped in on her, we'd go somewhere for a chat and a bite to eat. Walking through Central Park with her in that long ago, sun-burnished autumn, was for me like being in a dream. Three or four months before, I had been sitting in an aging classroom at St. Bon's. Now here I was in the city of my dreams, walking with Frank Sinatra's Manhattan secretary. When he moved his office to Hollywood, Marge did not want to go west at her age so she stayed on in the east looking after Sinatra's interests. When he later closed the New York office they came to an amicable parting of the ways. A very proficient woman, she soon became private secretary to a rising young New York actor, Montgomery Clift. It was when visiting her office one afternoon that I met Clift, who dropped by to see her about something.

In that long ago time, our conversations were as rambling and as absorbing as our walks. Of the pen pals Marge introduced me to in her Sinatra days, while I was in high school at St. Bon's, I was still writing to Beverly from Brooklyn, who was at a secretarial school. Irma, who lived with her sister at Woodside in Queens, was studying commercial art. Brian, who liked to compose songs as a hobby, worked with a firm of stockbrokers in the city and lived with his parents in Newark, New Jersey. Ellen Coughlan, a college boarding student, lived with her father, mother and kid brother in the suburban community of New Rochelle. I met Ellen in person for the first time on a platform in Grand Central Station, 26 September 1948. As our meetings increased, with many weekend visits to New Rochelle, which took less than an hour by bus from Pleasantville, via White Plains, our friendship grew. We even went to a lecture by the famous media personality Bishop Fulton Sheen, star of the TV series *Life Is Worth Living*.

I met the Bishop when he finished his talk and introduced Ellen to him. He was surprised when I told him I was a cousin of Mary O'Neill who had worked as an assistant in his New York office for several years. He said he was delighted to meet a relative of Mary and called her "such a beautiful woman and so dedicated to her job." My mother, who also found her extremely attractive, used to say Mary was the Grace Kelly of Newfoundland. Mary's father, Patrick, was an O'Neill from Witless Bay who married Theresa O'Neill, one of the O'Neills from Bay de Verde who were not related to the O'Neills of Witless Bay. Theresa was my father's second cousin, whom Dad first met in New York where she was living with her parents. In World War I, Patrick, who had been a member of the Newfoundland Constabulary since 1903, commanded one of the patrol ships in St. John's harbour under the direction of the Admiralty. He was awarded the Order of the British Empire (O.B.E.) in 1935 for police work and for command of a vessel patrolling the Strait of Belle Isle and the north coast of Newfoundland during the war. After the war, O'Neill returned to police duties as a detective until appointed superintendent of the Constabulary from 1922-1934 when he was promoted to chief of police and the fire department, a position he maintained under his sudden death in 1944. It was O'Neill who, while police chief, separated the St. John's police force and fire departments into independent units.
When Ellen and I got back to New Rochelle and told Mr. and Mrs. Coughlan of our chat with Bishop Sheen, they

were most impressed. At the time of his retirement from the media in 1969, Sheen was made Archbishop of the Titular See of Newport, Wales. Actor Martin Sheen, whose birth name is Ramón Gerardo Antonio Estévez, adopted his stage name early in his career, in honor of Fulton J. Sheen. In time, I came to think of Ellen as someone I loved very much. She had the sparkling quality that comes with disarming innocence and was lovely to look at, being tall, thin and blond. What especially appealed to me in those days was how she was ripening in both mind and body. Although a dedicated Frank Sinatra fan, who had even dined with her idol at Essex House in New York, she was no mindless bobby-soxer, but a serious student working for a degree at the College of Mount St. Vincent-on-the-Hudson.

One of my close friends in high school days, Bobby Ricker, was an American whose father was fire chief at the U.S. Naval Base in Argentia, a less than two hour drive from St. John's. I met him and his older brother, Eugene, whom everyone called Geno, when they came to St. Bon's as boarding students from Argentia. He often came to our house for dinner on a Saturday or Sunday and to sometimes spend a weekend. In turn, I went to Argentia various times to stay with him and his parents. Bobby's visits to our house always turned into a mixture of laughter and pillow fights, until Mother called for us to stop and go to sleep. During these visits, John would be banished from his bed in our room to one in the attic, which he loved.

During the war Mother went to visit her recently married sister, Margaret Roy, in Washington, D.C., while our father was very much involved in business matters in Bay de Verde. With no one to care for us in the city during her absence, she arranged for John and me to spend the fall term as boarders at St. Bon's. When the war was nearing its end, the Ricker brothers were returned with their parents from Argentia to the U.S.A. In 1948 when I went to study in New York, Bobby and Geno were living in Ellen's hometown of New Rochelle where they attended the Irish Christian

Brothers' school, Iona College. We got a kick out of the fact that some of the Brothers at Iona taught us at St. Bon's.

One Saturday, shortly after school began at the National Academy, I went to see Ellen in New Rochelle. Bobby joined us to go on a long walk and I took the opportunity to introduce him to Ellen's mother, Mrs. Coughlan. She invited us back to lunch at her house. Later that afternoon, Ellen, Bobby and I took the train to Grand Central. We said goodbye to Ellen in the station, as she had to take another train to get back early to her college on the Hudson. Bobby and I went sightseeing and had a marvelous time among the famous sights of Manhattan, especially Times Square with its blazing lights and throngs of milling people. We took a room at a cheap hotel where we stayed overnight. Next day, we got the ferry from Battery Park to the Statue of Liberty on Bedloe's Island. We climbed to the top, took in the fascinating view and returned to the base of the statue where we read the immortal poem of Emma Lazarus:

> Give me your tired, your poor,
> Your huddled masses yearning to breathe free,
> The hopeless refuse of your teeming shores,
> Send these, the homeless, tempest-tost to me,
> I lift my lamp beside the golden door.

Bobby Ricker and I met each other a number of times, usually in New York City where we stayed overnight at the usual cheap hotel and had a great time. To have a Newfoundland friend in New York, even though he was really an American, meant a great deal to me. Bobby and Geno later went to Tulane University in New Orleans, Louisiana. We corresponded for some years until finally the letters stopped. He is like many other friends I had who drifted out of sight with the passing years. I find friendships are islands of curiosity in the sea of life. We pause among them for awhile, enjoying the days, the months, the years, until we suddenly wake to the realization we have moved on, and old friends who were cherished forever are memories.

Before starting classes at the National Academy of Theater Arts in Westchester County I took the train to Washington, D.C. to visit my mother's sister, Margaret, and her husband Fred Roy, a widower with two children in their teens. They lived on Sligo Creek Parkway in Silver Spring, just over the Maryland state line. I was on roller skates for the first time when their daughter Betty, a few years my junior, took me to a nearby roller rink. In the next several days Uncle Fred showed me all around the American capital. There was the Supreme Court, the White House, Lee Mansion, Smithsonian Museum, Jefferson, Lincoln and Washington monuments, the grave of the Unknown Soldier and the spar of the battleship *Maine* in Arlington, Virginia.

Friday, October 7, I took the train back to New York, and crossed from Penn Station to Grand Central, where I caught the Mount Kisco local. Half an hour later I was on the platform at Pleasantville, the first stop after leaving the city of White Plains. Pleasantville was a small Westchester bedroom community of New York City. I took a deep breath and looked about me. On the far side of the station square a concrete building loomed above a small hill. A sign painted on the front read Clare Tree Major Theater Productions. I knew the place also housed her National Academy of Theater Arts. Beside it, on the sidewalk level, was Pleasantville's only claim to international fame, The Reader's Digest editorial offices and publishing plant. I realized the life I had chosen for myself was about to begin at last.

A taxi took me from the train station and deposited me at the door of Mrs. Guion's house where a room had been reserved for me by the school. Mrs. G. introduced me to the actor I was about to displace in her household, Winton Sedgewick, who, I gathered, was the apple of her aging eye. He was about to depart on a theatrical repertory tour of four plays by Shakespeare. His main role would be Romeo, in the National Classic Theater's production of *Romeo and Juliet.* Mrs. Guion did not serve meals, only provided a room, so after depositing my things, Winton and I made our way to the Rome Restaurant where most of the students ate, having rooms only and no board. It would be the first of many meals taken at the Rome, where we bought punch cards instead of using cash. At the restaurant, Winton introduced me to another actor, James Hillburn, who would be playing the title role in *Macbeth.* The National Classic Theatre also included in the tour *The Merchant of Venice* and *The Taming of the Shrew.* I little imagined then that Jim would become one of my closest friends for many years and, in time, my roommate in London.

That Friday evening Mrs. Guion took me with her to see one of the Clare Tree Major Children's Theater productions, *Poor Little Rich Girl,* giving its last dress rehearsal before leaving on tour next day. Unlike the Shakespeare Company, which had a repertory of four plays, the Children's Theater shows were so heavily booked, each company performed only one play. There was a car for the actors and a truck for the excess actors, scenery, costumes, props and luggage. Both vehicles were driven by an actor who received no fee, but was paid a $100 bonus at the end of the tour, provided he had no accident all season. The performance of *Poor Little Rich Girl* took place in the auditorium of St. Mary's Private School for Girls, an exclusive Westchester boarding school run by an order of Episcopalian Nuns. It was a place where I would perform a number of times in the coming months.

A formidable old lady, with her gray hair in a topknot, was seated like an Empress in the front row, notebook in hand. She was introduced to me by Mrs. Guion as Clare Tree Major. A hand was extended as her wrinkled face broke into a warm smile. "So you got here at last and all the way from Newfoundland. Welcome to our school." She explained to me she had invited Mrs. Guion to take me to the dress rehearsal to meet her where she was witnessing a performance by a departing company of players. The famous theatrical dowager reminded me we had an appointment to meet in her office at the school next day. She then called for the curtain to rise and bent to her task.

In the morning I went with Winton to the National Academy of Theater Arts where the Shakespeare Company was busy loading their belongings, costumes and scenery for the tour, which would be leaving in a few days. Flora Houghtaling, Mrs. Major's highly efficient, no-nonsense secretary, ushered me into the presence. When I had met the venerable old lady the previous evening, I was immediately struck by Mrs. Major's remarkable resemblance to Dame May Whitty, a favourite old actress of mine in movies such as *Mrs Miniver* and *The White Cliffs of Dover.* When I spoke of the resemblance to Jim Hillburn, he exclaimed, "Oh, my God! Don't mention her name to Clare. I'll tell you about it later." Over lunch he explained that, years ago, Clare, then an actress in New York, had been offered the lead in a mystery play by a young Welshman named Emelyn Williams, *Night Must Fall,* that was Broadway bound. As a Shakespearian actress, she found scaring an old lady almost to death on stage to be quite distasteful, and when she discovered the young author was also homosexual, that did it. She turned down the part, predicting disaster for the production, and was to spend much of her life in a fruitless task of weeding out what she called "fairies" from her own companies. Her English rival, May Whitty, accepted the part Clare refused in *Night Must Fall.* The play was a huge success. May Whitty, afterwards Dame May Whitty, became an international star, especially in the movies. Emelyn Williams went on to write many plays that were huge successes, especially *The Corn is Green.*

Thanks to Jim I was fortunate not to have mentioned to Clare her remarkable resemblance to Dame May during our face to face meeting. Like Gilbert & Sullivan's Koko, "I sat in solemn silence" and listened while she launched into a lecture about how well her school qualified an actor for acceptance by theatrical agents. Integrity and the quality of one's art must be jealously guarded. She believed only performers could teach the essentials of success to young would-be performers, so we were to be taught by nationally known actors and actresses. Clare reminded me that the board of directors of her school included Vincent Price, his actress-wife Edith Barrett, Mildred Natwick and the great Maude Adams. I call Miss Adams great because she was truly great as J.M. Barrie's Peter Pan, the role with which she was most closely identified and which she often reprised. Adams was the first of many actresses to play Peter Pan on Broadway. It was not sufficient these famous performers should occasionally lecture us at school, but through expert daily supervision, other teachers, such as the members of the board of directors, including Miss Adams, would prepare us for those values required by modern producers when we went to read for professional engagements.

Dorothy Major, Clare's divorced daughter, who had been an actress in several Broadway productions, lived with her mother in nearby Chappaqua, and taught at the school. One morning she appeared in the doorway of our classroom to say the Shakespearian players were waiting for her mother to begin a costume rehearsal in the small theatre downstairs. Clare Tree took me down with her and sat me beside her as she inspected the costumes of the actors appearing in *The Merchant of Venice*, which was about to go on a six month tour with her two stars, Forbes Francis and his wife Olga Baliss, whom I thought perfectly marvelous actors when I saw them in performance as Shylock and Portia the previous evening.

Clare Tree took exception to the costume worn by the actor playing Launcelot Gobbo, a servant to Shylock, and called for costume designer Marion de Pew, a dear woman, beloved by everybody. When Marion arrived, her dress full of pins, needles and thread, Mrs. Major beckoned the young actor to come to the front of the stage. She reached up, and began poking him in the groin with her finger, while demanding "Marion, what is that unseemly bulge? Can't you get rid of it?" Marion answered, rolling her eyes in her head. "That, Mrs. Major, is part of the young man's anatomy." Clare ordered her to get rid of it at once. "Outside of ordering a doctor to castrate him, ma'am," Marion said, with exaggerated impatience, "I have no idea how to get rid of it. He left his padded jockstrap at home this morning, but promises to have it for the full dress tonight at St. Mary's."

Clare turned back to the errant actor, and began to yank at his tights in order to smooth out the wrinkles that formed around the unseemly bulge. Suddenly, the tights were down about his ankles, and all was revealed, as he was not wearing underwear. Mrs. Major stared at the offending member, and cried out in her chilled English accent, "Young man, will you get your maturity out of my face?" Needless to say, we all found it quite amusing as the young man, his maturity in hand, fled to a dressing room. Just two weeks earlier I had been a green kid, fresh out of high school, in a remote North Atlantic seaport. Now here I was in New York, sitting beside a well-known director-producer, watching a company of professional actors prepare for a play they were about to tour. The whole thing boggled my mind.

Much of my first Sunday at the Academy, I spent with Winton and Jim at Jim's digs, feeding them their lines for the plays they were about to appear in on tour. Their digs, as actors always called their living quarters, were in a very attractive attic apartment consisting of a double burner hot plate in a window alcove, a fairly large living room with a sofa bed, and a bedroom with twin beds. I realized immediately it would suit me much better than the single room at Mrs. Guion's if I could find two people to share it. In any case, I spoke to Mrs. Hann, the landlady, and she agreed not to rent it to anyone else until I had a chance to find a roommate or two when the Academy opened.

Monday morning I met my fellow students as we gathered for our first class. There were to be eight men and three women with about a half-dozen students still to come, including Jane, Cynthia and Delores. From the moment I shook hands with one of the men, a thin, dark, good-looking fellow from Kentucky named Douglas Lynch, it was the beginning of one of my few very deep friendships and it was to last until his unexpected death in 2002. Like all the other men in the class, except me, he was an ex-serviceman, formerly with the U.S. Navy, attending school under the G.I. Bill. In the months and years that followed, Doug and I would become inseparable.

That first morning, we students met Raymond Edward Johnston, one of the most versatile and noted actors of the American stage in the '40s, who would be among our teachers. Mr. Johnston played Alexander Graham Bell in a biographical film, but it was his stunning performance on stage in another play, *The Patriots,* which won the New York Drama Critics Circle Award, (there were no Tonys in those days). These roles made him a star on Broadway. He was a star in my eyes for a much different reason. One of the most popular radio programs in North America in the '40s opened with a squeaking door and a low sepulchral voice speaking in slow, solemn tones: "This is your host, Raymond, welcoming you to the *Inner Sanctum...*" It was a program my brother and I huddled to hear each week with our parents during high school, on VOUS, the radio station on the American base in St. John's, Fort Pepperrell. The show was a creepy radio thriller and its host, Raymond, turned out to be our Mr. Johnston. We made him repeat the famous opening for our amusement that first morning. Later that day he cast me as Ivan (the John Qualan role) in Eugene O'Neill's famous one-act play *In the Zone,* which he was to direct.

After a few days the missing female students arrived, first Cynthia, then Jane, and finally Delores, who was to become one of my dearest friends. Delores Marshall was an attractive blond from Balboa, California, and a dead-ringer for the lovely French star Simone Simon, who thrilled me, my brother, and our group in the 1942 classic movie chiller *Cat*

People. Delores doubled once for Simon in a film, but her mother, who wrote the daily horoscope in the *Los Angeles Times,* and her father, owner of the world famous Trader Vic's, a restaurant in Balboa, sent her to New York to study acting.

When Delores arrived a few days after we started classes, another of our teachers, actress Betty Caine (wife of Raymond Johnston), cast Doug, Delores and me in a delightful one-act Japanese comedy, *A Dear Little Wife,* in which we played husband, wife and lover, respectively. Betty, who had her greatest Broadway success as Marguerite in *Speak of the Devil,* a dramatic version of *Faust,* began her career acting with Jessie Bonstelle in Detroit. I was later to discover Jessie Bonstelle had starred on stage in St. John's one night in 1902, and introduced a young actress in their company, Frances (Daisy) Foster, to sing a new song, *The Ode To Newfoundland.* Miss Bonstelle said the words were written by our Governor, Sir Cavendish Boyle, and the music by his friend, the great English composer, Sir C. Hubert H. Parry, who had written the music for Blake's hymn "Jerusalem," which is sung to this day at the last night of the Proms in the Royal Albert Hall, London.

Our dancing coach, who doubled as fencing master, was Richard Cressy, a leading dancer with the Le Meri Dance Company in New York. Of Indo-European extraction, he had been trained by the great Ruth St. Denis herself. From him we learned basic ballet training and techniques to help us in developing poise and grace on stage. I had no talent for ballet dancing, or dancing of any kind, but I did enjoy the fencing classes.

There is no doubt whatever, one of our favourite teachers was the elderly Viola Roache, who taught speech, or was supposed to teach speech and Shakespeare. We would no sooner have our books open than she would launch into one of her endless, fascinating theatrical stories from her own life when she was a Broadway star, stories that always held us spellbound. A charming and very dear woman, Vi ended a long and brilliant career on Broadway as Mrs. Higgins, the mother of Professor Henry Higgins, in the first New York production of *My Fair Lady* with Julie Andrews, and Rex Harrison as her son. When she went to Hollywood in 1951 to make her first feature film, *Royal Wedding*, in which she played the mother of Sarah Churchill, reporters who met her train at the station in Pasadena asked her for a statement. Vi stood on the steps of the train car, pulled up her skirt, showing a leg, and commented, "My God! Lana Turner at seventy-five!"

Miss Roache told us many unforgettable theatrical stories, one of which she used to illustrate her reason for never giving advice to any would-be players who came to her. Many years before, when she was appearing on Broadway with the popular Irish actor Tyrone Power, his son, Tyrone Jr., used to haunt her dressing room. Young Ty desperately wanted to be an actor and asked Vi to guide him. She told him what he must do was concentrate on the theatre in New York and get as much experience as possible. She worked with him on developing stage technique until one evening he told her that he had an offer to go to Hollywood. Miss Roache was shocked. She warned him to have nothing to do with Tinseltown, where he would be lost among the thousands of handsome young men like himself trying to break into the movies. She insisted his future lay on the stage, where his father, her co-star, was a famous actor, and to rid himself of all ideas of becoming a movie star. A few days later, she said, he decided not to take her advice and left for the film Mecca. The rest is history, as the saying goes. In Hollywood, young Tyrone Power became one of the biggest box office stars of all time.

On another occasion she was in a play with a burly young actor who had a dreadful Brooklyn accent, bumbled about the stage, and had a tough-guy face that looked as if it had been squashed, though he had a heart of gold. A talent scout from Hollywood spotted him in the play and offered him work in the movies. Vi told him to forget it. Whatever chance he had on the New York stage, she told him, he would have none in Hollywood where the camera would be merciless in showing up his faults. He thought about it for a few days but finally decided not to take her advice. The play was closing and he would be out of work, so he signed with the talent scout, and headed for California. William Bendix sprang to stardom after a meaty role in *The Glass Key* starring Alan Ladd and Veronica Lake. In the words of Leslie Halliwell, "His broken nose and Brooklyn accent later sustained many a mediocre film as well as adding to the flavour of good ones." The Bendix career reached its peak with the extremely popular TV series *Life of Riley,* in which he starred as Riley for five years.

With her endless supply of such first-hand stories, it is little wonder Viola's classes were always spellbinding. We did learn Shakespeare from her, as well as from Mrs. Major. Towards the end of our first term we did a student production of scenes from *The Tempest* in which I was cast as Prospero (the rightful Duke of Milan), Delores was Miranda (daughter of Prospero) and Doug played Ariel (an airy spirit). We had a strange fellow student from Montana, Raymond Posey, who was Caliban (a savage and deformed slave). Ray was a bit older than the rest of us and insisted we call him Mr. Posey. His mother came with him to Pleasantville and he used to scoff at the rest of us who were not so fortunate as to have our mothers with us. Sometimes between classes, when we would be having coffee in the lounge, Mr. Posey would break into a frenzied recitation of Edgar Allan Poe's *The Raven.* While quoting the raven's "Nevermore," his eyes would bulge and he would foam at the mouth. When some student nervously laughed he would threaten to shoot whoever did not appreciate his art. We reported this to Dorothy Major, but her mother paid little heed, until one night Mr. Posey went berserk in his rooming house, fired some shots from a revolver into the floor, and was carted off in handcuffs by the police. We never saw him or his mother again.

Most of the other students were rather run-of-the-mill, except for Duncan de Mille Elliott. He was from a wealthy society family and lived in a huge mansion in Greenwich, Connecticut, from which he commuted every day in his own large Buick convertible. He got the de Mille part of his name from his mother who was a first cousin of dancer Agnes de Mille. Their uncle was the great Hollywood film producer Cecil B. de Mille. Duncan had a resonant voice and afterwards did quite well as a radio commentator in London and Paris, from where I sometimes heard him reporting to North America on CBC Radio. One evening we students were invited to dinner by Duncan at his parents' mansion. We all squeezed into what vehicles were available and drove through the dark to a stately residence ablaze with lights in Greenwich. In the large living room, with a crystal this and that gleaming from sideboards, walls and ceilings, we were introduced by our host to an elegant couple who were his parents. They welcomed us with great charm. After drinks, served by a butler and housemaids, the butler announced dinner in the dining room. I imagine few of us have dined in such splendor since.

A fellow student, John Connally from Texas, was also among those late arriving for the beginning of the school year. He told us he was studying dramatic art, not because he wanted to be an actor, but because he wanted to be a politician and thought the techniques of voice projection and acting would help him. A big and very affable man, as well as a war hero, after graduation from the Academy he went home to Texas and sought election to the Texas governing body, while the rest of us joined road companies or haunted casting offices in New York. In spite of much research I cannot say if he was the John Connally who became governor of Texas, and was riding with John and Jackie Kennedy when the president was shot to death in Dallas.

Within a few days of my meeting Doug Lynch, he and I decided to take over and share Jim Hillburn's apartment at Mrs. Hann's when he left on tour. Mrs. Guion was shocked when I told her I would be moving out so soon after my arrival, but I arranged with Mrs. Major for a fellow student,

Delores Marshall, who had yet to arrive from California, to take my room. Delores was very pleased with it when she did arrive. Doug and I occupied the bedroom with the twin beds at Mrs. Hann's, while a troublesome fellow student, Russ, slept on the sofabed in the lounge. He went home to Connecticut every weekend, but the arrangement was not a success. We found him a difficult roommate, still suffering from the effects of a wartime breakdown, and having nightmares. He was as touchy as he was surly. Tensions mounted until we had a heart-to-heart talk with him, after which he agreed to move to another room in Mrs. Hann's house. Before the year was out he fell in love with one of the female students, Jane, and they were married just before graduation, but nobody at the school attended the ceremony.

Meanwhile, Delores, Doug and I, became an inseparable trio, spending many weekends at the movies in White Plains, or on three-mile walks to Chappaqua. At the end of an overgrown driveway on the Chappaqua road we discovered a huge abandoned mansion falling into ruin, rather like Rochester's Thornfield Hall in Charlotte Brontë's *Jane Eyre*, except that it had not been gutted by fire. The three of us made it our own secret place. We would take a picnic with us on sunny weekend afternoons, go there and sit on old broken furniture in the huge, empty library, with dark oak walls. A large window, with unbroken glass was beside a stone fireplace and overlooked the Hudson River. I see the three of us now in hallowed memory, lying back like lords and a lady of the manor, the late afternoon sun streaming down on the Hudson, a small fire burning in the enormous fireplace, as we didn't want the smoke to attract the neighbours. We sipped our soft drinks as we languidly fed each other lines for the parts we were memorizing for our next student production.

On one occasion we were summoned to Chappaqua on a Saturday evening to meet a member of the school's board of directors, an immortal of the American stage, the great Maude Adams. Unlike other mediums of art and entertainment, theatre is a place of truly magical moments that linger forever in the heart and memory. In my own years of theatre-going I have witnessed several such moments on the theatrical stage. There was one in the Tennessee Williams' play *A Streetcar Named Desire*, when the wonderful Jessica Tandy said in a beautiful voice, "I have always been dependent on the kindness of strangers." Another special memory is of Shirley Booth's marvelous line in *Come Back Little Sheba*, a play about alcoholism and a lost dog named Sheba who represented her doctor husband's drinking problem. At the end of the play, when he has been rehabilitated, she says to her him, "You know something, Doc? I don't think little Sheba's ever coming back."

I am told that a memory that has lived long among New York theatre-goers, as well as those who first saw the play in London, was a moment in the 1908 production of James M. Barrie's *What Every Woman Knows*, at the Empire Theatre. When Maude Adams, who became a star in another Barrie play *The Little Minister* in 1897, was asked by her husband, a clergyman, "What exactly is charm, Maggie?" playgoers often recalled the moment when Miss Adams looked at him during an electrifying silence and finally said in a soft Scottish accent, "Well, James, 'tis a sort of a bloom on a woman. If ya have it ya dinna need anything else. If ya dinna have it, it makes nae difference what else you have."

By 1948 Maude Adams was long retired and in her late 60s. One autumn evening that year she came to a dinner party held in her honour by Mrs. Major, who invited her students to her home as guests on her rambling estate in Chappaqua. We were all surprised when Maude Adams arrived to see she was wearing a cape and hat like those she wore in the first production of *Peter Pan* which she had starred in on Broadway forty-three years earlier in 1905. It seemed sadly ironic to us students that this wonderful star, like the boy Peter, did not seem to want to grow up or at least let go of her greatest role. Our meeting with this immortal of the New York stage was one of reverential awe at seeing the elfin-like personality of this sweet little old lady who was supposed to have been one of our teachers at the Academy that year but, sadly for us, she had retired. It is said all who saw her perform as *Peter Pan* never forgot that magical moment when the fairy, Tinkerbell, was dying, and to bring her back to life Adams came down to the footlights to plead for the audience to clap as loudly as they could if they believed in fairies. When she asked the question, the bewitched spectators always broke into thunderous applause as Tinkerbell was restored to vigorous life.

It was the same in 1950 when I had the good fortune to see that great Hollywood actress, and one of my favourites, Jean Arthur, play Peter Pan on Broadway, while Boris Karloff was Captain Hook. With those two leads how could it be anything but a huge success? Jean Arthur broke Maude Adams' record run and was the first Peter to actually fly on stage, even swooping out over the audience. Tinkerbell was a flashing light that darted all over the stage. In that production of the play, later turned into a musical for Mary Martin, I was surprised to see that the dog of the Darling family, Nana, was a black and white Newfoundland, as called for in James M. Barrie's script. The Landseer Newfoundland was a dog that got its name from a painting by Queen Victoria's favourite artist, Sir Edwin Landseer, who called his work "A Distinguished Member of the Humane Society." To this day, black and white Newfoundlands are known as Landseers. Nana is undoubtedly the most famous Newfoundland dog of all time, and known to generations of children all over the earth.

I saw Forbes Francis and his wife, Olga Baliss, in a dress rehearsal of *The Merchant of Venice*, at the Anglican girls' boarding school in Westchester, St. Mary's-in-the-Fields, where we did all our school performances as well as those of companies going on the road. Forbes Francis was Shylock and she Portia. Her "quality of mercy" speech was to me masterfully done in a quiet, controlled voice. I dreamed I would be among the Shakespeare players myself the following season. That dream came closer to reality one day in November when Clare Tree Major called me into her office to tell me she was sending me to join the National Classic Theater Company on tour in Connecticut where it would be presenting a single performance of a play called *The Bishop Misbehaves,* set in an English pub. A contractual agreement had been made the previous year with a group in New Haven, which the company was unable to fulfill due to the sudden illness of one of the lead actors, when the performance had to be cancelled. The sponsors insisted on rescheduling the play the following November. In order to do so, the National Classic Theater would take a break in its autumn tour to stage *The Bishop Misbehaves* in New Haven, even though the cast would be short one actor and one actress.

Mrs. M. told me she was sending me to take the role of that one actor, Frenchy, a small but important part in the popular 1935 English stage thriller. Her daughter, Dorothy, went with me to take the part of the actress who left the cast. We rehearsed in Pleasantville for two days. Although slapped together, and anything but a classic, the antics of the misbehaving bishop, played by my friend Jim Hilburn, in solving a crime at an English Inn were greeted in New Haven by a full house at Yale University. The reviews which followed next day, when Dorothy and I were headed back to obscurity in Pleasantville, we were told by her mother were quite full of praise.

My performance could hardly be called my professional debut, since I was an unpaid student, but it was my first appearance on stage with a professional company. However, it did boost my ego to have been picked from among my Academy classmates for the role. I possibly got it because I had the closest thing to an English accent among my colleagues. So delighted was Mrs. Major with reports of my acting in the play, she went so far as to promise me Laertes, in next season's production of *Hamlet,* in which I would have the opportunity for a sword fight with the melancholy Dane.

Nobody realized at the time that a terrible tragedy would lead to the 1948-49 tour of the National Classic Theater Company being its last. Shortly after Dorothy and I returned from New Haven, an ashen faced secretary, Flora Houghtaling, burst into class one morning when Mrs. Major was teaching us projection. We could tell at once, from Flora's look of alarm, something was terribly wrong. She whispered to Clare, who clutched her bosom and turned a bleached white. Almost fainting, she was helped from the room on Dorothy's arm. We turned to each other in puzzlement.

As we were all buzzing like bees, Dorothy came back in, and said we were to have the rest of the day off. She explained that, shortly after 8 o'clock that morning, the National Theater Company's car, carrying six of the actors, slammed into a bridge abutment in Pennsylvania. Unfortunately, a member of the Shakespeare tour company had been killed in the accident. We were in shock as Dorothy told us that although details were scanty, the performers left Harrisburg early that morning for their next engagement, which was a long drive away. They had gone only a short distance along the Pennsylvania Turnpike, then the only super highway in America, when, for some reason, the car suddenly went out of control and smashed into the iron trestle of a bridge which spanned a river.

When pressed for the dead actor's name, Dorothy said it was Tom Welbourn, whose antics a few weeks earlier as Lancelot Gobbo endeared him to us all. She was in tears as she gave us the dreadful details. Dorothy told us Eleanor Connor, who had become a good friend of mine in the short time I knew her, was riding between Tom and the unidentified driver, and was in hospital with a broken back. Those in the rear seat, Winton, Forbes and Olga, escaped with only cuts and bruises. Stunned at the news, we all stumbled from class. We found out the actor driving the car, whose name I sadly cannot remember, fell asleep at the wheel. Only a few nights earlier, on the eve of their departure, we had all been laughing gaily and singing together at O'Gorman's tavern near the Academy. It was, in fact, that night in O'Gorman's I had my first drink of alcohol. I would be twenty-one years old in less than two months.

Boozing was something many of us teenagers never thought of doing when living at home in St. John's. I suspected my kid brother of having taken his first drink long before me as he was a prankster. I have a group photo, taken by my first cousin, well-known press photographer Frank Kennedy, in which seventeen of us, nine girls and eight boys, are standing and sitting in the bay window of our house on Cochrane Street. The occasion was a farewell party thrown for me by my mother, on the eve of my departure for New York by ship. No liquor was served, or even thought of, although we were all eighteen to twenty years of age.

Frank Kennedy, a son of my father's sister Nellie and her husband, Captain Nicholas Kennedy, was a leading Newfoundland photographer who worked with the *Daily News* for twenty years and afterwards spent many years with CBC Television. It is said he made all *Daily News* readers laugh with his annual April Fool's Day newspaper photos which came out in the morning. His pictures were always published under the caption "April Fool" and many readers proved to be April Fools, especially in 1952 when he published a picture of an ocean-going ship, the *LOOF LIRPA*, with its prow on Water Street having been driven up Bowring's Cove from the waterfront. I know many people failed to read the name of the ship backwards, which told you that you were fooled into thinking it was a real accident, and had forgotten the date was the first day of April. A lady told Frank that she was in Conception Harbour when she saw the picture in the paper at her grocer's store. She immediately jumped on a bus that was leaving for St. John's and came in to see the ship in the middle of Water Street. When she got to town and told the driver where to let her off, he had to tell her the sad news that there was no ship on Water Street and the whole thing was an April Fool's joke. Frank said the bus driver told him at that point everyone on the bus broke into gales of laughter.

Chapter 8

An Actor's Life For Me

In the New York town of Pleasantville, a few nights after the National Classics Theater's awful car accident, Doug and I rid ourselves of our flatmate, Russ. We were evicted by the landlady, Mrs. Hann, not for anything we did but because her son was suddenly being discharged from the armed forces and wanted to live at home in our small flat. We moved immediately into a lovely attic bedsitter, in Mrs. Flynn's house, on the other side of Pleasantville. Her husband was an FBI agent in New York and always carried a revolver. The night of our move we were walking home from the local cinema and passing O'Gorman's Bar, when Doug suggested we go in and have a drink. I agreed and we entered the dingy tavern. When the bar girl asked what we would like to drink I was at a loss to know what to order. Doug saved the day by asking for two Manhattans. Although he had only had them a few times before, when in the navy, they became our immediate favourites. For years, Manhattans always held a special place in my life. With us, going to O'Gorman's "for a drink" was more likely a weekly thing, rather than nightly, and a drink usually meant one drink.

Jim Hillburn told us at the time of the accident that he and Winton were in the truck along with the driver and had no involvement. We were all extremely upset. Replacements were quickly found for Tom, who had died, and Eleanor, who was seriously injured and still in hospital. The remaining tour dates were still to be played by the Company, with Forbes and Olga as replacements for Tom and Eleanor.

However, the tragedy took its toll. Forbes and Olga were getting old and had filled in as a favour to Mrs. Major. They told her they had decided to retire from the road at the end of the season. Clare Tree then cancelled all bookings for the National Classic Theater next season. Sadly, the Company never toured again.

Meanwhile, three public performances were given of each of our student productions. First at the Threshold Playhouse, a 99-seat theatre in the Academy, then at the private girls' school, St. Mary's-in-the-Fields, and finally, at the New York State Prison for Women in Bedford Hills, where we men were always welcomed with cheers and whistles by the appreciative ladies when we came on stage. During our first term we performed in two or three one-act plays, such as Eugene O'Neill's *In the Zone,* the Japanese play *A Dear Little Wife,* Maxwell Anderson's tale of the French Revolution *The Feast of Ortelons* (small birds that were a French culinary delight), W.W. Jacobs' famous thriller *The Monkey's Paw,* and Lord Dunsany's *The Lost Silk Hat.* As we learned our craft we moved on to performing full productions, which included St. John Ervine's great Irish play *John Ferguson,* in which John Connally played the title role and I was his son. In its day the play had been the financial saving of the infant New York Theater Guild, the most exciting and responsible producing organization of the American stage. The Guild began as an outgrowth of Clare Tree Major's recently defunct Washington Square Players. Its heyday having passed, the Theater Guild's last official offering on Broadway was as co-producer of the unsuccessful musical *State Fair* (1996), after which it was dissolved.

The Yellow Jacket was a curious full-length Chinese fantasy, performed in the Chinese manner. Written and directed by a man named Benrimo, it opened first at the Fulton Theatre, 4 November 1912, and lasted thirty years in various Broadway revivals, the most famous being that by the Academy Award winning actor Charles Coburn at the Cort Theatre in 1916. He directed and toured the play for many years as well as playing the important role of Chorus. It also starred his wife, Ivah Wills as Chee Moo (Kind Mother), with Beatrice Wood as Due Jung Fah (Fancy Beauty). The part of Wu Hu Git (Young Hero) was played by George Gaul, who fights to regain the Yellow Jacket. Schuyler Ladd, in a repeat performance from his role in the 1912 production, was Wu Fah Din (Daffodil, who usurped the Yellow Jacket and thus the throne of the Emperor of China). In our student production, I was Daffodil, Wu Fah Din, Cynthia was Chee Moo, Delores, Due Yung Fah, and Doug, Wu Hu Git. We had great fun doing the production in the Chinese theatrical tradition.

At one point in the play, Chee Moo is ordered beheaded. The executioner comes to me and asks what he should do with her head. I cry out in glee, "To the pigs with the head of Chee Moo." It was a wonderful line and became an oft-repeated expression among the Academy students. For instance, if we arrived at the Bedford Hills prison and the stage helpers were not yet there, someone would say "To the pigs with the head of Chee Moo." In the Rome Restaurant, if a waitress mixed up an order, one of the crowd was apt to cry, "To the pigs with the head of Chee Moo." We got much laughter out of the expression, while strangers looked on in wonderment.

Any weekend I didn't stay in Pleasantville, I would leave after class on Friday and catch the train to Grand Central, spending Saturday and Sunday at the Central Park YMCA in the city. Sometimes Doug and/or Delores came with me but more often I went alone. In those days I passionately loved New York, including The Central Park Y, unlike Sloane House, the downtown Y, where the infamous Sloane House Marys (gay young men) prancing the hallways, were a hazard, especially if you bent over a drinking fountain. The first weekend I went to New York I stayed at Sloane House, near Penn Station. When I called Uncle Phil to meet me, I had tickets for Henry Fonda in *Mister Roberts* that night. He said when he met me that Sloane House was no place for an inexperienced lad from Newfoundland, still wet behind the ears, and that on Saturday night it would probably be necessary to defend my chastity "tanquam virgo assaulta" (like a virgin under assault). I survived the experience unscathed but never stayed there again. Whenever I was flush with a gift of money from home, such as after my birthday, I would take a room for $3.50 per night in a small, clean hotel, The Sharon, next door to an even more flagrant netherworld of licentious behaviour, the Everard Baths. It wasn't until much later, when the old Everard suddenly went up in flames one Saturday night, sadly extinguishing the lives of a number of the flamboyant young men frolicking there, that I became aware of its reputation as perhaps the most outrageous netherworld in Manhattan.

In the late '40s, New York was for me a place of legends spun from dreams. While a student at the Academy I often explored those endless legends on foot, by bus and by subway. Sometimes I was alone and other times with Bobby, Brian, Delores or someone else. My first impression of Greenwich Village, a negative one of littered streets, was gathered on a solitary walk through the district my first few days in the city. It was not until I strolled those streets again on autumn and spring days with close companions that I came to discover the enchantment found there by generations of pilgrims in search of their *Nirvana.* On my weekends in New York City I got to know Chinatown and Little Italy. I often ended the day eating Chinese food at a favourite restaurant on Mott Street, the Port Arthur, while the sun fell in a bank of red clouds on the Jersey shore. Other times I ate at Tofenettis on Times Square, or at the Automat, a favourite eatery in those days. It always fascinated me to look through the endless racks of tiny glass windows in the Automat, drop in some coins, open a window, and take out the plate of cooked food I saw inside.

One afternoon in the fall, sitting in Battery Park with Bobby Ricker, the son of the Argentia U.S. fire chief, we began talking about the happy days we spent in Newfoundland, and

I got my first whiff of homesickness. We were watching the ferry boats ply unceasingly between Manhattan and Staten Island and the other islands in the bay. As they threaded their way among the hulls of seagoing vessels, they plowed the ebb and flow of river tides until lost to sight. I was suddenly overwhelmed by the thought that somewhere out beyond that horizon lay home. I admitted to Bobby I felt an overpowering desire to be among family and friends we loved, in familiar places, but the mood soon passed. I recall that evening, after a show and saying good-night to Bobby, I wandered about New York City, waiting for the 1:10 a.m. train back to Pleasantville. Some nights I would walk through the darkness of Central Park, with the roar of Manhattan an echo among the trees. On one such night when Doug was with me, we climbed an outcrop of rocks in the park, and half hidden in the flickering shadows of thick shrubs, delivered Shakespeare soliloquies we learned from Viola Roache to puzzled passers-by. If it sounds silly now it is because in those days we were living in an awakening world. There was laughter in our voices then, and we believed what we said, when we talked endlessly of things we hoped to do in futures that would never be.

Some Sundays, when my finances did not allow me to spend the weekend in New York, I would go by bus from Pleasantville to White Plains where I changed buses, and on to Ellen's home in New Rochelle, for dinner with her family. My friend Bobby Ricker continued to join us, and after eating, we three would take in a band concert, or some event at Iona College. There were always things to do. On occasions such as Thanksgiving and Easter, it was Doug who came with me from Pleasantville to New Rochelle. On Friday afternoons Ellen would come home from college for the weekend. Mr. and Mrs. Coughlan would allow her to take the train to New York City Saturday afternoon, where we would meet under the clock in the concourse at Grand Central. I had first to gain her parents' trust and consent before such harmless trysts were permitted. From the railway station we would set off on foot to explore the city, doing the art galleries, the museums, the Hayden Planetarium, the world's great shopping emporiums, Tiffany's, Cartier's, Macy's, Altman's, Bonwit-Teller's and Bloomingdale's. At times we would take in a play. Balcony seats at the matinees were $3.50 or less, and that was how I saw Tallulah Bankhead in *Private Lives*, Katherine Cornell in *That Man*, Alfred Lunt and Lynn Fontanne in *I Know My Love*, and my favourite MGM star Ruth Hussey in *Goodbye, My Fancy*. Tallulah was also the star of a popular TV show which had as its theme "May the Good Lord Bless and Keep You," written especially for her.

In would have been unthinkable for Ellen to stay overnight in the city, so I would see her off home on the early evening train. When she was gone I would take the shuttle from Grand Central to Times Square, and sometimes take in a Broadway play alone, or meet Brian, my friend from New Jersey, for a show or a movie. He would come over by bus, meet me in the Astor Bar, and after our evening on the town, which generally meant dinner at the Automat, take a room at the Y where I was staying. Besides sharing a love of opera and ballet we were both lifelong devotees of Gilbert & Sullivan. On Sunday afternoons we often went to the G & S performances that used to take place in Jan Hus auditorium in The Bronx. Weekends, when Bobby Ricker was able to escape from Iona and join me in Manhattan, I would take a single hotel room at the Sharon which we would share to save the expenses he couldn't afford.

Cheap matinee seats for the plays were not main floor or mezzanine, but in the upper balcony, from which I saw many of the greats of the American stage. We were what the French so lovingly call young people in the far reaches of the theatre, "*les enfants du Paradis*"— the children of Paradise who were seated up among the gods. We would pay from $2.50 to $3.50 each for a seat, and if the performance wasn't sold out, we moved downstairs into the empty seats on the main floor after the first scene or act. Not once did an usher ask us to leave. That was how I saw Helen Hayes in *The Wisteria Trees*, Jane Cowl in *The Second Mrs. Tanquery*, Maurice Evans in *The Devil's Disciple*, Martita Hunt in *The Madwoman of Chaillot*, Thomas Mitchell in *Death of a Salesman*, Eva La Gallienne in *Mary Stuart*, and Katherine Hepburn in *As You Like It*. In her production there was an unknown young actress playing Celia with whom I was afterwards to become a friend when we worked together in summer stock. Her name was Cloris Leachman. Whenever we went to the opera at the huge old Metropolitan Opera House on 39th Street, we bought standing room tickets, and again moved into unoccupied seats after the first act. I can never banish from memory the excitement of attending my first live opera.

As a boy I often tried to listen to *Saturday Afternoon at the Opera* broadcasts on short-wave radio, but there was always static to cope with, and Mother asking, "Why don't you go out and get some fresh air?" My first purchase of an operatic recording was made at Dicks & Company on Water St., when I was fifteen and in ninth grade. One Saturday I went to their record department on the second floor and used most of my weekly allowance to purchase a 12-inch RCA Victor wax recording by Lily Pons. On the advice of store manager Ivor Thistle, whose aunt, Leonore Lily of St. John's had been my mother's best friend in girlhood, I bought the "Mad Scene," from *Donezetti's Lucia di Lammermoor*, the aria "Spargi d'Amaro Pianto," which in English was "Cast On My Grave A Flower." I still have the recording and sometimes play it for the memories it brings and the pleasure it gives.

I knew Sir Walter Scott's novel *The Bride of Lammermoor* from the previous summer when I found it among my father's matching collection of Nelson's novels, which I often plundered for reading matter during my mature summers at our house in Bay de Verde. They were a set of small great novels published by T. Nelson & Sons, Ltd., a forerunner of

Pocket Books. I read of Henry Ashton's determination to avenge his wrongs upon Edward Ravenswood, regardless of the pain it was to cause his sister Lucy, the bride of Lammermoor. Knowing she went mad and killed her bridegroom on their wedding day, I was so thrilled by the recording, I wrote the Divine Lily, in care of the Met, and told her of my rapture. To my utter amazement, she answered with a signed photograph, "To Paul O'Neill, Lily Pons." I still have the Scott novel, the old, scratched, 78 rpm wax recording, and the photograph from Miss Lily Pons, which is on my office wall.

Since tinkering with opera on radio as a boy on Saturday afternoons, I dreamed of attending a performance at the Met. That dream was to come true one weekend that autumn when I came to the city from Pleasantville, took a room at the Central Park Y, and met Brian at the Jersey bus depot downtown. I had obtained tickets for us to see an evening performance of Verdi's *Il Trovatore*, with the great Tito Gobbi, Robert Merrill, then at the height of his fame, and the Italian contralto Cleo Elmo in her signature role. She had a sumptuous voice and vivid presence (I had one of her recordings at home). She stayed only two seasons at the Met and returned to Italy where, for some reason unknown to the public, she abandoned her stage career.

There were other evenings to come when we sat among the gods in the old house, now but a fast-fading memory. The great, golden curtain from the old Met stage rose for the first time in the 39th Street house, 22 October 1883, on a performance of *Faust*, and fell for the last time, eighty-three years later 17 April 1966, at the end of a star-studded, gala evening performance which came to a close with everyone holding hands on stage and in the hall, while singing the pop tune "This Old House," followed by a tearful" Auld Lang Syne." RCA Victor purchased the curtain, cut it up, numbered the pieces, and sold it with a recording package of the farewell performance. I was among those who purchased the recording and my piece of curtain now hangs in a frame beside the pictures of several opera stars on my office wall. In addition to Lily Pons, there is a photograph of one of the world's greatest singers, Geraldine Farrar. She is pictured holding two dogs and on the back she has written in her own hand, "Thanking you for your appreciation of the early records. Geraldine Farrar." Another of the framed stars on my wall is Lucrezia Bori, the great Spanish soprano, who wrote on the front of her picture, "To Mr. Paul O'Neill, Sincerely, Lucrezia Bori."

One of my most memorable theatrical experiences in New York was not at the Met but in seeing Ethel Merman at the Imperial Theatre on the closing night of the long Broadway run of *Annie Get Your Gun*. I went alone, lined up for three hours, and got a ticket for $2.40 that allowed me to stand at the back of the seats on the main floor. That evening the house was all shouts and tears as audience and ushers clamoured for each number to be belted out by Merman and cast in encore after encore. As the clock began to approach midnight, Merman called for the audience to be quiet, and said, "How about this? We'll do each number three times if you'll let me get on with it, or we'll be here all night." Everyone cheered and each of her numbers was twice encored. Toscanini once said Merman was the greatest invention since the French horn, and she was, since her voice carried to the last row of the top balcony with ease. It was well after midnight when an exhausted Ethel, cast and audience, stood, held hands, and sang together the show's biggest hit, *There's No Business Like Show Business,* as the final curtain fell on Merman's greatest triumph. The clapping and cheering, through tears, continued for nearly ten minutes, while the object of our adoration stood center stage, deluged in hugs, kisses, flowers and paper streamers flung from the audience.

What was perhaps my most moving evening of theater in New York involved the marvelous black singer and actress Ethel Waters, who was making a comeback from many years of heartache and obscurity, helped by the recent publication of her autobiography *His Eye Is On The Sparrow.* Bobby came in from New Rochelle and met me as usual at that popular haunt of actors, the Astor Bar. We each sipped a Manhattan, because it was the only drink either of us had enough self-confidence to order, or even liked to taste. Except for a cool beer at O'Gorman's Bar in Pleasantville on hot summer nights, I knew little or nothing about alcoholic spirits, although I was nineteen. After we had dinner at Tofenetti's, we strolled down Broadway to the St. James Theatre where we had tickets for a play both of us were longing to see. It was *The Member of the Wedding*, adapted by Carson McCullers from her own book, and starring Ethel Waters.

The evening turned into one of pure theatrical enchantment as we watched the charming and sentimental play. What made *The Member of the Wedding* so extraordinary were the performances of the three leads, Ethel Waters, Brandon de Wilde and Julie Harris. Ethel played a black housekeeper, Bernice Sadie Brown. I will never forget her sitting in a rocking chair on stage in the semi-darkness, her arms around the two children, singing the spiritual "His Eye Is On The Sparrow." One of those children, eight-year-old John Henry, was played by little Brandon de Wilde. He was so touching in the play that when little John Henry died on stage, people all over the theatre, including myself, were sniffling and wiping away tears. Brandon de Wilde will forever remain etched in movie-goers' memories as a small boy crying out a heartbroken, "Come back, Shane," in the final moments of Alan Ladd's classic movie, *Shane.* Brandon later starred in other movies such as *Blue Denim.*

The most remarkable performance in the play, however, was that of thirteen-year-old Frankie, a lonely teenage girl played by a skinny young actress in her mid-20s, Julie Harris. When Ethel Waters took her curtain call that evening she said to the audience, "Ladies and gentlemen, I would now like to introduce you to the next great lady of the American stage." She went offstage and led on Julie Harris, looking so small and fragile. She was given one of only two standing ovations I was ever to see on Broadway. The other was for Patricia Neway, utterly stunning as Magda, in Gian Carlo Menotti's opera, *The Consul.* Neway was later to win a Tony Award for her portrayal of the Mother Abbess in the original production of *The Sound of Music.* Ethel Waters was right about Julie Harris, however; she did indeed become one of the great ladies of the American stage, screen and television.

Musicals, such as *Annie Get Your Gun*, were at the top of my theatrical menu in those days, and I thoroughly enjoyed them, starting with Beatrice Lillie's antics in John Gunther's *Inside U.S.A.*, which I saw with another pen friend, Irma, my first week in New York. Many funny stories are told about Queen Bea, as Miss Lillie was called by her fellow thespians. She was married to Sir Robert Peel, an Englishman and direct descendant of Sir Robert Peel, founder of the London Police known as bobbies. A story told about her I especially enjoy concerned when she was appearing in Chicago. She went to see her favourite hairdresser, whom we shall call Gladys, for a clip and curl. While Bea was sitting under the hairdryer, Mrs. Swift, dowager wife of the millionaire meat packing czar, walked in. The Swift woman demanded Gladys do her hair immediately, and was shocked to be told she would have to wait since Gladys was occupied with Miss Lillie. The dragon lady of Chicago demanded to know who this Miss Lillie was. When told she was the star of a show playing in a downtown theatre, the society matron huffed in a loud voice, "Tell Gladys to hurry up with that actress woman. Say Mrs. Swift is waiting." Afterwards, when Bea was paying her bill in front of the perturbed society matron, she turned to Gladys, and said, in that equally loud and famous voice of hers, "By the way, Gladys, you can tell the butcher's wife that Lady Peel is through."

I was utterly enthralled by Cole Porter's *Kiss Me, Kate*, with Alfred Drake and Patricia Morrison, which I saw just six weeks after its opening. All the songs were fresh, dazzling and very exciting. I was also quite overwhelmed by Mary

Martin washing that man right out of her hair in *South Pacific,* which I saw with Mother's brother, my Uncle Phil. After I watched Ray Bolger with Judy Garland in the movie *The Wizard of Oz,* he became my favourite scarecrow. In his hit Broadway musical *Where's Charley?* He asked the audience to join him in singing a chorus of the show's hit song "Once In Love With Amy." Doug, my roommate, and I joined our voices with the rest of the audience and the result was a night to remember. The show was a musical version of the old Brandon Thomas chestnut, *Charley's Aunt,* and because of Ray's performance, it now has a special page in my book of outstanding theatrical events. I was also captivated by a fantastic unknown when I saw an actress named Carol Channing on stage for the first time. I was sure I was seeing the birth of a star, but I was wrong. She was to become a super nova when she sang "Diamonds Are A Girl's Best Friend" in the stage hit *Gentlemen Prefer Blonds.*

Sonja Henie had been a secret passion of mine as a kid. The Brookfield Ice Cream Company in St. John's used to hand out 8" x 10" coloured pictures of movie stars in exchange for the covers of Dixie Cups, those small tubs of ice cream you bought for a nickel. I collected enough Dixie Cup covers to get a picture of the honey-haired Olympic figure skating champion from Norway, who had stolen my affections in *Sun Valley Serenade.* When I went to the Brookfield office on LeMarchant Road, after getting out of school one afternoon, the man I talked with wanted to give me a picture of Bobby Breen that was lying on the counter. I hated Bobby Breen and his teen movies in which he had a golden voice, behaved perfectly, was kind to old people, etc. I told the man he was a sissy, and insisted on a photo of Sonja. Grumbling, the fellow went off to search for her picture and returned with one. Over the years that picture of Sonja Henie, pinned to my bedroom wall, slowly faded. After going to New York I went to see her skate in the flesh, as star of the Broadway musical, *Howdy, Mr. Ice,* which brought my boyhood dreamgirl back to life.

Like people everywhere who grow up with the ocean's ebb and tide at their doorstep, I found I missed the nearness of the Atlantic when I was living in Pleasantville, Westchester County. The untamed sea was in my blood, and the Hudson was no substitute. I had grown up with the North Atlantic growling outside my window. It was the breast that nursed generations of my family. Sometimes in Pleasantville, whenever I felt a compulsion for the sights and sounds of the ocean, I would go to the city and take the subway to the beach at Coney Island, where I could breathe with an unbroken view of the Atlantic.

I first heard of the world famous amusement park, Coney Island, from my mother who sometimes went there in the 1920s when she lived and worked in New York as a governess. She spent weekends and holidays on the Spalding's large summer estate at East Hampton, a refuge of the wealthy, at the far end of Long Island. Like nearby Jones Beach, or the Boardwalk in Atlantic City, Coney Island was the subject of numerous turn-of-the-century song and dance numbers I had watched endlessly at Saturday movie matinees in St. John's in company with my boyhood friends, Ron O'Brien, Tom Cahill, and of course, my brother John. We would sit entranced by Alice Faye, Betty Grable, June Haver, Vivian Blaine, Doris Day et al, as they strutted about the screens of the Capital, the Nickel, or most often the Star theatre, belting out Gay '90s song hits in sugar-coated, Technicolor musicals.

I remember the first time I rode Coney Island's famous Thunderbolt roller-coaster with Doug on a warm spring afternoon. After arriving at Grand Central in the city, we took the subway to the beach where we strolled about in unaccustomed sunshine, kicking the warming sand with naked feet, our shoes hung around our necks. We visited what peep shows were open for the season, until we came at last to that monster roller-coaster. When I staggered off the Thunderbolt at the end of a hair-raising ride, I threw up immediately. It was embarrassing in front of Doug, but then moments later he, too, was sick. I always suffered terribly from motion sickness. The giant Ferris wheel, on the other hand, provided an entirely different sensation. It was exciting to sit in one of the open gondolas and be whisked up through the twilight to the stars. From atop the wheel you looked towards the lights of Manhattan coming from far away. It was like someone peering over a balustrade and seeing a great ballroom being slowly lit up.

Another place on Long Island I sometimes visited for a weekend with Doug or Brian was Fire Island. A workmate of Brian's, also from Jersey City, had taken a house which he shared at the Pines with two friends for the summer. They had given him an open invitation to stay overnight whenever he wished, and to bring a friend, as they had spare sleeping bags. Fire Island, unlike Coney Island, was a real island, on the outer banks of America. You took the train from Pennsylvania Station to Sayville, beyond Amityville, a community that was later to become the scene of the most infamous horror hoax in America. Amityville was almost halfway from Manhattan to Montauk, the northern tip of Long Island. In those days, Sayville was a delightful village of white houses with painted shutters, basking in the shade of elm-lined streets. At the wharf you caught a ferry across the shallow water to the slim sandbar that was Fire Island, now a national seashore.

In that long ago autumn of 1950 the Pines was still a place where the nights were filled with little more than the flutter of sea breezes, gentle music and sounds of laughter. Doug and I had gone to Fire Island, wide eyes gleaming with wonder, and drank in the enchantment of soft lights, gentle music and the embrace of friends. In the dark, the reflection of lights on the water trembled like the beautiful illusions that lit up our lives. We would sit on a weather-beaten deck above the sands, discovering the delight of a gin and tonic over that of a Tom Collins. For me, life was still a strangely compelling fantasy and a glamorous legacy of adventurous ideals. A year earlier, back in St. John's, I had been sitting in a dusty, old classroom at St. Bon's, trying to get my Grade Twelve certificate. Now I was entirely on my own, becoming slowly absorbed in what I imagined would be the rest of my life.

Fire Island was in those days a collection of shacks occupied by poets and other writers, which as writer Andrew Holleran says, became "a Malibu, mobbed each summer by hordes of youths quiet as deer coming to your hand for salt." As time went on, those hordes, quiet as deer, turned into wild, profligate mobs, who glorified their defiance of convention in orgies of unbridled sex, booze and drugs, becoming as jaded as the ancient queens who flapped among them like death's heads, until all were smothered in clouds of angel dust and devastated by the plague of AIDS. As this lifestyle was directly opposed to the one that appealed to me, we soon stopped going to Fire Island. I never returned there again.

To be young, full of unpruned dreams, and with a city like New York as your oyster in the late '40s and early '50s, was like entering a sun-blazed valley where the shadows were merely an enhancement of the beauty. You didn't ever think of going back to anything that had been before, only of following your rainbow. It is always exciting to do things you have never done, think thoughts you have never thought, go places you have never gone. That is the joy of youth in every generation, just as it is the pain of age to know, when you have done what you must do, thought what you must think, gone where you must go, the rainbow remains forever elusive.

One weekend after we came back from touring *Toby Tyler*, I met Ellen Coughlan for dinner at the Candlelight Restaurant in Yonkers which was owned and operated by a Newfoundland woman, Patricia Murphy from Placentia. The Candlelight was, for many years, one of the popular New York eateries for tourists and locals alike. While we were dining, Ellen knocked the stars from my sky by telling me she was about to become engaged to a young man she had been seeing for several years before we met. He was someone she loved very much and would be marrying, and that was that. I realized as she was talking, she looked upon me only as a good friend, while I had come to consider her as someone special in my life. Sad to say, having gotten the hint, I never contacted her again. I also lost touch with Brian, who was called up by the Draft, and even Bobby Ricker who went to a southern university, as I moved about North America and Britain with touring companies before finally settling at home in St. John's where the best things in life were yet to be.

Andrew Moore and Elizabeth (O'Neill) Moore of Bay de Verde.
My great grandparents on my mother's side.

Grandfather John O'Neill of Bay de Verde.

James O'Neill, Paul O'Neill's father.

Paul and brother John.

Paul and John.

John O'Neill and son Paul O'Neill.

Paul and Mom.
Graduation from St. Bons.

Paul, John & Josephine.

56 Cochrane St. home.

Paul O'Neill.

Paul in Bowring Park.

Paul leaving by ship for America with Mom and Dad.

Paul O'Neill and Mother Theresa.

Chapter 9

The Wind Blows, The Sea Flows

William Butler Yeats says, "No art can conquer the people alone. The people are conquered by an ideal of life upheld by authority." This ideal of life, Yeats tells us, is found in the arts — music, drama, poetry, painting and literature — all of which draw us closer together. Culture evolves from an impression of the senses of sensitive people. The arts are the means whereby our values, one might even say the moral element, is injected into the social order and becomes part of life, not as the subject of study, performance and exhibition, but as a revolt of individualism because our traditions have been downgraded. Society, the interaction of men and women within the state, must restate the traditions in constantly changing forms if they are not to be lost. The more formal they grow, the more empty they become. It is the role of the creative artist, not politicians, to keep us in a state of perpetual revolt, but one rooted deeply in our past, as deeply as modern Christian worship is rooted in ancient pagan rituals. We cannot inspire culture in everyone but we can share a simple understanding of who and what we are. It is not sentiment, with a few thoughts and feelings thrown in, that inspires a people. That is often the way of the politically unmotivated. The imagination is roused with curiosity among those people involved in the arts who have a need, indeed a destiny, to be among the most curious.

Perhaps it is just as well we sometimes make an end to special friendships. I will always see the blond-haired Ellen as young, beautiful and beloved, the auburn-haired Brian as handsome, prepossessing and sincere, the copper-haired Bobby Ricker as amusing, eternally devilish, his lithe body full of remarkable energy. Ellen was the more beautiful for the impatient smile she wore when we were trying to make up our minds to do something or go somewhere. Brian was the more good-looking for the sarcastic grin with which he tried to mask his true sentiments. Bobby was the more cherished for his endless pranks and irrepressible laughter, still echoing after many years. There was to be one more woman with whom I hoped to entwine my life and love, but I had yet to meet her.

In those days I was very good at impressions and had I kept at it might have had a career as an impersonator. I remember on one autumn visit to Coney Island, with Ellen and Bobby, when the three of us sat on the sand at the end of the season, and I had the two of them rollicking with my impressions of Walter Brennan, Ethel Barrymore, Thomas Mitchell, Peter Lorre, Maria Ouspenskaya, Robert Newton and others. We sat like crows, in a kind of arc, with Ellen in the middle, trying to fascinate each other with chatter, watching the sun reflect on waves that rolled in with boring regularity, hearing the poignant sounds of summer coming to an end around us. Men were hammering shut their concessions. As the sun was setting and we grew quiet, a scattering of sprightly children ran past, turned back and shouted to us, but their words were unintelligible in the breezes. The thought never occurred to me then, as it has now, that one day we too, like those children racing across the sand, would stop, turn back and shout to each other, but our voices would be no longer heard, having become lost in the winds of time.

Where I come from,
Nobody knows;
And where I'm going,
Everything goes.

Ellen interrupted me as I began to murmur the tuneless ditty.

"What's that...a poem?" She asked.

"It's 'Jennie's Song' from the movie of Robert Nathan's novel — *Portrait of Jennie.* A new movie starring Jennifer Jones that recently opened."

"Where I'm going, everything goes..." Bobby mused. "I once read a Robert Nathan novel, *One More Spring.* I really liked it, even if it was a bit pretentious, and didn't make a hell of a lot of sense to me."

"Books sometimes make sense only in your imagination," I answered.

"OK. It was beautifully written." He gave me a smile.

"I've corresponded with Robert Nathan, and I know his wife," I announced, pausing a moment for the impression this information would have on my two friends.

"You corresponded with Nathan?" Bobby was riddled with disbelief.

"And you know his wife?" Ellen voiced her surprise.

"Well ... I don't actually know either of them," I confessed, "but I have corresponded with him several times, and once with his wife, Janet. They live in Truro, Massachusetts. I loved *Portrait of Jennie* and another of his novels, *One More Spring,* but it wasn't until I read *The Sea-Gull Cry* that he became my favourite author. I wrote and told him I was going to become an actor, and if ever they made a movie of *The Sea-Gull Cry* I would dearly love to have the chance to play the young professor. He amazed me by writing back and telling me that a few years earlier, he'd had a letter from a fifteen-year-old school girl in Alabama when *A Portrait of Jennie* was published. She hoped to become a movie actress, loved reading *Jennie,* and felt she was destined to play the part on screen. He said he wrote to try and dissuade her from trying her fortune in Hollywood, a place of endless disappointments, but she didn't listen. Neither did she get to play *Jennie.* However, he said, he was amazed to run into her years later in Hollywood, where she was going into her first big movie role. She reminded him of the letter she had written as a schoolgirl ..."

"Who was she?" Bobby cut me short.

"Let him finish." Ellen demanded and asked me, "What was the movie?"

"The picture in which she was about to appear was *The Best Years of Our Lives.*"

"Damn you, who was she?" Bobby kept insisting.

"A young starlet under personal contract to the producer, Samuel Goldwyn," I said.

"Teresa Wright." Bobby pounded the sand with glee, delighted to have beaten me at my own game. "I saw *Best Years* and one of the stars was Teresa Wright."

"I'm sorry to rain on your parade, smarty, but Teresa Wright was already a star when she made *Best Years,*" I added with mocking disdain. "In 1941 she won an Oscar as Best Supporting Actress in *Mrs. Miniver.*"

"Please tell us who she was." Ellen begged.

"Cathy O'Donnel," I smirked. "She had her first major role in *The Best Years of Our Lives* playing the high-school sweetheart of double amputee Homer Parrish, played by a real-life World War II amputee veteran, Harold Russell, whose parents were Newfoundlanders."

Ellen nodded with a smile.

"Cathy O'Donnel is now starring in a new movie with Farley Granger." Bobby said. "*They Live By Night.*"

"I saw her in *Your Red Wagon,*" Ellen offered. "She must have made that after *Best Years.* She was never a big star..."

"May I finish my story?" I interrupted sarcastically.

"What story?" Bobby had lost track.

"I was telling you what Robert Nathan said to me in his letter."

"About Cathy O'Donnel... Go on, tell us."

"She's not the point of the story, Bobby," I exclaimed.

"Then what is the point?" Ellen was by now also losing patience.

"Robert Nathan said, when he met Cathy O'Donnel on a studio lot when she was about to become a star, the experience taught him never again to discourage anyone from going for their dream. 'Who knows?' Nathan wrote to me in his letter, 'Someday you might get to play the professor in a movie of *The Sea-Gull Cry*.'"

"What did Mrs. Nathan write you about?" Bobby was inquisitive.

"Mostly it was about her husband's new novel, *Long After Summer*. She said it was a Cape Cod or sea book, and those who enjoyed *Jennie* would be equally pleased with it. Do you want to know something? If I wasn't going to become an actor I would most probably be a writer. It's something I've wanted to do even longer than to be an actor... I'd like to write beautiful prose like Robert Nathan, and poetry, too."

"I always wanted to be a dancer," Ellen said, in a rather wistful voice. I knew that, as she had written me about it several times. "But the more I study for my business degree the more I realize my wish to be a dancer is little more than a fantasy. My parents would never allow it. I know now I'll end up in an office somewhere."

"I want to write songs," Bobby said with a grin like a Cheshire cat. "So what am I doing trekking into the city every day to work in a brokerage firm? Ambition... hah! What's it get us?"

"I told you," I insisted. "Harold Russell's parents came from Newfoundland. They moved to Nova Scotia where he was born. The family afterwards settled in Boston. Russell, who lost both his hands during the war, won an Oscar for playing himself, a handless former U.S. Navy man in *The Best Years of Our Lives* without ever thinking of becoming an actor. In fact, he won two Oscars that year, Best Supporting Actor and an honorary Oscar for bringing hope and courage to his fellow veterans. I ask you, why should his dreams be any more potent than mine?"

"He never dreamed of being an actor, you just told us that," Bobby took the wind out of my sails. "Just imagine, he got the part because he was a wounded G.I." Bobby's answer sounded cynical, but it was to the point so he went on. "You have to have a gimmick going for you in show business these days. What's yours?"

I fell silent and never answered him.

The last time I saw Bobby was just before Christmas 1950, when I got back to New York, from the *Toby Tyler* tour that ended in the American West. Feeling a bit homesick, I decided to fly to St. John's from New York City to spend the holiday season with my family in Newfoundland. Although I had no intimation of it then, I would never again work in America, and would only visit the country as a tourist. I did have in mind some thoughts of going to London.

When I saw my friend Brian for the last time, it was at a café near the American Airlines terminal in downtown Manhattan, where we had arranged to meet. As we dawdled over lunch, he looked preoccupied. I asked what was wrong. He told me he had been drafted into the United States Army, was to report to boot camp in a few days, and feared being sent to fight in the Korean War. We were both pacifists who hated war and we had often discussed the subject. That afternoon he confessed he didn't have the guts to register as the conscientious objector he was. He told me if he did so, his father would be utterly shamed to have a son unwilling to serve his country, although that had nothing to do with his decision.

The same thing happened to the actor who played Captain John Smith in a play we were touring about Pocahontas, a fellow named Ted Stephens, who like Brian was also from New Jersey. When a draft call came for him, while we were touring on the road, our producer, Clare Tree Major, managed to get him deferred until the end of the tour. Ted also hated war, but felt it would be considered un-American not to let himself be drafted and shipped out with bugles blaring and banners flapping in the breeze. I never heard from or of him again.

Brian and I never met again either. I had one letter from him at an Army Post Office address, to which I sent a reply but never received an answer. I don't know if he ever went to Korea, or if he ever went and came back alive because, strange to say, we never corresponded again. I feel sure he was badly wounded or died in that awful war, probably on some lonely, snow-swept Korean hillside. Much to my own regret in after years, I never returned to New York from that Christmas flight home, except as a tourist. The major reason for my coming home was that I would also have had to register for the draft had I returned to America because of my status as a permanent resident of the United States. And so events that had absolutely nothing whatever to do with either of us, half a world away, changed the course of our lives. Instead of returning to New York to resume my career after my Christmas holiday in Newfoundland, and because the Korean War had begun in June 1950, I went to London, England instead.

Whenever we were on tour a part of my heart always remained behind in New York City, a place where anything can happen to anyone and often does. In one of his show tunes, Leonard Bernstein wrote, "New York, New York, it's a hell of a town." To me in the late '40s, without a serious social conscience, it was anything but a hell of a town. It was magic. When Rudolph Bing was asked why he moved from the refined elegance of London's Royal Opera House, Covent Garden, to take over as general manager of the Metropolitan Opera House in Manhattan, amidst the hectic pace and babble of the great city, he answered simply, "Because New York is where it's at." For me, even after all these years, New York and London are still the only two places on earth "where it's at." My memories of New York and London are of two very wonderful cities that came at a marvellous time in my life that I will never again be able to repeat.

Chapter 10

Those Who Dream Dreams

A year at the National Academy meant a full year with only brief holidays at Christmas and the beginning of summer. Graduation was in early September. Within a week after our graduation, the next group of students began their year. The graduation ceremony for the Class of '49 was held in the garden of Mrs. Major's estate in Chappaqua, a few miles from Pleasantville. Family and friends, including my mother, came from near and far to witness the events, including our student production of scenes from *Macbeth* in which I played the title role. Next day, those of us who wanted a theatrical job and agreed to employment in one of Clare Tree Major's five touring companies of the Children's Theatre of America, were cast in various plays, rehearsed with other actors she hired, and sent on the road for eight months playing in theatres and auditoriums from New York to California and back. Male actors were paid $40 per week while females got $35. The reason given was that male actors toted about scenery, costumes, etc. while the actresses had only to take the costumes down from where they hung in the large costume box, iron them when necessary and put them back on hangers in the box after the show.

10 September 1949, after being given a sendoff wave by Mrs. Major, the *Toby Tyler* Company headed west for California. Our play, based on the 1880 children's book, *Toby Tyler, or Ten Weeks with a Circus* by James Otis Koler, was the story of a small boy who runs away from home and ends up in a circus act with a monkey. Our first engagement was September 15

at the Delft Theatre in Crystal Falls, Michigan. The stage on which we gave our first performance, a matinee, was terrible and we were forced to cut a lot of the business and scenery. However, the sponsors thought it all went over well. We generally played to full houses and sometimes, such as at St. Paul, Minnesota, we played to 5,000 people. Our matinee performance at Huron College, Huron, South Dakota, went over extremely well. The auditorium in Aberdeen, South Dakota, had a skating rink attached. While we were playing to kids and their parents on one side, the skating show *Icelandia,* from Iceland, was playing to kids and their parents on the other side of the wall.

Since starting our tour in September, we had been through thirty States by September 29 when we arrived in Miles City, Montana. We were the first theatre company ever known to play on stage in Miles City. Our matinee and evening performance went over well. During the evening show on September 30 we had a mishap on stage. Among the many wonderful newspaper reviews we got were a few which I'm going to quote since they refer to me. One Montana reviewer wrote, "The clown portrayed by Paul O'Neill furnished plenty of action and elicited much laughter." Another said, "The clown Boser was played by Paul O'Neill who delighted his audience with pranks and pantomime, all lent a true feeling of the sawdust circle to the production."

The Miles City Sunday paper observed, "The clown, in his antics, was a casualty, when he slipped on the stage floor and cut his chin quite badly. With the idea, 'the show must go on,' however, he finished the play and then went to the hospital for treatment." I remember leaping on stage and slipping. There was a barrel in front of me with a metal hook around the top. As I went down my chin struck the hook and I was knocked out for several seconds. When I came to and was helped to my feet, I discovered a gash just under my chin that was spilling blood on my costume. With the help of chin wraps of some sort I finished the performance and was taken immediately to Holy Rosary Hospital where they let me go after stitching the unfortunate cut. It was the first and only time I suffered such a mishap on stage. The stitches were removed about a week after my accident. In Butte, the capital of Montana, I was able to call in at the Irish Christian Brothers school and find two of my teachers from St. Bonaventure's College in St. John's teaching there, Brother O'Dwyer and Brother Dunphy.

I don't remember much to catch the eye in Wyoming except Yellowstone Park, where we saw the world famous geyser, Old Faithful, shooting its water into the air right on time. I liked Wyoming and found it had the atmosphere of cowboy days long past. In Pinedale, we made an overnight stop that was to be quite meaningful for me. After the show we returned to the Park Hotel where, to my surprise, a supper was laid out for us in the dining room and in the middle of the table was a cake with 21 candles burning on top. The company had discovered my secret, that October 26 was my 21st birthday and were throwing a party for me that is today an enchanting memory.

The worst performance I recall us giving was in Logan, Utah, where we played in an almost empty theatre while a major snowstorm howled outside. All that was on anyone's mind was that raging blizzard that almost drowned us out, yet the Logan *Herald Journal* critic said of my performance, "The clown, brilliantly decked in green and red stripes, was endlessly amusing with his lithesome tumbling and prankish tricks." I remember our having to cope with numerous blizzards and snow storms in the American west. In Ogdon, Utah for example, we were half an hour late arriving at the theatre due to the worst blizzard we were to encounter but strangely enough, the show was our best to date. At the Fox Theatre in Spokane, Washington, we gave two performances and had standing-room-only audiences of 2,300 at each. November 21 we finally caught our first sight of the Pacific Ocean at Tillamook, Oregon, 71 days after leaving New York, completing our trek across the continent.

It is amazing the things actors sometimes have to cope with. For example, it came as a shock to us in Washington State when our company manager, George Scutt, who was in his 60s, went missing. I telephoned the police on behalf of the other players to report his absence. They told me they were holding him on a charge at the police station and that I should come to the jail to discuss the matter. I was speechless when they said he was arrested for sexually molesting a teenage boy that afternoon in a movie theatre. To tell you the truth, I don't remember now what I did but somehow I got him out on bail after several days of meeting with the authorities. Meanwhile, we had three or four performances immediately ahead of us so we were puzzled as to how to cover for him. We ended up having me play most of George's scenes in addition to the clown and somehow managed to get through the performances without the sponsors being any the wiser, although a few did ask, "What happened to Mr. Scutt?" He had been in earlier performances of Children's Theatre of America where they got to know him. After four or five days we were finished our engagements in that area so we picked up George at the hotel where he was hiding out and fled to southern California. We were never bothered again by the incident.

I generally enjoyed touring. Though the pace is always hectic, there are some periods of three or four days when you have no performance and can enjoy where you are. However, I recall one place where we gave two shows which were oversold even though we couldn't perform in the theatre, which was under repair, so we played in the most ridiculous of circumstances on the University of Oregon's gym floor to two howling, disinterested audiences. We were forced to use microphones and I can tell you plenty went wrong. Around that time four of our company informed George they would be leaving the show in Los Angeles where they hoped they would find work in movies. The four characters, who would have to be replaced by other actors, were Toby Tyler, the Fat Woman, the Thin Man and the Bare Back Rider.

I recall most of us who had never been to California really looked forward to arriving there. That was to happen on December 15 when we drove down the Oregon coast in a nuisance rain. At 6:30 p.m. we entered California where we found huge single rooms at the old Central Hotel in Eureka and next day we drove on to San Francisco where we parked our car and set out for "the top of the Mark." This is the famous tourist spot on the top floor of the Mark Hopkins Hotel. After a few drinks, we went on to dinner at the extremely popular Fisherman's Wharf. December 23 we gave a performance at the San Jose State College to a theatre that was almost empty. I expect it was too close to Christmas. After the show we stored the truck, loaded with the costumes and other stage properties, in Bakersfield and kept the car for our own use. Some of the actors went to spend the holidays with friends and relations while the rest of us put up at the luxurious St. Moritz Hotel on Sunset Boulevard in Hollywood.

Christmas Day, my second Christmas away from home, Doug and I were invited to Delores Marshall's home in Balboa, even though we had never met either her father or her mother. They proved extremely pleasant and generous people. Sadly, Delores was touring with the *Sleeping Beauty* Company, performing on the East Coast. Trader Vic's was a beautiful seaside bar and a sort of nightclub in Balboa and very popular with film stars, although there were none there on Christmas Day because the place was closed to the public so that Mr. and Mrs. Marshall could entertain Doug and me. It was indeed a memorable occasion and I shall never forget Balboa.

As we were going to be staying for some days in Los Angeles, we moved to the less expensive Stowell Hotel. George Scutt, our *Toby Tyler* company manager, back on the job, was forced to seek replacements for Mary Elizabeth Thompson, Buddy Holcombe, Muriel Sweep and Doug Lynch when all four resigned from the company. I assisted George in hiring replacement actors from the famous acting school, The

Pasadena Playhouse in nearby Pasadena. The replacements were auditioned and we arranged for those hired to come and see us give our second last performance with the original cast in San Bernardino on January 10. It was one of the best presentations of the tour. The new actors were introduced as Andrea (Bobbie) Blayne, who would be replacing Mary as Lily Treat, the Fat Lady (although she was herself quite thin), Tyler Glen Duff, who was replacing Buddy as Mr. Treat, the Thin Man, (a part once played in an earlier CTA company by film star John Dall of *The Corn is Green* fame), Elizabeth Fillman was replacing Muriel as Ella, the bareback rider, and Robert Hallgren, replacing Doug in the lead role as the runaway boy Toby Tyler.

The 10th of January 1950 is important to me because on that day I met Andrea, who would become, and forever remain, the greatest love of my life. She was an actress who, after all these years, still stirs romantic longings in me. Andrea's stage name was not her real name. It was fashionable in those days for performers to adopt pseudonyms. Her real name was Blayne Andrea Beatty, from St. Paul, Minnesota. Thinking Blayne Beatty sounded too masculine, she switched her first and second names, becoming Andrea Blayne, and dropped her surname Beatty. Anyway, we all called her by her nickname, Bobbie, which I shall do forever.

January 14 we did our last show, a matinee, with the old company at the Methodist Auditorium in Pasadena. Next time the curtain rose on *Toby Tyler*, strangers would be playing four of the parts. When we finished loading the truck, we said our parting words accompanied by hugs, kisses and a few tears. Doug and I had said our goodbyes in the room we shared at the Stowell that morning. In the time we had known each other we had become more like brothers than merely friends, so parting was no simple matter of a handshake and trading good luck wishes. In the year we were roommates we shared our lives. In that hotel room the wonderful reality of our relationship, its ups and downs, was suddenly ending, almost as if it never happened. St. Augustine says, "A friend should be loved freely for himself and not for anything else." That is exactly how it was between us and not for anything else. We would later share our friendship again in a far away country, but neither of us knew it then. With every fibre of my being I wanted to stay behind and take my chances on finding success in the movies, but I was compelled to complete my contract out of loyalty to Mrs. Major, and seek success on the New York stage where I was certain my true destiny lay, not in the movies.

Before our final show, George Scutt and I went back to the Pasadena Playhouse to have a read through with the replacement actors we hired from the auditions. When our afternoon chore was done, George returned to the hotel while I stayed over in Pasadena to have dinner with Bobbie and a few of the other actors. I was delighted when she invited me to come see her that evening as one of the leading actors in the Playhouse production of *The Young and Fair*, a popular Broadway hit of the time. I found her an inspired actress who totally captivated me with her grace and presence on stage and off. She was beautiful, elegant, and utterly charming. Although I did not know it then, a feeling of romance was already beginning to bloom.

Everyone was up early for breakfast on Monday morning after which we picked up the new actors at their lodgings and headed east after a morning rehearsal of the show at the Playhouse. With Tyler Glen Duff, a good-looking, if somewhat moody, young actor as my new roommate, we entered Arizona on January 16, viewed the Grand Canyon and drove on to Prescott, a place that struck me as a remote town high in the mountains where we spent the whole of the next day rehearsing the new company in the ballroom of the Hotel St. Michael. From Prescott we took alternate U.S. Highway 89 to Clarkdale, a community that was smothering in sulfur fumes, and on the verge of becoming a ghost town. There, on January 18, the new cast gave its first performance at the Civic Auditorium. As was to be expected, much went wrong. However, the sponsors were pleased and we knew things would shape up in the next few days.

From Prescott we wove our way through masses of cactus, over deserts alive with rolling tumbleweed, to Phoenix, where the company put up at the St. James Hotel. I was invited to stay with the Van Zants, parents of my friend Susan, a fellow student in Pleasantville, who was on tour with the *Cinderella* Company, which included another of my lifelong friends, Evelyn Bohn of Harrisburg, Pennsylvania. The Van Zants owned a Mexican restaurant, Pancho's Patio, where they entertained our whole cast at dinner. Following the meal Bobbie and I went to the Ann Lee Theatre where the great and marvelous Jane Cowl mesmerized us in her 1947 Broadway success, *The First Mrs. Fraser.* In 1923, she had made Broadway history by playing Shakespeare's Juliet in over 1,000 consecutive performances. Critic George Jean Nathan once declared Jane Cowl was "not ... the best Juliet that I have seen, but she is by all odds the most charming." After playing matinees in Roswell and Artesia we arrived in Carlsbad, New Mexico, where we stayed overnight, and for $1.50 toured the world famous caverns. At the 750-foot level you could buy lunch for 50 cents. Then it was on down to the 900-foot level and back up to the top by elevator.

By the time we gave our next performance, in the Ilfeld Auditorium at Highlands University, Las Vegas, the new actors had the play down pat, and it was a great success. After that we had a few days off in the enchanting New Mexico city of Santa Fe. We crossed Texas with stops in Roby and Dallas. I was by then quite smitten with Bobbie, who seemed to be responding to my ardour. We broke Mrs. Major's cardinal rule of "no twosing" in her companies, and spent much of our spare time together. From Dallas I took the car with Bobbie, Tyler and Betty and drove to Shreveport, Louisiana, on our way to our next engagement in Arkansas. George and the rest of the cast followed a different route in the truck. Had we given a performance in Shreveport, who knows, perhaps a teenaged Elvis Presley might have come to watch and ask us for our autographs, as he was living there at the time.

It was January 28 and the beginning of spring in that part of the country, with flowers and trees in bud. We navigated terrible roads through the bayous of Louisiana and the cotton fields of Arkansas in order to reach Pine Bluff, where we rejoined the others for one performance and a three-day stay. During our Pine Bluff layover we began rehearsals for a new play for us as the *Toby Tyler* tour was coming to an end. The new play we would be touring was Ouida's classic fairy tale, *The Nuremberg Stove.* Kentucky roads were in flood as we made our way north. Numerous detours took us to bookings in Paducah, Hopkinsville, and Bristol, a town whose main street straddled the Tennessee-Virginia state line. Dry on the Tennessee side, it was wet on the Virginia side, with plenty of bars.

In Richmond, Virginia, we found Mrs. Major ensconced in a beautiful suite at the handsome old Jefferson Hotel. She was as imperious as Queen Victoria, whom she greatly resembled. We were booked into the more modest Martha Washington Tourist Home. The grand dame was in town to rehearse us for three days. *The Nuremberg Stove* tells of a family who, falling on hard times, are forced to sell a beloved heirloom, a stove hand-painted by a Renaissance master. An English writer of sentimental, romantic novels, Ouida was best known for *Under Two Flags* and the children's classic *A Dog of Flanders,* which has been filmed a number of times. I was to play the Austrian emperor, Franz Joseph, and Bobbie was the Empress Elizabeth. The new actors all impressed Clare Tree with their acting talents and she invited the whole company to dine with her at the Jefferson Hotel before she returned to New York by train.

We gave the last performance of *Toby Tyler* for six weeks February 13, in Annapolis, Maryland, and departed for Pleasantville, arriving in a snow storm. Tyler Glen Duff and I took the room I shared with Doug at Mrs. Flynn's. She had not rented it again after we left. The first performance of

The Nuremburg Stove was given in Huntington, Long Island, February 17. From Huntington we were off to Meriden, Connecticut, where we performed in the high school auditorium.

There we parted with the obnoxious Judy, the monkey in *Toby Tyler*, whom Mrs. Major had purchased from a pet store to play the role of Mr. Stubbs, the monkey on stage in the show. Doug volunteered for the chore of looking after her, which meant feeding "Miss Poo," as we all called her. She was not only a nasty lady but dropped smelly reminders after her. Muriel Sweep gave Judy the name Miss Poo. She slept in a cage in Doug's and my bedroom which the company provided rent free. Her six weeks' vacation was spent in the monkey house at the children's museum, a sort of zoo, in Hartford, Connecticut, where George had taken her. While our *Toby Tyler* primate co-star was on holiday in Hartford, *The Nuremburg Stove* company played in such places as Philadelphia, Newark and Doylestown, where we had charming rooms (for a change) at the Bucks County Inn.

Since the beginning of the tour, the truck, which we called "Bertha" (the car was called "Tallulah"), had been giving us nothing but trouble and we were involved in one breakdown after another as we crossed the continent. The account I kept of our tour mentions the truck breaking down endless times; once, when we were high in the Rocky Mountains late one very snowy evening, the actors had to be rescued by the highway police. Another time we had to be diverted to Denver for a week while truck repairs were being carried out. Finally Mrs. Major's man-of-all-work, Joseph, was sent to meet us in Newark with a replacement truck that we exchanged for the old one in which he was towed back to Pleasantville for repairs. With our replacement truck from the Children's Theatre of America fleet we were quickly back on the road giving performances at the Capitol Theatre in Dover, Delaware and the Virginia Theatre in Alexandria, where the roof blew off the new truck in a wind storm, and rain soaked our scenery, costumes, props and luggage. Passing through Pleasantville, we returned the new truck and got the old one back, Mrs. Major having had it properly repaired.

My Aunt Margaret and Uncle Fred, who lived in nearby Silver Spring, Maryland, drove over to Alexandria, Virginia, March 11, where they became the first members of my family to see me perform on stage as a professional actor, at the Virginia Theatre. My mother's sister, Margaret had emigrated from Newfoundland to New York in the early 1920s and married Fred Roy, a widower with two teenage children. He was an accountant from Maine, who worked for the federal government in Washington. As the next two days were free of any performances, George let me take the car and drive over to Silver Spring, where I stayed for a couple of days with Aunt Margaret and family.

Another performance took place in Frankfurd, Pennsylvania, a suburb of Philadelphia, where I had the truly heart-warming experience of playing to my first cousin, who drove to Frankfurd from Philly. Mary Cronan was the daughter of my mother's sister, Elizabeth Cronan, whom we all loved dearly. It was Mary's twelve-year-old brother who was blown to bits on the S.S. *Viking*. She herself had been working in theatre since she came to America in the mid-1930s. She had been in the chorus line of *Sally Rand's Nude Ranch* in the 1939 World's Fair. Mary was one of those "heart of gold" people who I was fortunate to have as a Godmother.

With "Bertha" repaired we set out for Boston March 12 and, to everyone's delight, it was our headquarters for the next eight days. As soon as we were settled at the Earle Hotel, behind the State House, I called my brother John who was studying business administration at Boston College, a Jesuit university in the suburb of Chestnut Hill. Next day the cast drove to Concord in a snowstorm and did something that was a bit unusual. On March 13 we gave a very good performance to a very good audience, in a very good theatre at the Veterans Building in Concord. When we got back to the hotel that night, John was there waiting for me and I was reunited with my dear brother. We sat in my hotel room and talked until the wee hours.

During the next few days, which we had free, John joined Andrea, Betty Barstow and me in doing the town of Boston and the nearby countryside. We took in some movies we'd missed while on tour and dined in the evenings at Durgin Park, a famous Boston restaurant owned by cousins of John's girlfriend, Justine Rogers, whom he later married. John and Justine had four children, Sheila, James, Paul and Irene. Sadly, they both died young: Justine on 25 August 1979 at the age of 48, and John on 26 July 1984 at the age of 54; so few short years after his beloved wife. It was hard on their children as they had no immediate relatives on their mother's side and only me on their father's side. It was hard on me, too, but I lovingly became their surrogate parent. In later years, I was blessed to become the surrogate grandfather of my brother John's nine grandchildren, and great grandfather to five great grandchildren all in Boston.

A memorable performance on the tour for me was a matinee we gave at the old Opera House in Calumet, Michigan. The audience was already lining up when we arrived at the theatre with our truck full of scenery and car full of actors. The thing that made it memorable was a simple statement by the theatre manager: "Sarah Bernhardt played on this stage many years ago." I thought to myself, "Here I am, a kid from Newfoundland, playing on the same stage the immortal Sarah Bernhardt once played on."

The smallest audience we played to was 25 people, mostly children in a backwater town in Oregon. The largest audience we had was one of standing room only at the Auditorium Theatre in St. Paul, Minnesota. I recall it was a good show and the sponsors told us afterwards everyone loved it. They even invited the cast (the actors were their own crew) to a buffet dinner in one of their homes. An unforgettable performance was the one we gave in Glendale, California, when Miss Poo the monkey jumped off the stage and ran through the howling audience of parents and children. She darted under seats and across aisles until someone finally trapped her and put her back on stage. Needless to say, it was some time before the cast and audience got back in a mood in which the performance could continue.

St. Patrick's Day we drove out to the town of Andover, where we gave a benefit performance of *The Nuremberg Stove* to a full house at Memorial Auditorium. A stagehand, not one of our company, hung one of the doors to the throne room in the Emperor's Palace so that it unfortunately opened inward instead of outward. Nobody knew it had been hung the wrong way by the stagehand until the moment when I, as the Emperor Franz Joseph, commanded Tyler, who was playing a courtier, to bring before me the waif found hiding in the potbelly Nuremberg stove. Tyler marched to the door and gave it an imperious push. It failed to yield. Not realizing it was wrongly hung, he then shoved the door much harder. For a moment or two, while we watched in breathless horror, the set swayed perilously this way and that, and then, its ropes having come undone at the back of the set, it pitched forward piece by piece. All the flats had broken loose from their tie-lines and fell onto the stage, one by one, like a house of cards. As the palace walls tumbled about us the audience gasped in stunned amazement.

There were two huge pillars made of papier mâché to look like marble. They stood on either side of my throne. As they began to collapse Bobbie and Betty each grabbed one and prevented their falling. Not knowing what to do I cried, "Earthquake" as the curtain fell. This broke up the audience, as well as the cast, and everyone howled with laughter. When the flats were laced back together and the curtain rose once more we could not go on with the play because of the audience laughter and applause. It took some time for the mirth to abate and the cast to regain its composure. When we finally got the play back on track it was a smash hit. I have never known such an understanding audience.

Only once before had the cast broken up in a similar fashion. "Breaking up" is the theatrical term for uncontrollable laughter on stage. When we were playing *Toby Tyler* in the charming community of Doylestown, Pennsylvania, the slim and curvaceous Bobbie, who played Lily Treat, the overweight fat lady of the circus, was wearing tons of padding to give her great bulk. There was a scene in which Mrs. Treat, who has taken Toby to her heart, comes upon the villainous Job Lord, who runs the concession stand where Toby Tyler works. She finds Lord, played by George, beating the hapless runaway lad with his cane. She grabs it out of his hand, flings him to the stage floor and, standing with her foot on his stomach warns him never to lay a hand on the lad again, while the audience clapped loudly. At that point the elastic holding up Bobbie's enormous red bloomers broke, and folds of red cloth flooded over poor George, nearly smothering him, while the audience shrieked with laughter.

Soon the whole cast, especially Bobbie, who stood on stage with her bloomers spread under her like a huge, collapsed tent, was also drowned in helpless laughter. We were unable to continue with the play and had to bring down the curtain for five minutes while the Fat Lady repaired the elastic in her bloomers. In the wings, some of the cast laughed until tears ran down their faces. On a long tour of mainly one-night stands, when everyone is overtired from constant travelling and performing, a mishap on stage can easily become hysterical. When we finally brought up the curtain we were able to get on with the performance but it was agony to say our lines without breaking up every time we looked Lily Treat in the face.

Betty had a somewhat similar experience on another occasion, one that caused the cast on stage to break up completely. Playing the beautiful, young circus bareback rider, and dressed in a brief, frilly, costume, she ran on stage to be greeted by a teenaged audience who filled the theatre with the loudest chorus of whistles we ever heard coming from an audience. Amazed at her reception she asked under her breath what the fuss was about. Tyler, who was playing the Thin Man, whispered out of the corner of his mouth so we on stage could hear, "You forgot your pants, darling." Poor Betty was mortified until she realized from our uncontrollable laughter it was a joke.

While in Boston March 18, we did a performance in John Hancock Hall and that gave my brother his first opportunity to see me performing with a professional company. He afterwards came with us for a play date in Portsmouth, New Hampshire. On the way we stopped in Gloucester and saw the fisherman's statue, erected to honour "They that go down to the sea in ships." After the evening performance, John, Bobbie, Betty and I drove up to Ogunquit, Maine, for a late night supper. We wanted to see the famed Ogunquit Playhouse, a popular summer theatre where the girls and I had ideas of looking for work when the tour ended. After we drove back to Boston, I said a lonesome goodbye to my brother. I don't know which of us felt sadder as we drove off in different directions, he to resume his studies at Boston College and I to start a hectic couple of weeks beginning with four performances in Hartford, Connecticut.

After the four performances in Hartford, we headed for Buffalo, New York, where we gave a good show at a beautiful theatre in the suburb of Orchard Park. Later that afternoon, four of us drove to Niagara Falls, but I couldn't cross into Canada as I had forgotten my border-crossing card. That meant I had to drive back to our hotel in Buffalo, get my border crossing card and return to rejoin the others. We then drove to the Falls, which were an amazing sight. They actually consist of the Horseshoe Falls on the New York side and Niagara Falls on the Ontario side. The gorge in front of them is 160 feet deep. After seeing the waters all lit up, we crossed over Rainbow Bridge on our way to St. Catharine's for dinner.

It was the first time I entered Canada as a Canadian citizen. I found it remarkable that I was visiting the country of which I was a citizen for the first time at the age of twenty. I never wanted to be a Canadian and never would want it, but if I must belong to someone else's country, Canada is the one in which I could take pride. I tried explaining this to my American travelling companions but it was not easy. They wondered why I hadn't become an American. I did not have the heart to tell them I wanted that even less than I wanted to be Canadian and let the matter drop. The only time I had ever been in Canada previously was for the few hours on the *S.S. Fort Townshend* when she called in at Halifax on my way to New York and I was still a Newfoundlander.

After playing two more New York dates, Aurora and Batavia, we drove to Toronto for a few days while George took the truck to Detroit where we rejoined him for a performance on April 4 in front of a large audience at the Masonic Temple. We also did a show in Bay City, Michigan, where a friend of Tyler's from the Pasadena Playhouse joined us. We let him play a small part in the performance, which gave us all great amusement.

The Easter break (eight days) came in Detroit where the Thomas Mitchell touring company of *Death of a Salesman* was playing. They were staying at the same hotel as we were, the Earle. We were all given "professional courtesy" (free tickets) at the theatre, a thing which acting companies used to extend to each other in those days. We went backstage afterwards to meet Mitchell and the cast. Tommy Mitchell was a wonderfully brilliant actor whom I first saw on film as Scarlet O'Hara's father in the immortal *Gone With The Wind.* Mitchell was the first person to win an Oscar, an Emmy and a Tony Award. They were well deserved as he gave many quite marvelous film performances, usually in a character support role, but nothing he did in motion pictures, as far I am concerned, matched his work on stage as Willy Loman. The young, unknown actor who played the son, Biff, Darren McGavin, later became a major film star through television. He took a shine to Bobbie and invited her out for an after-theatre dinner that evening.

There was no reason for Bobbie not to take McGavin's offer, but when I saw her leave with him, I was nipped by the green-eyed monster for the first time in my life. Although we were just close friends at the time, and not romantically involved, I felt crushed at seeing her walk away on Darren McGavin's arm. It was Easter Saturday, and although I had said nothing to Bobbie before going to see *Death of a Salesman*, I had hoped to myself we might go somewhere after the show. Instead I returned to the hotel more than somewhat miffed. Who was this Darren McGavin that he should ruin my secret plans for an evening with someone I was beginning to care for rather a lot? When I heard her return to the room she shared with Betty just after midnight, I took the basket of Easter eggs I'd bought for them and placed it outside their door, with a note that read, "With love from Peter Cottontail." The song "Here comes Peter Cottontail" was then quite popular and on the hit parade.

Easter Sunday morning, when I got back from breakfast, there was a note under my hotel room door in Bobbie's familiar writing. It read:

> Here came Peter Cottontail
> Hopping down the bunny trail...
> He hopped his way to the Earle Hotel
> But Bobbie and Betty they could tell...
> They knew he wasn't a bunny at all
> But a really great guy whose name is Paul.

It wasn't up to T.S. Eliot's standards but I treasure it to this day.

From Detroit we went on to Ohio for play dates in places like East Liverpool and the state capitol, Columbus, where we were again given professional courtesy to see the woman many considered at the time the leading actress on the American stage, Katherine Cornell. She was appearing in a play called *That Lady*. Seeing the great Cornell was for me a dream answered as I sat entranced by the aura of this incredible performer. Known as the greatest American stage actress of the 20th century, Katherine Cornell was nicknamed "First Lady of the Theatre" by her friend Helen Hayes. She began her career with the Washington Square Players, as did Clare Tree Major, Lawrence Langner and Theresa Helburn.

Our own performance at Memorial Hall in Columbus went well in spite of the fact everyone broke up in an important scene when I pointed to the statues of the kings on the stove and they weren't there. In Springfield we gave our last performance of *The Nuremberg Stove.* I was to go from being the Emperor of Austria to being a circus clown in *Toby Tyler.* Mrs. Major's man, Joseph, met us in Toledo with a truck full of sets, props and costumes for *Toby Tyler.* Chirping beside him, in her cage on the seat of the truck, was her nibs, Miss Poo, back from her Connecticut vacation.

With the obnoxious primate garnering most of the accolades from our young audiences, we resumed playing *Toby* April 17 and 18 in Monroe, Michigan. Tyler Duff, the Thin Man, who was having personal problems with some of the actors, announced he had a call for a movie part from his agent in Hollywood and would be leaving us after the performance at Keith's Palace Theatre in Akron, Ohio, on April 21. In a panic George, our company manager, advertised in the local paper for an actor. Auditions were held at our hotel in Akron and an amateur actor, Joe (Marty) Martinek was hired. During the next four days, as we drove west, through Indiana and Illinois, to Salina, Kansas, we rehearsed with Marty in hotel dining rooms and lobbies every evening. He gave his first performance April 25 in front of a huge, appreciative audience at Memorial Hall in Salina. After the performance we all drove over to see the famed Indian Burial Pit. It contained the remains of 146 Indians which had been left exactly as they were placed many centuries ago.

From the burial pit in Salina we drove to Abeline, a once booming town where cattle were driven up from Texas and shipped east on a newly built railway that put an end to use of the famed Chisholm Trail, a feature in many a cowboy movie. In Abeline we saw the house in which General Dwight D. Eisenhower's mother lived, and where he was taken soon after his birth. It is a typical mid-western home of a middle-class family only a few blocks from Main Street. We all walked together in the dust and sagebrush of what was left of the old Chisholm Trail. In Dodge City, the next stop on our tour, we visited the Beeson Museum of Wild West memorabilia and even went to see Wyatt Earp's home. On Boot Hill, we saw the graves of some of the famous cowboys and bad men who died with their boots on. That same beautiful afternoon, at a place where the wagon ruts of the old Santa Fe Trail ran along the banks of the Arkansas River, just west of the town of Cimarron, we were having a picnic in a tumbledown shed when the cowboy who owned the place rode up on his horse. We told him we were actors from New York reliving the days of the Earps, Doc Holliday, Wild Bill Hickock, the James boys and Billy the Kid. He laughed and said we were a bunch of East Coast nuts, but we looked harmless and he rode on, leaving us alone to enjoy our picnic under fading western skies.

On our way back to Santa Fe, New Mexico, for performances at the Lensic Theatre and Seth Hall, we played in Lamar, Colorado, at the Pioneer Theatre, a small theatre with the smallest stage we ever played on, and in Las Animas, which received its name from "the river of the souls lost in purgatory." We had a couple of days off in Santa Fe during which Bobbie ran into a friend, Johnny Sands, whom she had worked with in several plays at the Pasadena Playhouse where the young teen idol was sent to improve his acting skills. He told us he was making a movie in the nearby pueblo settlement of San Ildefonso. Sands became a teenage heartthrob when he played his first part in the 1946 movie hit *Till the End of Time*, with Robert Mitchum and the lovely Dorothy McGuire, who lived in Pleasantville, where Doug and I met and talked with her several times in our local supermarket. After *The Bachelor and the Bobby-soxer,* with Cary Grant and Myrna Loy, in which Johnny was Shirley Temple's love interest, he was destined for stardom. The picture he was making near Santa Fe was *Two Flags West,* with Linda Darnell, Cornel Wilde and Joseph Cotton.

Johnny said if we turned up on the set some morning he could get us a day's work as extras since local extras were in demand every day. Bobbie and I took our company car and drove out to the set next morning. On the set she ran into another Playhouse friend from Pasadena, a former school-teacher who took up acting, Dale Robertson. Dale had a small part that would lead to his becoming a movie idol of much greater magnitude than Johnny Sands, who disappeared from the screen within a few years. Dale became especially famous when he starred in the television western series *Tales of Wells Fargo,* from 1967 to 1971. It turned out afterwards that he was a close friend of the father of my dear friend in New York, Terri Duffie, an actress I was to meet later that year in summer stock. Terri told me Dale used to spend much of his time when in Manhattan with her mother and stepfather, the songwriter Russell Robinson, whose biggest hit was the song "Margie." Russell helped the young actor in his early days of struggle in movie town. I met Dale a second time at the Robinsons', when I revisited New York some years later and went to see Terri, but by then he was an important movie celebrity as well as TV star.

The trip to the set for *Two Flags West* resulted in Bobbie and me being hired as extras for the next day's shooting of wagons rolling. Johnny introduced us to an assistant director who, short of a few crowd extras, wanted to know if I could drive a covered wagon. Remembering the old days with our horse and carriage in Bay de Verde I said I had often driven wagons but not since I was a boy. We were signed up, completed the necessary union exemption papers, and I drove a covered wagon in a scene with Bobbie beside me wearing a western bonnet. It was my first film bit, known in the trade as "a cough and spit." A stuntman had recently been killed on the set when detonating an explosion during the filming of an attack on the fort by Indians. Johnny Sands told us Linda Darnell did not like Joseph Cotton, her co-star, who had a rather superior attitude towards her. A few days previously, in a scene in which he was to sweep her into his arms and carry her off into the sunset, she filled her dress with lead so that when he went to sweep her into his arms he couldn't lift her, giving the cast a big laugh and him some embarrassment to Darnell's great amusement.

Two Flags West was released, and if we didn't blink we saw ourselves flash past in a wagon. Johnny Sands afterwards made *The Admiral Was a Lady*, and *Target Unknown*, before his budding career wilted in 1951 with a stinker called *The Basketball Fix*, after which he sank permanently from sight. Likewise, our late colleague, Tyler Glen Duff, who resigned from the company in Akron, Ohio, later surfaced in the support lead in a 1953 movie as Glen Tyler, playing a bad man in *The Kid from Oklahoma*, starring Will Rogers, Jr., and Nancy Olsen. It was a modest western about a genial plainsman who becomes sheriff of a small town and uncovers its mayor as a killer. I never again heard of Tyler in the Hollywood swim. Acting is a profession that yearly chews up thousands of talented, as well as untalented, hopefuls and spits them out into oblivion.

Of all the hundreds of actors and actresses I have known, only three ever attained real stardom. They were Joan Collins who was in class at Royal Academy of Dramatic Arts (RADA) with my roommate Jim Hilburn and came to our London flat for the odd party; Rosemary Harris, whom I met through Anna Moremon, a fellow RADA student from Australia who, like Jim, boarded in the house where I boarded in Chelsea. Rosemary was to win the coveted gold medal at RADA in the public show. She went on to achieve mega-stardom on stage in New York and London as well as in the movies. In the 1994 film *Tom & Viv,* she was nominated for an Academy Award. A few years later she won the Tony Award for her performance as Eleanor of Aquitaine in *The Lion In Winter.* Rosemary has been nominated for and won a number of film and stage awards, including two Oscars. At the time this was written, she was one year older than me, at the age of 82, and still being deluged by rave reviews for a play in which she was appearing on the New York stage, *The Royal Family on Broadway.* It was a revival of the 1927 comedy by Edna Ferber and George S. Kaufman, and has nothing to do with any Royal families but is a glittering drama about the Cavendishes, a fictional theatrical family based on the real-life Barrymores. It originally starred John, Lionel and Ethel Barrymore.

As for the third of my triumvirate of famous actress friends, Cloris Leachman, I have a long-treasured photo of her sitting on my knee in a dressing room when we were appearing together in *The Second Man* at the Norwich Summer Theatre in 1950. Cloris won an Academy Award for Best Supporting Actress in the 1971 film *The Last Picture Show.* She was a contestant on Season 7 (2008) of *Dancing with the Stars* at the age of 82 and was the oldest contestant to dance on the series. The following year she was Grand Marshal for the 2009 New Year's Day Tournament of Roses Parade in Pasadena, California, and also opened the annual Rose Bowl Game that day.

After a break of several days in Santa Fe, we continued playing dates in New Mexico and Kansas, including two performances in Great Bend, where we braved our first cyclone. We didn't need the Wizard, or Toto's bark, to tell us we were in Kansas. When we reached Topeka we discovered that the hotel, where rooms were booked for us, had been blown away like Dorothy's house by the cyclone winds of the previous day, after first being gutted by a fire that incinerated our payroll. Such was life on our yellow brick, theatrical road.

My first cousin Agnes Cronan, a sister of my Godmother, Mary Cronan of *Nude Ranch* fame, went to New York as a young woman and lived with our Aunt Margaret. She married a man from Indiana and moved to the city of Anderson which was close to Indianapolis. While the Company put up at a hotel in Indianapolis, George let me have the car to drive over to to Anderson to spend a few days with Agnes and Jim who were about to move into a new house which Agnes took me to see.

On Bobbie's birthday, May 10, we were in Portsmouth, Ohio. After doing two shows we gave her a surprise party at the Mae-Bert Motel. Our gift to her was a beautiful pair of earrings Betty and I had chosen a few days earlier at a very good antique jewelry shop in St. Louis, Missouri.

When we arrived in Cincinnati, we once more got professional courtesy to see a hit play on tour from New York. This time it was the incomparable Martita Hunt, outrageously marvelous as *The Madwoman of Chaillot*, with Ellen Corby and Neva Patterson. Bobby and Betty had both worked with Miss Corby at the Pasadena Playhouse. I knew her from seeing her in endless movies as prissy spinsters and nosy neighbours, but especially memorable as one of the aunts in *I Remember Mama*, with Irene Dunne. Backstage, Ellen Corby, whom I knew, introduced us to the queenly Martita, an actress I fondly recalled playing the eccentric Miss Havisham burning to death in her wedding dress in *Great Expectations*, the version with John Mills and Jean Simmons. Ellen came with us for a meal and we talked theatre for hours. Years later, Ellen Corby was to have a tremendous success as the beloved Grandma Walton in television's long running, smash hit, *The Waltons*.

We racked up a few more performances in Kentucky and Ohio until we reached Hillsdale, Michigan, where on May 13 we gave the final performance of our tour. For me it was No. 153 as Boser the Clown in *Toby Tyler* and doubling as circus owner Mr. Castle. It was not unusual in road shows for actors to sometimes take two parts, a major and a minor role. In addition to *Toby*, we had done 34 performances of *The Nuremberg Stove*. That season I had given a total of 187 performances in the two plays since leaving New York in September. Once we reached Pittsburgh on our way back to Pleasantville, and nosed our vehicles onto the famous 180-mile Pennsylvania Turnpike, which was then the only freeway in America, I felt homeward bound. We had an overnight stop in Harrisburg where I again stayed with the parents of my very dear actress-friend Evelyn Bohn, just home from the Children's Theatre of America tour of *Cinderella,* in which she played Cinders. We have remained close friends for life.

Next morning, May 15, we drove the rest of the way to the George Washington Bridge, over the Hudson River, in a heavy rainstorm, and up Westchester County to Pleasantville, where we parked the car and truck and got our final pay, after which we were out of work. There was no such thing as unemployment insurance to look forward to in those days. All we had to live on was what we saved from our $35 or $40 weekly pay. I had around $200 in my pocket and got a bonus of $100 for driving the car, accident free, throughout the tour. Bobbie, Betty Fillman, Bob Hallgren and I decided we would share an apartment in New York City while looking for work. We took the train to Grand Central and got rooms for the night at a modest, theatrical hotel, the Ashley, on West 47th St., half a block from Times Square. A night clerk at the hotel mentioned to us that the penthouse was vacant. We smiled at him with no thought we could ever be able to afford a hotel penthouse in Manhattan but we did ask to see it.

The penthouse at the Ashley was small, but roomy and charming, consisting of a tiny entrance hall, a kitchen with a table for four, a nicely furnished living room, with a door opening onto a terrace, actually the tarred roof of the building next door. We were close enough to Times Square to see Father Duffy's statue half a block away. There was a single bedroom with twin beds. The whole apartment rented for $200 per month. We asked what it would cost for a bedroom on the same floor with twin beds and were told $120. After some negotiation we got the apartment down to $180 and the bedroom on the top floor down to $100, so Bob and I took the penthouse, while Bobbie and Betty took the cheaper bedroom next door, but they had full use of the apartment and were given keys. We agreed we would share meals and kitchen expenses. It was a wonderful, youthful impulse that would take most of our savings, but we were hoping to have jobs in summer stock theatres by the time the month was up, else we would face eviction. A summer stock theatre is a theatre that generally presents weekly stage productions of different plays only in the summer time and often features visiting stage and film stars. I rushed out and had some stationary printed with my address, The Penthouse, Hotel Ashley, and began circulating theatrical agents with CVs and professional photographs I'd had taken in Detroit.

As soon as word got about among our friends that we were living in a penthouse, half a block from Times Square, they descended on us "from Scarsdale to the Rockaways," or wherever, when they came to downtown Manhattan to do the daily rounds of agents and producers. Looking back, I realize I had and still have many dear friends from my National Academy days, and from touring companies of the National Classic Theatre and Children's Theatre of America. In those companies while touring coast to coast, I began to realize how tough a career was acting, but we were doing the thing we all loved to do. Bobbie, Betty and Bob had numerous friends from their Pasadena Playhouse days who dropped in on us in New York where they were looking for work. We had to stretch the dollars we had saved on tour, so when friends stopped in at mealtime, or even for a cup of coffee, we quickly learned to charge the automat prices. What wonderful days they were as we dreamed dreams of theatrical success that, for most of us, was never to come.

Chapter 11

When I Was One And Twenty

As soon as we were settled in the Ashley penthouse, Bobbie and I went to see the Broadway production of George Bernard Shaw's *The Devil's Disciple,* with Maurice Evans, Marsha Hunt and Victor Jory. She had appeared in a couple of plays with Jory at the Playhouse in Pasadena and knew him quite well. Born in Dawson City, Yukon, he was one of the most respected Hollywood and Broadway performers. He toured with theatre troupes and appeared on Broadway, making his Hollywood debut in 1930. Initially, Jory played romantic leads, but later was mostly cast as the villain. He made over 150 films and dozens of TV episodes, and also wrote two plays. His long career in radio included starring in the series *Dangerously Yours.*

Vic, as we called him, was a founder of New York's American Repertory Company. The night we saw him perform in *The Devil's Disciple* we invited him back to our apartment. Vic came, and brought with him his stage co-star, Marsha Hunt, a charming woman who played leads and second leads in various movies. She signed her first movie contract with Paramount Pictures at the age of 18 and afterwards starred in films produced by MGM. As late as 2008, at the age of 91, she appeared in a film, *The Grand Inquisitor.* After his first visit, Vic often dropped in at our place after a performance for a chat, a beer or coffee. Another frequent caller at the penthouse was my mother's brother, Phil Flynn, president of the New York Harbour Pilots Association. He really seemed to enjoy the attention Bobbie and Betty always gave him, as well as the company of actors like Vic Jory. Uncle Phil listened bemused as we actors shop-talked, having been on ships all his life.

One evening, an actor from my student days at the National Academy, Richard, a friend of mine and a transvestite, arrived at our apartment. He had a female persona called Theodora, after the Byzantine actress and wife of Emperor Justinian I. He was still in his chorus girl costume and rather inebriated as well as seemingly depressed when he came to our door. He had not gone on tour with us but chose to work as a drag queen in the village. We paid little heed to poor Dick that night as he wept and talked of suicide. Suddenly he bolted from the room, rushed out and scampered across the roof terrace from which he flung himself over the brick wall apparently into the street below. His scream stopped as he fell. A look of horror froze on the faces of our stunned visitors, especially when we showed no reaction. "My God!" several gasped as they got up and ran to peer over the edge of the wall into 47th Street below. When they did, they found Richard sitting quietly on the roof of an adjoining building half-a-floor below our terrace. He had begun his roof-fall act one night several weeks earlier. After seeing him perform it several times we paid him no heed. On the other hand, our horrified guests were quite shaken.

The month we spent at the Ashley was truly, in the words of the student prince, a month of "golden days in the sunshine of our happy youth." The warm neon nights of early summer, stretching out to the south, were crowded with talk as we sat out on that small roof terrace, heedless of the stench of gasoline fumes or the roar of Manhattan traffic filling the air around us. We sometimes talked until the first light of dawn over Manhattan, aware only of arguing acting theories and our visions of what the theatre should be. Some nights we told jokes that quite literally made us laugh until tears ran down our cheeks. Other nights we would articulate our private emotions, and what personal conflicts we felt in our lives and careers as we each reached for our own *Kismet.* We were young, full of hope, and nobody had a reason to fear the truth. Like children holding pieces of a broken mirror, each of us thought we had the whole of it. On wet days we read scenes from Shakespeare and other playwrights, or used our creative imaginations doing improvisations. There has never been so wonderful and bewitching a time in my life as that one, in great part because I was sharing it all with Bobbie and my other friends from the tour.

Often when we returned from fruitless visits to the offices of agents and producers, Bobbie and I would take off on our own, for a walk through puddles of afternoon shadows in Central Park, or a stroll along Riverside Drive, while flotillas of stars spangled the evening sky over the restless metropolis. Bobbie had a delicacy that was an evocation of my dreams. Away from her, I felt an almost physical loss. I see now she was the summing up of my youth and innocence. To me she was all crimson and lapis lazuli, fire and blue ice, with lively, flashing eyes and a remarkable, feminine vitality. When we were together I knew a happiness I was never to know again with any other person, male or female.

It was years before I was able to admit to myself that I spent my youth haunted by ghosts of my Catholic upbringing, and the sense that all pleasures of the flesh were evil in God's eyes. I laugh in anger at the nonsense that was drilled into me by my teachers, the Christian Brothers. I am not without strong feelings of resentment over the anguish caused to a timid, impressionable youth groping his way through the religious agony of physical desires. Bobbie, too, was the product of a strict Episcopalian upbringing. The natural and instinctive things we both felt were choked in religious sentiments that troubled our minds and inflicted wounds that for me took years to heal. My soul still bears the scars. The heart does not grow nobler under the touch of sorrow and denial. The risk of being embraced and loved is not taken without the risk of being rejected and having one's energy wasted. I had been told life is a trial marked by our deepest loves and our deepest hurts but, as Houseman said, "I was one and twenty, what use to speak to me?" By the time I was able to break through the petty conventions imposed on me in God's name by priests, teachers and parents, something very meaningful was already slipping away. Sad to say, by my indoctrination and education, I had become a changeling, and only a likeness of who I really was remained. Had I waited too long a time before breaking the sorcerer's spell?

One evening Victor Jory announced over his cup of coffee that he had arranged an acting job for Bobbie during the summer months with his friend Herbert Kneeter, owner and producer of what used to be called an alfalfa playhouse, in Norwich, Connecticut. It was actually a summer theatre where the company rehearsed all week with a stand-in reading the leading part. On Monday morning a Broadway or Hollywood name would arrive, rehearse with the cast, open that night, and perform all week until Saturday, departing with his or her loot for the next engagement on the star's circuit. Next day Bobbie came back to the apartment from her meeting with Kneeter feeling she had muffed it for some reason. While the director, Ted Post, seemed to like her, she felt Herb Kneeter did not. However, a few days later the telephone rang. I was alone and answered the call. It was Mr. Kneeter to say she had been accepted for the company.

I boldly asked Mr. Kneeter if he had any positions still open for actors. He told me most of his company was complete but that they needed a few players for small, but important parts. I felt like quoting the old chestnut, "There are no small parts, only small actors," but held my tongue. In truth, I wasn't really interested in doing minor roles, but with money running out, I asked for an audition. When I got to his apartment he introduced me to his sister-in-law, the movie star Jean Hagen, who is best remembered for her

Academy Award supporting role nomination in *Singin' in The Rain*. With her was Ted Post, who was directing the plays that summer at Kneeter's theatre. He afterwards became a well-known director in films and TV. Post found lasting fame as director of the *Planet of the Apes* movie series. When I was halfway through the audition, Ted Post engaged me on the spot. He said he would have used me as juvenile lead except he had already hired a young actor, Peter Brandon, who was to make a bit of a name for himself on TV.

That was how Bobbie and I found ourselves playing at the Norwich Summer Theatre in the summer of 1950. She was not due to arrive until three weeks after the season began for a reason that soon became apparent to me. The ingénue, who was already hired, but not terribly good, had to be given a month's notice that she was fired. It all became a bit messy when the actress got her notice and appealed to Equity, the Actor's Union in New York. We opened with a once big but fading star, Kay Francis, in *Goodbye, My Fancy*, which I had seen on Broadway with one of my film favourites, Ruth Hussey. Miss Francis was one of my mother's favourite stars, because she always made "women's pictures" in which she suffered nobly.

The star arrived at the Norwich Summer Theatre, located in the Masonic Temple in Norwich, on the morning of our opening. Before we commenced our dress rehearsal Miss Francis complimented the designer, Randolph Gunter, on his beautiful set and asked to see the lighting, which was heavy on pink. The scenic and lighting technician, Leland Watson, recalled another aging star of the previous year, Mariam Hopkins, who demanded he re-light the stage with pink gels. Gels were transparent material of various colours used to cover stage lights. Lee had to completely redo his lighting as the pink gels entirely washed out the wrinkles that were in Miss Hopkins face so she could get away with playing the young Catherine Sloper in the 1949 stage hit *The Heiress*. In the movie version, Miss Hopkins played Catherine's aunt. Lee brought up the lights for Miss Francis, who scolded him, "You've been a very naughty young man. Do you really want me to act in a pink fog? I know why you put so much of it in those gels, and thank you, but I really would prefer you lit the set the way you want to and should." He immediately began changing the lighting.

Herb Kneeter bluntly warned the cast the glamorous Miss Francis had drunk herself out of pictures and we were to be on our toes and see that she didn't sneak a bottle of old John Barleycorn into her dressing room. On opening night, as the play went on, we noticed the star's words becoming more and more slurred. She always had a slight sibilance, and was never able to pronounce the letter R in her movies. She talked of wabbits, twucks, the color bwown, and so on. By curtain call that evening the pronunciation of more than just the letter R was giving the former screen enchantress trouble. While she was on stage, Herb searched her dressing room high and low but found no sign of the demon. It wasn't until her dresser, Helena, one of the young apprentices, was about to empty the jug, from which she drank water throughout the play, to soothe a "sore throat," that Miss Francis cried out in alarm for her to stop. Herb grabbed the jug and discovered the water it contained was actually firewater, gin or vodka.

That evening, at the reception to mark the opening of the season, I found myself seated alone in a corner of the downstairs Green Room with the star who was in her cups. She was becoming morose, and cried on my shoulder, telling me she had always been attracted to young men. I pretended not to know what she meant, and lost my opportunity to have Kay Francis among my souvenirs. She did say, "Where is it gone? The fame...the fortune...Where is it gone?" Since I hadn't a clue I made no attempt to reply. A photographer from the local press came over and asked if he might photograph her. She agreed. When he asked if she would mind telling him her age, she smiled broadly. "Listen, young man," she said, "it took a lot of boozing and a lot of whoring for me to get to where I got in the movies, which accounts for every line on my face. I'm 47 and proud to have made it to this age." To me at 21, she was over the hill. Her frankness, while probably said in inebriated fun, left me a little speechless. It was my first close encounter with a former dryad of the Hollywood tree, and hearing even a falling star admit to such human foibles as drink and whoredom was heady stuff indeed for a boy from little old St. John's, behind whose ears it was still somewhat damp.

After the photographer left, Miss Francis asked me to get her another gin. When I returned with it she looked at me a little unsteady, and said, "Carole killed herself, but that's no answer. Is it?" I knew she was referring to Carole Landis, who committed suicide over a love affair with Rex Harrison that had gone sour. Kay Francis, Carole Landis, Martha Raye and Mitzi Mayfair toured the volatile front lines of Europe's battlefronts in World War II for the USO. It was incredible that four Hollywood stars would defy the Germans and take their show to the boys on the front lines. One Saturday afternoon, when I was a schoolboy, I went with my close boyhood friends Tom Cahill and Ron O'Brien to see a movie at the Star Theatre called *Four Jills in a Jeep*, based on the ladies' wartime adventures. I thought to myself if Tom or Ron could see me now, trying to comfort one of the four Jills, actually sitting with and consoling Kay Francis, they would be utterly amazed.

In spite of her problem with the sauce, Kay proved a warm and wonderful woman who won all hearts the week she was with us. Fay and Garson Kanin's play *Goodbye, My Fancy* is about a congresswoman who returns to her old college for an honorary degree and falls in love with a photographer sent to cover the event. I had seen one of my favourite stars, Ruth Hussey, do the play on Broadway. There were a number of young actresses playing college girls in our production, including the reigning Miss Connecticut. Kay Francis had great fun telling them to go ahead and upstage her (steal the scene) if they could, because they were the stars of tomorrow, and they must make audiences take notice of them. One actress the audience did take notice of was a very plain looking, funny woman in the permanent company, Florence Stanley. Florence took the part of the congresswoman's wise-cracking secretary and played it to the hilt, almost walking off with the show. Kay Francis was delighted and foretold a brilliant career for Florence. It was many years later before her prophecy came true, when Florence Stanley played Bernice, the wife of Sergeant Phil Fish (Abe Vigoda) in the popular television comedy series *Barney Miller.* Florence and Abe were two of TV's most popular stars. They later had their own spin-off series, *Fish.* Then, like fading stars, they both vanished. That Saturday night, after Miss Francis kissed everyone goodbye and left, taking her share of the week's proceeds with her as she drove away, a Norwich catering firm arrived with hamburgers and soft drinks for the players and backstage crew, compliments of our beloved Kay Francis. It never happened again that summer.

Herb Kneeter worked everyone so hard he soon became known as "the Beast of Belsen," the name the press had given the man who ran the notorious death camp for the Nazis. Everyone in Norwich was looking forward to the second week of the season when we would have as our star the wonderful comedienne Eve Arden, the endlessly amusing actress of the acrimonious but engaging high-school teacher *Our Miss Brooks.* She was booked by Herb to take part in Ruth Gordon's humourous play *Over Twenty One,* based on Miss Gordon's own wartime domestic problems at a seedy tourist motel, near the military camp where her husband was doing his basic training. Eve Arden was bringing her own leading man, an actor named Brooks West. He was her off-stage romancer and turned out to be as supercilious a snob as she turned out to be a nasty star performer. When she saw the set, we stood around eagerly awaiting her first humourous remark. Instead we saw her screw up her face and call our designer, Randolph Gunter, to the stage "What's this?" she demanded of him in bitter tones, "a garbage dump? You can't expect me to play in anything so decrepit looking as this." Randy replied with dignity, "If you read the script, Ma'am, you would find the set described as a very run-down motel room at the edge of a military base, and this is a very run-down motel room on the stage of the Norwich Summer theatre." The war between the two, which was to last all week, had been declared. The star said she did not appreciate Randy's sarcasm and ordered him to repaint the set immediately, in colours that would compliment her wardrobe. Randolph, a rather portly man, quietly placed the paint gun he was holding at her feet, saying, "There you are, lady. Go right ahead but be quick. The dress rehearsal is scheduled to begin 30 minutes from now." With that he turned and calmly walked back to his workshop, leaving Eve Arden to throw down the gun and stalk off to her dressing room fuming.

When Florence Stanley, a member of our Summer Theatre troupe, came on that evening in *Over Twenty One*, playing the small part of a motel neighbour, the audience remembered her great performance from *Goodbye, My Fancy* the previous week and gave her a loud ovation. As the ovation began to die away, a very miffed Miss Arden hissed in Florence's ear, "How much did you pay them to start that racket?" Later in the week one of the actors, Michael Lipton, found an old papier-mâché skull in the prop room. He packaged it like a gift, with ribbon and bow, and placed it on the dressing room table of Arden's friend and co-star, the arrogant Brooks West, as being from the actors and crew of the summer theatre. When West opened the package he was roused to anger.

On Saturday night when Eve Arden was preparing to drive off to her next engagement, she gave the theatre apprentice who was her dresser for the week $5 saying, "I wish it could be more." Young actresses in the Company took turns as dressers for the visiting stars and usually got $50 from them for their work. I must say for Herb Kneeter, when hearing about the $5 bill, he became furious, saying he had just passed the star a cheque for over $2,000 as her share of the week's take. Kay Francis had given her dresser $100, and her admission take was half that of Eve Arden's. The few who were not completely disillusioned by the famous comedienne's behaviour gathered at the stage door of the theatre as she was leaving on Saturday night, and called out to her as she climbed into her car, "Goodbye, Miss Arden." She turned to Brooks West, who was driving the car and said, "I wonder if these people know how much they bore me?" and they drove off.

The next play, *Angel Street*, was a package show. That means all the actors with speaking roles as well as the various props came for one week to a summer theatre. The cast usually featured one or two movie stars as drawing cards. Minor roles were filled by actors and actresses with the playhouse. *Angel Street* had been filmed years before as *Gaslight*. It gave Ingrid Bergman one of three Academy Awards she won over the years. A young actress with Bergman in *Gaslight*, Angela Lansbury, was brought over from England at the age of 18 to play the conniving cockney maid. It was her first movie appearance and one for which she received an Academy Award nomination but not the Oscar.

Our next star, Laraine Day, would be bringing her entire cast with her except for two minor roles. In the summer theatre production of *Angel Street*, she had as her co-star Ernest Cossart as Inspector Rough. The veteran old actor made his American debut in 1903 and was one of the original actors of the Theatre Guild. The part, played by Charles Boyer in the film version, was taken in Laraine's summer theatre production by Ferdie Hoffman who had played in *Angel Street* on the New York stage for a record breaking run. Two smaller parts, as London bobbies who come on stage to arrest the husband at the end of the play, were taken by actors Bob Youdelman and Paul O'Neill. Laraine Day, a practicing Mormon, neither smoked nor drank. She didn't even take coffee, which struck me as very odd for a Hollywood celebrity, especially since she had a much publicized romance and marriage to baseball manager Leo Doruche of the Brooklyn Dodgers.

Laraine Day had been well known to our boyhood group from 1939 to 1941 when we took in all seven of her performances as Nurse Lamont in the Dr. Kildare movies. On Saturday afternoons my brother and I would sit with friends in the old Capitol movie house on Henry Street and watch her assist Dr. Kildare, a character who first appeared in Paramount's 1938 gangster melodrama *Interns Can't Take Money*, starring Joel McCrae and Barbara Stanwyck. The medically sophisticated yet socially naïve *Dr. Kildare* was later to appear in a highly successful television series where he was played by Richard Chamberlain. The Kildare movies were a nursery for such starlets as Lana Turner, Ava Gardner, Marilyn Maxwell and Martha O'Driscoll. Needless to say, I was thrilled to be doing even a walk-on part with Laraine Day, the charming Nurse Lamont I so loved from the many Saturday matinees I attended.

Angel Street had originally been called *Gas Light*, but because an English film of the play had been made titled *Gaslight*, the play had been renamed when it came to the U.S. When the play was later made into a Hollywood film, the old British film title was restored. Without consulting Miss Day, who had agreed to take the Bergman role, the theatre owner Herb Kneeter decided to advertise the play on our summer theatre stage by the Hollywood title. His action made Laraine very angry and it began a week of bizarre happenings. In addition to the aging Ernest Cossart as Inspector Rough, her package included a Broadway actor, Ferdie Hoffman, as her husband. Betty Underwood was the maid, Nancy, while a dear old actress in her late 70s, Elfrida Derwent, was the housekeeper. Elfrida was the sister of Clarence Derwent, who with Teresa Helburn and Armina Marshall ran the Theatre Guild. At the time of her appearance with us, her brother Clarence was the president of Actors' Equity, the American performers' union.

The evil vapours created by the name change increased on opening night when, after waiting more than ten minutes for the signal to bring up the curtain from Herb

Kneeter, who was raking in money in the box office, Laraine grew impatient and ordered the stage hand to pull it up without delay. *Angel Street* begins with the evil husband offering to take his already distracted wife to the theatre to see a comedy or a tragedy. As he hopes, she is unable to make up her mind. In a state of nerves, verging on insanity, she wanders to centre stage and muses, "Shall it be the comedy, or the tragedy." Laraine Day did not get beyond the words, "Shall it be the comedy...", when the curtain suddenly came down with a swoosh. She rushed off in alarm, thinking Ernest Cossart, who was not all that well, had suffered a heart attack.

Instead of finding the old actor prostrate, she ran into the theatre's owner, Herb Kneeter, who rushed at her, fuming, "How dare you give orders in my theatre." We saw she was totally flabbergasted by his accusation. He ranted on, "I give the signal from the box office when I want the curtain raised, not some baggage from Hollywood." She recovered her wits and turned on him. The gentle Mormon was replaced by an outraged actress, aghast to think he was petty enough to haul down the curtain in the midst of a scene. A slanging match ensued in which Elfrida Derwent became unnerved and began to swoon. Bob and I had to help her to her dressing room where she kept her smelling salts. After about five minutes, calm returned and everyone took their places. Herb rushed around to the box office, pushed the bell, and the curtain rose a second time on Laraine Day, standing in the middle of the stage where she had been, and continued with the line, "...Or the tragedy?" the words she was about to say when the curtain came down suddenly. The audience may have been puzzled by this, but backstage we were all doubled up with laughter.

Next afternoon the Norwich Fire Marshal appeared in the theatre to do an inspection. He threatened to close the place down for that night's performance if a partly inoperable fire door he discovered at the back of the stage was not put in working order by curtain time. Herb was again fit to be tied. Poor Miss Derwent, who happened to be passing, said "I was worried about that fire door." Herb rounded on the innocent old lady, "So you're the bitch who reported me to the fire department." She turned out to be not quite so helpless as we thought. After weathering a tongue-lashing by Herb she made her way to the telephone and called her brother Clarence in New York, and lodged a grievance against Herb with Equity. The door was fixed and the evening performance went ahead, but not before we heard Laraine give our employer a real dressing down, telling him he was the most unprofessional man she had ever come across in her career. In return, he characterized her as a Hollywood female canine, "with a capital B." Next morning, Clarence Derwent, in answer to his sister's call, sent Equity snoops to the theatre. They poked about and took statements from us as they investigated Herb's operation and his abusive treatment of performers. Here I shall have to draw the veil on the whole sorry affair, because I do not know the outcome of the charges and counter-charges involving the actors' union.

There were more personality conflicts the following week, when we were doing S.N. Berman's sophisticated comedy, *The Second Man.* The star, Franchot Tone, brought with him an utterly charming co-star, Margaret Lindsay, who was as ladylike in person as she was in her numerous Warner Brothers film roles, such as *Dark Victory*, with Bette Davis, and the Ellery Queen pictures she made with Ralph Bellamy and William Gargan. As boys, my friends and I would rush off to the movie matinees on Saturdays to watch her as Nikki Porter, Ellery Queen's secretary. With Equity on his tail from the previous week, Herb had few qualms about taking on the elegant Franchot Tone, a *bon vivant* film star and reputed womanizer, who seemed to us a strangely quiet man, the opposite to his newspaper persona.

Franchot was fresh from having made scandalous headlines after a public brawl in which he and actor Tom Neal had fisticuffs over a sexy starlet named Barbara Payton, whom Franchot married the following year. She made headlines around the world. Her hard drinking and hard living ultimately deformed her once enviable beauty and destroyed her physically and emotionally so that she died at 39 years of age after following a road of self-destruction and unrelenting destitution from which she could not get untangled. Herb warned Mr. Tone to keep away from the young actresses in the company. The star was furious. Angry words were exchanged. I heard Franchot say backstage, "I'm sure that man's insane. How dare he speak to me that way!" We found Franchot Tone a charming, easy to talk to man.

Herb's heavy hand was, in fact, causing a great deal of unrest. Several of our own performers quit the company and there was grumbling among apprentices. Our talented director, Ted Post, was among those who quit. He got into a row with Kneeter over constant interruptions to rehearsals and his interference with production. Ted called him "a Philistine, the Attila of summer stock." Herb retorted by calling Ted, who limped from a war wound, "a pathetic cripple." That did it! Ted walked out the door never to be seen again by us. Henry Weinstein, who had been his assistant, was made director.

In *The Second Man*, the ingénue was played by Cloris Leachman, a young actress of vibrant personality. I had seen her give a vigorous performance on Broadway, playing Celia to Katherine Hepburn's Rosalind in Shakespeare's *As You Like it.* There was a scene in *The Second Man* in which the butler brought out a bottle of champagne. Normally this would have been ginger ale, but Franchot wanted the audience to hear the cork pop and see the bubbly flow when he opened the bottle. He insisted on, and paid for, the real thing. As soon as it was poured into the glasses, and the cast raised them in a toast, the curtain came down. There was a very quick costume change as all the actors but Cloris, who was not in the next scene, rushed off stage to change. Those of us who were standing in the wings quickly hurried out and joined her in quaffing down the glasses of champagne. Cloris became quite a famous star, with an Academy Award for film. After starting out in TV's *Mary Tyler Moore Show,* as Mary's friend, Phyllis, Cloris had a long, successful career as a star of her own comedy series, *Phyllis.* Of all the virtual unknowns I have worked with along the way, Cloris became the most successful star.

When Kneeter announced an actress named Andrea Blayne would be joining the company the following week and playing female leads beginning with the next play, *The Spider,* starring Victor Jory, there was much consternation voiced by the resident company. I kept my mouth shut, knowing what had gone on behind the scenes between Vic and Herb. Angry words passed between Mr. Kneeter and the ingénue, who handed in and played out her notice, and then filed a grievance with Equity, an organization which by then must have been quite familiar with the Norwich Summer Theatre's problems. I was looking forward to being reunited with Bobbie. After all, she was my reason for being in the Norwich Company, instead of that of Ogonquit, or Dennis, or Cape Cod. I physically trembled with excitement when I embraced her again in Norwich. She arrived unaware of the backstage tumult caused by her becoming the ingénue.

Victor Jory shook my hand and said how pleased he was to see me again, while introducing me to his wife Jean, their son Jon and daughter Jean, who were all playing roles in *The Spider,* a play about a magician, Monsieur Chartrand, which required twenty-five actors. On stage Chartrand is performing magic tricks when the theatre lights go out and a revolver blazes in the darkness. The house lights come up to reveal a bloody corpse lying at centre stage. At first the stunned spectators do not realize it is part of the play. Actors and actresses planted in the audience help sustain the illusion of reality. When Chartrand asks if there is a doctor in the theatre, an actor rises in his seat and is asked to come on stage where he pronounces the man dead.

The local police, who have been called, are actually actors. They rush in wearing uniforms and forbid anyone to leave the playhouse or even their seats. Jean Innes, sitting down front and disguised as a member of the audience, gets into a loud argument with a policeman, and insists she be allowed to go home and feed her baby. He refuses to let her go and when she becomes a nuisance, he chases her around the theatre where she is handcuffed and taken away, to the stunned amazement of the audience. On stage there is pandemonium while the stage manager, Maloney, played by me, tries to control the actors and reassure the audience. Finally, more actors arrive dressed as plain clothes detectives. They calm down the audience and a séance is held on stage by Chartrand to discover who committed the murder. The audience, knowing by now it is all part of the play, joins the fun and holds hands, singing "Shall We Gather at the River" and "In the Sweet By and By" as the theatre lights go slowly down. When the place is in virtual darkness, there are cries by actors sitting in the audience that astral insects are swarming around the theatre. At that point actors on stage and in the audience hurl handfuls of puffed wheat on the unsuspecting playgoers sitting in the darkness.More panic ensues as audience members scream in alarm and imagine they are feeling strange insects crawling over their faces and bare arms. After more tricks and magic the murderer is caught.

Martin Masters, the Norwich newspaper critic, unimpressed by such hokum, thought "Victor Jory and a fine supporting cast are a redeeming feature in an otherwise weak vehicle." After praising Paul Stevens as Inspector Riley, Masters added, "Speaking of talent we don't want to overlook anyone, because the whole cast is outstanding: especially Sandy McCauley, Andrea Blayne, Paul O'Neill, Pat Tobin, Jean Jory, Norbert Edwards, Rodman Montgomery and Louise Williamson." It was nice to be thought of as outstanding even if only by the local critic. Masters also wrote in his criticism, "Herbert Kneeter is rapidly gaining recognition as a 'straw hat' (summer theatre) producer who is presenting shows of unusual merit, never before produced in summer stock and the Norwich Summer Theatre is becoming one of the most outstanding in the straw hat circuit."

Bobby and I were delighted to be reunited with our famous friend Victor Jory, and that's when we found out Herb Kneeter had given her the job to please him. I have a feeling Vic may have been a silent partner in the Norwich theatre venture. It was a pleasure to meet the Jory family, especially Jean Innes, one of America's finest character actresses. Her Broadway career went back to the history-making production of *Abie's Irish Rose*, and her 30 motion picture roles included parts in *Pinky*, *Edge of Doom*, and *I'd Climb the Highest Mountain*. I little thought their son Jon Jory, who had a bit part in the play, would grow up to take over the helm of the Actors Theatre of Louisville, a small regional theatre in Kentucky when it was just a few years old. Under his leadership, it has become one of the top theatres in the United States, distinguished as one of the few regional companies in the country which operates three diverse theatres under one roof. It became the birthplace of so many Broadway hits and modern American playwrights. Jory is still making headlines at the Actors Theatre of Louisville.

Within days of Bobbie's arrival, I realized my close relationship with her was in difficulty. One hot night after the show we sat outside the theatre and talked. She told me that when she was alone in New York — our roommates Betty and Bob having gone off to work with other summer theatres — she made up her mind to establish her career before making any emotional commitments. She asked that we think of ourselves only as dear friends for the time being. I hid from her just how shattered and unnerved I was by this. Up to that point all my thoughts were absorbed in loving her, but perhaps it had been only in my mind. To her it was a love without debts that grew from the kindness we felt for each other, rather than from emotion. While there were to be other loves in my life, none would ever affect me as had my feelings for Bobbie, who is loved to this day. Even now the glow lingers among the ashes of my years as I look at a photo of her I still have on a desk in my office.

I had a nice part in *The Show-Off* with Eddie Albert, a surefire, satirical comedy which was made into a movie four times. The play told of a girl's bumbling, boastful new husband who alienates his in-laws and nearly wrecks her family. Eddie arrived with wife Margo, the beautiful Mexican-born actress Maria Marguerita Guadalupe Teresa Estela Bolado, who went by the single name Margo in New York and Hollywood. She is long remembered in the Ronald Coleman classic film *Lost Horizon* as the lovely girl who obtains the High Lama's permission to leave Shangri-La. As she walks down the long passage that will lead her out into the world, she begins to age. When she reaches the end of the walk, she is a withered old crone. When I saw it at the Star Theatre in St. John's as a school kid, I was blown away by the scene. Margo first won acting honours on Broadway in 1935, with a memorable performance as Mariamne, the heroine of Maxwell Anderson's verse play *Winterset*, with Burgess Meredith.

At the Norwich Summer Theatre, there was a sort of leading lady in the Company, Pat Tobin, who played second leads after the visiting star, whoever she may be, and was in her second season at the theatre. We expected Pat to be playing Clara in *The Show-Off*, the top female role, but it was Bobbie who opened in the show opposite Eddie Albert, with the redoubtable Florence Stanley as her mother. Pat remained with us for several more shows before giving her notice and walking out. Martin Masters, the local critic, after praising Eddie for playing the perfect show-off, said of Florence Stanley, "The tremendous ovation given her was equal to that of the star and with due reason." The future Bernice Fish spent the summer winning all hearts, except Eve Arden's, each time she appeared in a production. The critic added, "Three of the resident cast not too often seen this summer, proved themselves born actors, Andrea Blayne (Clara); Paul O'Neill (Mr. Gill), and Bob Youdelman (Mr. Rogers). These three young thespians really fired the play and their respective performances were enthusiastically received."

Margo generally sat backstage during the week of performances, chatting to cast members while they waited to go on. Closing night, Eddie invited Florence, Bobbie, Bob and me to dinner with him and his wife after the play. I couldn't believe I was seated next to the wonderful actress I saw play the old hag in *Lost Horizon* at the Star Theatre many years before. What an incredible life I was beginning to lead. I again thought, if my friends could see me now. Margo was in the last stages of pregnancy at the time, and complained during the meal of the expected baby who was kicking the daylights out of her. We had only to look and see the action. When I went to the movie *Butterflies are Free,* years later, and the star, handsome young Edward Albert came on screen, I whispered to the person sitting beside me, "I knew that guy before he was born." My friend thought I had flipped out, and said disdainfully, "How could you have known him before he was born?" I smiled and kept the secret. His performance in *Butterflies* won him a Golden Globe Award.

One morning during the week of *The Show-Off,* I got a telephone call from Mrs. Major in Pleasantville offering me a three-month job with the Children's Theatre in the production of a play about the daughter of American Indian Chief Powhatan, called Pocahontas, who is believed to have established peace between the Indians and Europeans in America by marrying an Englishman, John Rolfe. When I accepted her offer she sweetened it by adding, "You will also be company manager." That meant my giving Herb Kneeter my notice as rehearsals for *Pocahontas* would be starting September 3, a week before the summer theatre closed. There were still five plays to go to at the Norwich Theatre but I was feeling tired after a year of touring and summer stock so I gave Herb two weeks' notice. I told him a touring outfit in New York I had worked for before was offering me a job as company manager of a road tour, which was true, and that I would be needed in about three weeks. He said our director, Henry, had a good part for me in *Blind Alley* with

Zachary Scott, if I wanted to stay on, which was what he would like me to do, but he said if I wanted to go I wouldn't have to work out my two weeks' notice and sent me on my way. In a bit of an emotional dither I said goodbye to Bobbie and the others and took the train back to Manhattan that Sunday.

I saw Bobbie only once after that, a year or so later in New York City. She told me she was going to marry a man from Argentina, and would be living in Buenos Aires. A mutual friend said she did just that. I never saw or heard from her again. The wind that blows from those abandoned days carries with it restless whispers of half-forgotten voices. They are heard now like stringed music coming from afar. I still think of us strolling hand in hand along the drifting sands of our ambitions, unmindful of the swirl of gentle waves that were pulling us apart. Had some observer in the shadows seen us pass we might have seemed like wanderers lost in dreams, but in my eyes there glowed misty visions of my own Hebrides. Time changed the signposts into ghosts and bleached out the islands of desire, so that what was dreamed became irrelevant.

Clare Tree Major herself chose and directed the actors in *Pocahontas* beginning the day after Labour Day in 1950, assisted by a former Indian chief and sometime professional actor who went by his Indian name, Lone Bear. Rehearsals for the tour took place in the theatre at the National Academy in Pleasantville. Our September to Christmas performances in *Toby Tyler* were a great success with almost every sponsor. It seemed both children and adults loved the backstage setting of the play when Toby ran away from home and joined the circus. I was surprised when rehearsals for our three-month tour of *Pocahontas* had no performers from our *Toby* tour. The play, written by Mrs. Major, began outside the *yehawken* (home) of Chief Powhatan at Weromococo in Virginia where the girl lived with her father the Chief. Lone Bear taught us genuine Indian songs, dances, and the proper pronunciation for words and names that appeared in the play. We found having him as assistant director proved to be a great boost to our involvement in *Pocahontas.* I recall my first line when I came on stage from my tent to where Indian males and females were dancing to the beat of the medicine man's drum was, "*Muchee werawa ta coga norah witsee,*" after which we all spoke English which had Indian words and terms spliced into it.

Theodore Stephens was Captain John Smith, an English colonist. He formed the settlement of Jamestown, Virginia through alternating periods of failure and success. Smith is said to have saved Pocahontas from death, although there is some dispute about the fact. It was Smith who urged the settlement of New England. Pocahontas herself married an English settler, John Rolfe, who in the early 1600s introduced the regular cultivation of tobacco in Virginia. The part of Pocahontas was played by an American actress of Italian legacy, Florence Carabee, while her husband, Rolfe, was played by John White. Their marriage established peace between the English and the Indian people.

Pocahontas had three performances before leaving on tour. In addition to the usual one at the Threshold Playhouse, the place we rehearsed all Children's Theatre of America touring companies and St. Mary's-in-the-Fields girls' school where we always performed, we gave a third performance, at the Bedford Hills Correctional Facility for Women, which we referred to as the Women's State Prison. With our truck loaded with scenery, props and costumes, we set out Saturday, September 9, for Iron River, Michigan, 121 miles away. We reached Iron River on the thirteenth. It may not seem like a long distance but the truck was heavily laden and the car had to follow behind the truck. Thursday, September 14, we opened *Pocahontas* with a performance in Crystal Falls, Michigan, with a matinee at City Hall. There followed three months of continually playing and travelling.

On October 17, the *Sheraton Press* in Wyoming reported, "Audiences from Sheraton and vicinity sat in trance as incidents from the lives of the Indian princess, Pocahontas,

Captain John Smith, Powhatan and John Rolfe unfolded at three matinee performances." Speaking of the actors, the newspaper noted, "All combined in presenting the high quality drama characteristic of earlier plays here." In Kalispell, Montana, the paper *Inter Lake*, in announcing the sale of tickets for *Pocahontas* said, "Last year the production of *Toby Tyler* was so successful that the Flathead County High auditorium could not accommodate all those who wanted to see the play. For that reason two performances were engaged this year."

I liked the way the Polson, Montana, *Flathead Courier* announced our arrival for a show there. Under the heading "*Pocahontas* Has All Star Cast," the article began, "Word has been received in Polson that the big truck carrying the scenery and other properties for the show *Pocahontas* is on its way and should arrive in Polson at the Lincoln school building November 1." It then goes on to name the characters and the actors playing them.

Sometimes our itinerary indicated driving at night after the show and a start very early next morning. Regardless of the condition of the weather and the roads, we had certain distances which we had to make in order to be on time for our next performance. Sometimes this meant driving in snow and/or rain storms, which I must admit were, at times, a bit scary on steep mountain highways. In Montana we played such towns as Butte, Miles City and Helena. Our Wyoming dates included Casper, Anaconda and Rock Springs in addition to places in such states as the Dakotas, North and South, Utah, Oregon and Washington. The latter two of these states landed us on the shores of the Pacific Ocean, which I had seen the previous year when I was on tour with *Toby Tyler*. A big plus for touring is the places and things you get to see that you would never have seen had you not gone on tour. I have been in 49 of the 50 states of America thanks mainly to the tours I went on. The only state I have not been in is Alaska. I even stopped off in Hawaii on my way to visit friends in Australia and New Zealand.

It was not unknown for us to be invited to teas and dinners at a sponsor's home after a performance. We enjoyed these opportunities to get to know people in various States of the Union. Sometimes there would be a conflict between an invitation and our itinerary, for example, when we played two performances in Polson, Montana, Flora Houghteling at the head office in Pleasantville sent a note with our itinerary stating, "Contact Mrs. Karlsgodt regarding the hour of performances and auditorium. Cast has been invited to a buffet supper. Have written Mrs. Karlsgodt that it will have to be at an early hour since you have to drive to Kalispell that night so would have to leave Polson at 6:00 or 6:30 and that if the weather is bad you will not be able to stay over for the supper, but will have to leave immediately after the second performance." I think the above information combines a number of our touring problems. The immediate date of the next performance meant we must drive after the show to get near where we are headed. Also there is the problem of an invitation to a reception or a meal by a sponsor which must be cleared away with embarrassing haste. Sponsors usually included such things as a school board, Parent-Teacher Associations, the American Association of University Women and various town or city halls. Tour information and bookings were made through the Pleasantville office.

The last three performances of *Pocahontas* took place with matinees on December 8 and 9 in Salem, Oregon, the state capital with approximately 43,000 people in 1950. It was by no means the largest city in Oregon since nearby Portland had three times the population. The final performance of the tour took place in Salem on the evening of December 9. A newspaper critic in Anaconda, Montana had written of us, "*Pocahontas* presented by the Clare Tree Major Players of New York enthralled 2,000 Anacondans and sponsoring American Association of University Women members reported an excellent performance. Authenticity and beauty of the dances were outstanding conveying definite moves of various phases. Nathan Pollock as Osianimo, the Medicine Man, was very convincing and became the hero for most of the small boys who saw him. Powhatan played by Paul O'Neill was impressive and dignified. The part of John Smith was done with restraint which subordinated it to the Indian characters. Pocahontas, the Indian princess of history, really came to life under the able touch of Florence Carabee. Her vivacity was hardly in accord with the accepted ideas of Indian austerity but she struck a responsive chord in the audience. Mateo and Opossoquionie clearly represented interesting types of women, the one foolish and embarrassed, the other constantly fearful."

Next day we began a week of driving to get us from Oregon back to New York. There were no incidents to report, not even a truck break down. We ended our journey across America in Hackettstown, New Jersey, where we took Route 8 to and over the George Washington Bridge and up the east shore of the Hudson River to the turnoff for Pleasantville. When we arrived at the company headquarters, Mrs. Major and others came out to greet us and welcome us home. After the Christmas holidays, which were about to descend on everyone, most of the actors with our company would be going on a winter and spring tour with another Children's Theatre production. In her itinerary for the week ending December 9, 1950, Mrs. Major wrote of our journey from Oregon to New York, "If you have reasonably good weather it should take you about a week to get here. Drive carefully but as many hours a day as possible. The company will be disbanded except that those that wish can go out again in 'Prince.' This we can talk about when you reach here. Share the driving as much as possible on the way home. Send us a wire each night saying where you are in case any one of you is needed." The "Prince" she refers to is her production of *The Prince and the Pauper.*

Chapter 12

When I Remember Bygone Days

Not having taken Mrs. Major at her word and offered to go on tour with *The Prince and the Pauper*, I decided I had enough of travelling on the road for the present and made up my mind to go home to Newfoundland for Christmas. My parents were so delighted to know that I would be spending Christmas with them they sent me an airline ticket as a gift. I was feeling so tired after a season touring in *Toby Tyler*, a season in summer stock in Connecticut, and a half season touring, that I welcomed the chance to take a rest.

This time, instead of going by land and sea, I flew home on a Pan American jet which stopped in Gander before beginning its flight to Europe. From Gander I made my way via Air Canada to St. John's, where my father and mother were waiting at the airport to take me to the house on Cochrane Street in which I grew from boyhood to manhood. I recall the joyful looks on the faces of my dad and mother while we were decorating the Christmas tree. I had already decided I would not be going back to New York after Christmas, but overseas to London where I wanted to experience working in English theatre. My brother John, who had left home to attend Boston College that fall, would be spending Christmas in Silver Spring, Maryland, with Aunt Margaret and Uncle Fred. Unlike me, he had never met Uncle Fred and he was a toddler when he last saw Aunt Margaret, when she stayed at our house in St. John's.

My first chore after arriving from the U.S.A. in 1950 and spending Christmas at home was to try and find somewhere to stay when I reached London. I wrote a friend of mine and classmate from boyhood, Jimmy Greene, who was Rhodes Scholar for Newfoundland in 1949 and attended Oxford University where he was studying. He was to marry an English girl, Cherry Midwood before returning home and becoming a lawyer and partner with the St. John's law firm of O'Dea, Greene, Neary and Puddester. Later, in 1960, Jim, who was a Progressive Conservative member of the Newfoundland House of Assembly, became Leader of Her Majesty's Loyal Opposition in Newfoundland, a position he was to hold for the next six years. The boarding house he found for me in London was located on a street called Sloane Gardens, about three or four buildings from Sloane Square, where I had a lovely private room. It was a prime location and the landlady, Florence Weewill, had two servant girls who served us two meals a day in the dining room, breakfast in the morning and dinner in the evening. It was more like home than a boarding house to her fourteen or fifteen boarders. A charming woman, Florence had a military officer living with her, Captain Barrett, whom she suddenly up and married. We were all invited to the wedding feast which amazed the boarders, men and women from Ireland, Australia, New Zealand, as well as myself and another Canadian from Halifax, Jane Palmer who, oddly enough, worked at the American Embassy.

A close American friend of mine, James Hillburn, who had been a student at Clare Tree Major's drama school and toured with me in several of her companies, arrived in England before me. Jim came to London wanting more knowledge of the theatre and acting so he auditioned at the Royal Academy of Dramatic Art where he was accepted as a student. He was living two blocks from RADA. I went to see him there and met one of his two roommates, Joe Ortin, a lad of about 17 from Leicester. His other roommate, Lawrence Griffin, was out. Jim complained that the quarters were cramped and they were paying £2-5s for accommodations only. I said I was paying the same for a single room with breakfast and dinner included in my digs just off Sloane Square.

A friend called for Joe Ortin and we were introduced. His name was Ken Halliwell. He seemed to be around 30 years old but Jim afterwards told me he was a fellow student not yet in his mid-20s. I recall he was almost bald and that probably gave the impression he was older. Ortin and Halliwell went out and Jim and I followed a few minutes later, walking from Gower Street to a pub off Charing Cross Road where we spent the evening. The following weekend I asked Jim over to my place for a meal which Florence told me she would provide for him as some of her boarders went different places on the weekend. Jim told me Ortin was there at loose ends and asked if he could bring him along. I mentioned the matter to Florence who had no objections. Weekend dinners were served at midday and the boarders were left to cook for themselves in the evenings on the gas rings in their rooms on Saturdays and Sundays. After we ate our meal, Jim and I talked about our experiences touring with *Toby Tyler*. I could see Ortin was becoming bored so I suggested we go to see the nearby ruins of the bomb shattered Royal Court Theatre, which was still boarded up and looking derelict. Jim wanted to know if it was the same theatre where many of Shaw's plays were first staged. I told him it was and that a bomb, which destroyed Sloane Square Underground Station next door, had seriously damaged the structure. Repairs were just beginning. I believe this was the first time Joe Ortin ever saw the famous building that housed the premier presentation of his plays *Crime of Passion* and *The Ruffian On The Stair* and led him to fame.

Within a couple of days of Jim's visit, two women from New Zealand who occupied a large bedsitter at Florence's facing Sloane Street, set sail for their home in Wellington. Not having his telephone number, I wondered if Jim would like to move in and rushed over to 31 Gower Street to tell him of the vacancy, after first checking with my landlady and obtaining her blessing for him make the move. He was delighted and we took the bedsitter. As we had little money we would need a third roommate to help pay the rent. I asked Joe Ortin if he would like to come to Sloane Gardens with us. He declined, saying he was about to move into a house which his well-off friend Ken Halliwell purchased. The day I went to help Jim carry his belongings from Gower Street to Sloane Gardens, Halliwell and Lawrence Griffin were there taking one of the spare sofas which he owned. Jim got another American student from RADA, Donald Mork, whose home was in a Boston suburb, to share with us. We set up three beds at one end of our sitting room where there was a wash basin, and turned the other end into a sitter with armed chairs but no sofa. There was a gas fireplace which was coin-operated. We constantly fed it shillings for the next two years.

We decided to throw a few parties as the sitter end of the room could accommodate six to eight people. These parties were tame affairs by modern standards. The only liquor was a cheap bottle of wine which we purchased from a spirits dealer we knew on King's Road in Chelsea. Many of the people who came to our soirees were RADA students or friends I made while touring or working at the film studios. Most of those who came to our flat were performers in search of work. Our guest list would today be a sparkling gathering of celebrities who have grown from nobodies to stars. This was especially true of Rosemary Harris. When I first met her, Rosie was a student rooming with an American, Amanda Steele, and another American student at RADA, Jacqueline Brookes. Jackie had cousins in Newfoundland, Chris and Barbara Brookes, and that seemed to give us one small link. Jackie afterwards scored several successes on the Broadway stage and was featured for some years in the popular TV soap opera *Another World* and on *As The World Turns* for nearly four years.

Other members of the group, who would gather at our apartment from time to time, were Ian Holm, a brilliant actor in many roles on stage and screen, Audrey Dalton from Dublin who found stardom with Richard Burton in *My Cousin Rachel,* and Sylvia Syms who recently played the Queen Mother in the movie *The Queen.* There was also Richard Coleman, whose real name was Ronald Coleman, which of course he had to change. He chose to call himself Richard instead of Ronald. In spite of the name problem, he had a highly successful career on the London stage. Joan Collins, another RADA student, whose sultry good looks were about to start her on the road to movie stardom, came several times to our flat. Another dear friend was the wonderful former child star Joan Dowling. To our shock and horror, she cut short her great promise by committing suicide a year or two after I first met her. John Berry turned to directing and became one of England's best, while Suzanne Holman tried to emulate her mother, Vivian Leigh. She had been awarded to the custody of her father, Herbert Holman, whom Leigh divorced to marry Laurence Olivier, and of course there was Joe Ortin.

A member of our group who met a tragic death was the student Amanda Steele. Mandy, who returned to the United States after graduating from RADA, was fortunate to be chosen for a leading role in the first season of plays at the Shakespeare Festival in Stratford, Connecticut. While driving up from her home in New York to Stratford, the car in which she was a passenger became involved in a serious collision and Mandy was killed. Sheila Ward, another of my dearest friends, kept in touch with me for years and became a popular novelist in England while her husband was a successful playwright. Sheila wrote me in one of her last letters, "...the burden of talent is frustration and the burden of fame is pain." She died shortly afterwards.

I have a special memory of Rosemary Harris, who gave me a 22nd birthday party at her flat. If anyone wanted anything to drink at the party, you brought it yourself as Rosie's budget could barely cover the cost of the food. Drugs of any sort were unknown to all of us. In fact, only a few smoked as we couldn't afford the pleasure. The thing I remember about Rosemary is her very expressive eyes. Her great rival at RADA was Anna Moremon. Anna, too, had eyes in which you could drown. When it came time for the public show at the end of their studies, the prize part, which Anna desperately wanted to play, went to Rosemary who ended up as Catherine Sloper in *The Heiress.* Anna would have made a brilliant Catherine as she had studied the part with Peter Finch in Australia and it was he who urged her to come to RADA. Needless to say, the Gold Medal was awarded to Rosemary instead of Catherine. Anna was totally miscast as an American woman in a scene from Ben Hect's frivolous play *See Naples And Die.* She returned to Australia so wounded in spirit that she eventually abandoned the stage and died young.

As soon as I was settled away I began looking for work. My first job was an appearance in a play on the BBC Home Service, *S.S. St. Pedro,* a radio adaptation of a book by James Gould Cozzens, produced by Archie Campbell on *Saturday Matinee.* I auditioned with Campbell, who gave me the part of the ship's steward. After that I managed to acquire an agent, a difficult but necessary task for every performer looking for work. Without an agent, it was virtually impossible to get a part in a play or film. I convinced a well known London agent to help me in my quest. She was Phyllis Payne.

One morning Phyllis telephoned me and asked how I'd like to do a partial repertory season in Manchester. I told her I would be delighted if I could get away with the English accent. She said they were planning to do several American plays and wanted a Canadian actor as it was too difficult in Britain to get work permits for American actors. I reported to Phyll's office 10 o'clock next morning and read to a man from Manchester who was sitting there. When I finished my reading, he said, "Can you be on the train this afternoon?" I felt it was impossible but told him I could be on it in the morning. He agreed and we signed some papers. As I got up to leave he said, "Your first part will be Stanley in *A Streetcar Named Desire.* It opens Monday night." Truthfully, I was shocked that Phyll had been able to obtain so important a part with such a reputable company as that of the great industrial city of Manchester for an unknown like me. When I mentioned this later to Phyll, she said, "It's your accent got you the job. The actor they first hired for the part had gone into a West End production and you are to be his replacement."

It turned out the Manchester Repertory production was the second time *A Streetcar Named Desire* had been performed in Manchester. The first run was Laurence Olivier's production starring his wife, Vivian Leigh, and the popular American star, Bonar Colleano. Our production, with me as Stanley and Joyce Parry as Blanche Dubois, was as fully acclaimed by the press and was as well received by its capacity audiences as the first had been years before. The *Manchester Guardian* called our venture "a really worthwhile production." So rarely do you find a drama that gives its actors so much scope on stage. It is realistically outspoken and presents in its story of the decay of one woman's mind the whole tale of the fall of southern aristocracy. It affords both the actors and the audience a really invigorating evening of theatre. We opened on Monday night and played to packed houses all week.

There was one memorable experience when I was on stage in *Streetcar.* A man who was blind sat in the front row with his seeing-eye Alsatian dog lying in the aisle beside him. On stage we had no idea there was even a dog in the theatre until the famous scene in which Stanley threatens to rape Blanche. She faints in his arms and he carries her to the bed while the curtain discretely falls. When we came to the scene and I began to tear the dressing gown from Blanche, there was a sudden dreadful roar as a snarling dog leaped on stage from the audience and Blanche and I found ourselves surrounding by yapping jaws. She fainted as I grabbed a chair with which to defend myself. Within seconds the owner was barking a command at the dog who immediately ceased his attack and leaped down on the floor at his master's feet. I picked up the inert Blanche who was still somewhat unconscious and staggered with her to the bed as the curtain mercifully descended. When it rose again we got a standing ovation from members of the audience who were laughing and even cheering.

In another review dated July 16, 1952, the *Guardian's* critic wrote, "*A Streetcar Named Desire* must be steered carefully if its course is not to become simply an appalling psychopathological shambles. The strokes must be laid on with calculated and graduated fineness, the nerves lacerated rather than battered. In the Chorlton Repertory Theatre Club's production, Eric Hillyard's hand is a fairly steady one but not enough time is allowed in some of the later scenes for all the nightmare poetry and queer symbolism to develop fully, and the difficult problem of faking uninhibited violence on a relatively small stage without further emphasizing the lack of space is not quite solved. The total result, however, is convincingly harrowing." My spirits were a little down after my return to London until one morning Dennis Price called to say he was to star in a film about the Royal Air Force and had recommended me to the producer for the part of a young airman. I went to see the producer and was given the part which turned out to be a very good supporting role that could lead to something big.

The Air Force story script was sent to me within a few weeks of its completion. I got a call from the producer's secretary telling me to make sure my passport was in order as the movie would be filmed in Switzerland in six or seven weeks. The plot, said to be a true story, concerned the crew of a Royal Air Force bomber shot down over Germany. They escaped into Switzerland with the help of a band of smugglers who drove cattle across the border from Germany with jewels in their hollowed-out horns. I was to play the wireless operator, a Canadian youth. When I told Dennis I had a supporting role, he was delighted but warned me the producer was an alcoholic and suffering from blackouts so I should check everything with his secretary. Blackouts indeed! I was amazed one afternoon, before filming ever got started, to read in the *Standard*, which I purchased in the underground station at Charing Cross, the producer had suddenly died of a stroke. I sat stunned as I rode the train to Sloane Square. His death resulted in work being delayed on the film. It was never to start again and the movie was finally cancelled. With it died my hope of getting a large movie role that would bolster my career.

Dennis Price, who had recommended me for the young airman part in the cancelled film, was the one friend I had who was a major star in English films. When I was trying to make up my mind as to whether I should study drama in the U.S.A. or go to England, I wrote letters to several English actors asking their advice. I received replies from Ralph Richardson, Dennis Price, Valerie Hobson and Laurence Olivier. Price had recently completed his first major film with Alec Guiness, *Kind Hearts and Coronets.* It was one of the great British films and it made Dennis a superstar around the world. To me, Price was quite chatty so I wrote him again telling him bits of gossip I heard or read about some of his co-stars. I was quite surprised that such a celebrity would waste his valuable time corresponding with someone in Newfoundland and sharing bits of trash. When I chose to go to the National Academy of Theatre Arts in New York rather than the Royal Academy in London, he wrote of his surprise and promised to get in touch with me on his next visit to the Big Apple, N.Y.C. He lived up to his promise and wrote me he would be staying at the Sutton Place Hotel across the street from Central Park and wanted me to come to lunch with him there on such-and-such a date, which I have forgotten.

Utterly amazed that such a big star would be sharing lunch with me, I took the train from Pleasantville to Grand Central and made my way to the hotel by taxi. We chatted through lunch like old friends until the time came for an appointment he had with a New York producer. The next time I saw Dennis Price was in London where I had gone to work and live. I gave him my address in Sloane Square along with my telephone number. We met several times at a pub he told me was a favourite of his. One day as we were chatting in the pub I mentioned how I always enjoyed horseback riding with a few of the actors I toured with when we were in the American West. I was amazed when he called me at the house a few days later to say he was coming to take me horse back riding at Richmond.

Dennis came in his car and got me next afternoon and we drove down to Richmond to ride the horses. As we were trotting across the park, a woman rider, accompanied only by a man who rode a few paces behind her, came up to where we were sitting and idling on horseback. She halted her horse and called in a cheerful voice, "Good morning, Mr. Price." To which a surprised Mr. Price replied as he attempted to get down from his horse. "Your Royal Highness! How very nice to see you out riding on a morning like this." The woman replied, "Please, don't either of you dismount," as she rode up to us. Dennis turned to me and said, "May I introduce you to the Duchess of Kent, Princess Marina, and you, Madam, to a Canadian friend of mine from Newfoundland, Paul O'Neill." We bowed to each other. When she found out I was from Newfoundland, she told me her late husband the Duke had visited there. I said that he rode past my house with the Governor on their way to Government House half a block away but did not confess I had taken a picture of him passing our doorway in a convertible. After a brief conversation she rode on without ever introducing the gentleman who stayed in the background. I imagine he was some sort of guard.

Another distinguished English lady I met through Dennis was Anna Neagle who was yet to be created Dame. I went with Dennis to the screenwriters' club next door to the Dorchester Hotel on Park Lane. As we were going in the door I bumped into a friend of mine, Pennington Richards, coming out. He told me he was directing a picture instead of filming it for a change. I seemed to remember it was *Tom Brown's School Days.* Anna Neagle and husband Herbert Wilcox were there, seated at a table, and asked Dennis and me to sit with them and have a drink. Dennis introduced me as a Canadian actor from New York who was in London seeking film engagements. He told me afterwards he said that in order to bait Herbert Wilcox. Wilcox took the bait and said to me, "Phone my office tomorrow and perhaps I'll have something for you soon," and handed me a business card. I thought to myself as we sat chatting, if only my mother could see me now, having a drink with Anna Neagle, as she was one of her favourite stars since seeing her in the 1933 film of Noel Coward's *Bitter Sweet*. She also appeared in the American film *Irene*, singing " Alice Blue Gown," an international hit. Looking back, I don't know why I neither phoned Wilcox or went to see him. Something else must have come up.

I was anxious to meet Dennis' wife, the actress Joan Schofield, and their two daughters but the offer never came. I discovered later they were being divorced at the time. Not knowing that, I accepted an invitation to lunch at his apartment. I was puzzled when I got there to find there was no sign of a wife or children. Puzzlement turned to shock when he made what I considered improper advances and urged me to hop into bed. Instead I hopped to the door while he cursed me for leading him on. Believe me, I had done no such thing. What I had done was mistake his leading me on as friendship. I never heard from or met him again during my London days. At a time when homosexuality was still considered a criminal offence in Britain, I discovered he strived to lead an ordinary life but failed, becoming instead a serious alcoholic which ruined his career. In April 1954 he attempted suicide and in 1967 was declared bankrupt. He died in 1973 at the age of 58 on the island of Sark where he sought refuge.

Sadly, this was not to be my only experience of such a nature in Britain. I read in *The Stage*, a weekly theatrical newspaper, that Gilbert Harding, the most famous radio star in England, was about to embark on a tour of Great Britain in the American play *The Man Who Came To Dinner* by

George Kaufman and Moss Hart, which made Monty Woolley a star on Broadway in 1939. The story of the cranky and meddlesome man who came to dinner was afterwards made into an enormously popular movie in which Woolley played his famous role. What possessed Gilbert Harding to want to revive the play in England more than ten years after its original success I do not know. I did, however, see in *The Stage* that he was looking for actors with American-type voices for his tour. I wrote him telling of my work in the arts in America and my long touring experience.

One afternoon in the BBC canteen, I was idly listening to Margot Davies chatter while looking about to see if there were any celebrities in the place. I saw none until the door opened and in came the famous, irascible host of BBC radio's extremely popular show *Twenty Questions*, Gilbert Harding. My favourite of these shows was the night when the popular singer, Anona Winn, one of the permanent guests on the panel, was asked the 20th question, "What is a sporran?" The program was live on air. Gilbert pompously informed Anona she had it wrong and was about to give the correct answer when she excitedly blurted out, "No, no, Gilbert. Don't say it. I know what it is ... it's that hairy thing that hangs down between a Scotsman's legs." For a moment there was stunned silence, then there was such an uproar of continuous laughter from the panel and studio audience they could not go on with the show. The producer had a technician fade the sound and play the ever ready broadcast excuse, "One moment please." It was many moments, in fact many minutes, before the program returned to the air.

I whispered to Margot, that afternoon in the canteen, "Look! It's Gilbert Harding."

As Harding passed where we were sitting, he smiled, "Good afternoon, Miss Davies."

While chatting to him she introduced me as a very dear friend from Newfoundland, which she called her home. When he asked what I was doing in London, I said, "Looking for work, I'm an actor."

"Theatre is not an easy profession to be trying to find work in these days," Harding said. "I mean, with so many actors back from the war, and all seeking jobs."

Having made that disheartening observation, he excused himself and was gone before I had a chance to mention his coming tour of *The Man Who Came To Dinner.* Some days later I returned to my boarding house in Sloane Gardens just off the Square to find Florence, my landlady, in a bit of a dither. That afternoon, when she and her chum from over the way, Lady Cadoogan, were having their usual sniff of the cork, a telephone call had come for me while I was out, from Gilbert Harding. She handed me a number on a piece of paper and I wondered if this call was to announce my big break.

When I called the number he gave Florence, Harding, who answered the phone, said he remembered meeting me at the BBC, and that he would like me to come for lunch and an audition. When I asked him where, he answered, "the Savage Club," which I knew to be a place for huntsmen opposite Canada House in Trafalgar Square. I passed it often on my way to and from Canada House, and always imagined it as a place where would-be great white hunters sat among stuffed heads of lions and tigers, along with elephants' tusks and their disembodied feet. In my imagination, I saw them sipping gin-and-it while reminiscing about the glory days of Empires in Africa and India. It seemed to me a strange and musty place to have lunch.

When I got to the Savage Club on the appointed noon, I was greeted by an aging concierge, asking if he could help me. I told him my name, and said I had an appointment with Mr. Gilbert Harding. The fellow bent over a ledger, ran his eyes up and down the pages, smiled and said, "Mr. Harding is awaiting you in Room 223 on the second floor." I took the open cage-lift and found the place, which turned out to be a bedroom, in which my host was waiting in a dressing gown. His noon-day attire rather put me on my guard and I began to feel slightly uneasy. It was beginning to look like

Dennis Price all over again. Seeing my uncertainty, the great man gave me a bear hug and told me to relax, adding that most actors were nervous at an audition, and that I should kick off my shoes. He also suggested I take off my tie and open my shirt, as he handed me some sides (lines) from the play. That way I would feel more relaxed.

When he opened a bottle of whiskey and poured two drinks I knew there was going to be more at stake during my audition than a part in *The Man Who Came to Dinner*. He handed me a raw whiskey, which I knew I would never be able to get down, and began to read the play script. Mrs. Major warned us at school in New York there would be times like this, especially for the girls. However, she said, these days boys were also becoming an endangered species. She felt it was her duty to let us know in advance what we must do in such a situation and not allow ourselves to become flustered.

The Dean of the Academy in New York, Wendell Whitten, once told us Mrs. M. was paranoid about what she called "fairies" getting into her road companies. At one Manhattan audition for actors, she got a hotel room at the end of a long corridor, where she and Wendell could watch for "swishy young men." Each time the elevator door opened, and an actor got out, she watched as he came walking towards them. Wendell said she would turn to him and whisper, "Mr. Whitten, do you think that fellow coming towards us is a fairy?" He said he kept answering her, "I have no idea, Ma'am." Finally, when she asked him for the seventh or eighth time, he turned to her in exasperation and said, "Mrs. Major, I have no idea, but if you like, I'll take him to bed in the other room and find out!" Horrified, she never asked the question again. Unknown to her, there was a "Tinkerbell" or two in almost every one of her touring companies, and every class at her school, including some of her most admired students.

After about seven or eight minutes of reading, in which I felt Mr. Harding's hand creep up my leg from the knee, he put down his script and told me the part was mine. He would be in touch later when he finished casting and let me know about a contract, and rehearsals details. Then he suggested perhaps I would like to lie down on the bed and rest a bit after the ordeal of the audition. Alarm bells were ringing in my head so I said that first I would like to use the bathroom. Once inside, with the door locked, I heaved a heavy sigh. Oh, dear! I knew if I did not lie on that bed and let him have his way, I would never go on the tour, but if I did lie there, it would not be the end of things. *The Man Who Came to Dinner* would be the man who became a nightmare.

There was a knock on the door and I heard Harding's voice asking, "Are you all right?" "No," I said, opening the door, "I've come over all strange. I expect it's something I ate." With that I grabbed up my tie, and not waiting for a reply, hurried out the door and down the stairs. I was never to see inside the Savage Club again, nor did I get the part. My flight was not a vain gesture however. As things turned out, Mr. Harding's health declined and he was not up to touring so the play was cancelled. He died in 1960 at the age of 53, collapsing outside Broadcasting House, the London Headquarters of the BBC. He was about to climb into a taxi when he was felled by an asthma attack.

One afternoon while I was still waiting for a reply to a letter I had written to Harding, I got my first telephone call from Margot Davies. Margot was the hostess of a BBC program, *Calling From Britain To Newfoundland*, a program which started in World War II when she began interviewing Newfoundland soldiers, sailors and airmen stationed in Britain who were delighted at the opportunity of sending a live message home. The show was sent by shortwave twice a week to CBC in St. John's where it was recorded and later broadcast. It proved to be extremely popular and had numerous listeners all over Newfoundland. When the war ended the program continued for many years afterwards, using Newfoundland tourists as guests.

Margot was the daughter of a man from Wales, Daniel James Davies, who had been appointed science master at the Methodist College on Long's Hill. Soon after her father and mother arrived, around 1920, and settled in St. John's, she arrived as a newborn infant. Although Margot spent her early years in St. John's, her voice and everything about her was extremely British. She began her schooling locally at Bishop Spencer College and when her parents returned to England in the mid-1930s, she continued her studies at Southlands, Harrow-on-the-Hill. While at Spencer in St. John's, she was introduced to the stage and began thinking of it as a career. Home in England, she worked with the Dublin Gate Theatre Company, which was doing a season in London. That got her a job with the Oxford Repertory Company. Margot had one sibling, a sister Lena, who was married to Lord Bagg. Margot and Lady Bagg were quite close.

It seems to me I had only just arrived in England when Margot was on the telephone asking me to appear on her program. Someone must have informed her of my trip to London or it could have been on a passenger list for the S.S. *Newfoundland*, sent her by Harvey's, as she was unbelievably well informed about the goings and comings of the Newfoundlanders in England. It makes little difference now as meeting Margot and our becoming close friends was one of the highlights of my time in England. After my return home in late 1952, Margot came on a long visit to friends in Newfoundland and we had many good times together.

One of the most exciting radio plays in which I was cast was one written by Margot, *A Long Way From Home*, about a young Newfoundlander who returns from St. John's to London where he served in the military during World War II, and finds it a city of many changes. It was first broadcast in England on the BBC International Service. Margot told me when she handed in the script to the producer, she suggested he audition me for the leading role. I did the audition and was given the part. My parents heard the play when it was rebroadcast by the CBC in St. John's. I appeared in several radio plays in England as well as two TV movies produced in 1952 by the BBC and featuring a young actress, Joan Hart, for whom stardom was predicted. The films, based on biblical stories, were the *Red Sea* and *The Story of Ruth.* Sadly, I never heard of Joan Hart again.

I also recall appearing on Radio Luxembourg, a broadcast company that operated a radio station in London, doing several commercials for Buckley's Cough Mixture. I am not sure why it was, but Radio Luxembourg made commercials for European stations. Their studios in London were at one of the most fashionable addresses in the city, Park Lane. My grandfather on my mother's side was Thomas Buckley but he had nothing to do with the cough syrup company. I remember doing commercials at the Radio Luxembourg in London which were played on air in parts of Europe and on the company's own DJ shows. The good thing about the station was that it paid actors well for their work, which was a small but thankful addition to their income. I recall several times being called on to play a Mountie in what they called, "The bitterly cold and frozen North of Canada."

A few days after the birthday party Rosemary gave me, I got a call from the BBC where I went and auditioned for a part in a radio play. I never heard from the broadcasting corporation but shortly after that I got what we used to call "a cough and a spit" in a film with Dirk Bogarde, then in his prime as a movie idol, and the American star, Yolande Donlan, whose comic talents I admired. As it turned out, when we were at dinner in Florence's dining room that evening, I mentioned I would be filming next day in a movie called *Penny Princess.* Anna's mother, who had come from Australia with her, said "I can't believe it. Anna, tell him your news." Anna smiled and said, "I also have a part in a movie." I was about to congratulate her when she said, "It's called *Penny Princess.*"

Next day, before dawn, we made our way to Sloane Square Underground Station and took the train to Elstree where we boarded a bus which deposited us at the studio gates. As it turned out, we were to play a scene together. It began with Anna and me coming into a hotel lobby and lining up to register behind the female star, Yolande Donlan. We were followed into the lobby by Dirk Bogarde, the male star. In the scene, Donlan clewed up her reservations at the desk and stepped back only to trip over our suitcases, but instead of falling on the floor, she fell into Dirk Bogarde's suddenly outstretched arms. The incident, which would develop into a romance between them, was the basis for the flimsy plot.

British films beckoned me and I appeared in several, the first being *The Gift Horse*, which starred Richard Attenborough. In *The Brains Trust* with Alastair Sim, I was an army recruit. There followed a number of small movie parts for me in which I was unaccredited. In *You're Only Young Twice*, the film version of James Barrie's play *What Say They*, I was a university student and was also to take a part in Pinewood Studios Technicolor film production of Sir Walter Scott's *Ivanhoe*. The classic story tells of the chivalrousness and daring stand the disowned knight, Ivanhoe, takes when he joins the brave-hearted and high-minded Robin Hood, the Valiant of Sherwood Forest who wants King Richard to rule the kingdom instead of the evil Prince John. Thanks to Phyllis Payne, who got me the part, I was one of about twenty horsemen who got extra pay for riding onto the scene and up to a stand on which were seated Joan Fontaine, Elizabeth Taylor and Robert Taylor (no relation) as Ivanhoe. We exclaimed as we pulled the reins of our horses and stopped in front of the stand and shouted in a loud chorus, "Long live King Richard! Long live Ivanhoe!" During the several days we were filming that one scene I had brief chats with both Elizabeth Taylor and Joan Fontaine and found them quite charming women.

One evening a friend of mine, James Whitely, who was hoping to marry a fellow student at RADA, Audrey Dalton, came to our room at Florence's to tell us the good news that he had found a backer for a play he was interested in staging in the West End called *Double Bend*. It had been written by a friend of his, Donald Madgwick, and consisted of five characters, two males, two females and another male called simply An Actor. Jimmy asked me to play one of the male parts called Peter, and I was delighted to accept. After a week of intensive rehearsals, the play opened Tuesday, August 19, at the Gateway Theatre, London. While the actors were praised by critics, they slashed the play to pieces. One London critic wrote, "No doubt if the clouds of obscurity surrounding the play could be pierced, it would be revealed as a remarkable piece of work, but it is not a good play." After denouncing the play he went on to write, "Great credit is due therefore to the producer and the cast in pinning the play down in such a way that it is possible to present it concretely." He praised The Actor played by David Tudor-Jones. As for the rest of the cast, he summed us up in a few lines saying, "The others are mere ciphers with little to do but speak their lines, which they do with commendable clarity."

Another London newspaper critic began his review of *Double Bend* by saying, "'Metaphysical clichés' muttered a playgoer angrily on Tuesday of this new play and this on-the-spot stricture hit the nail on the head. The play has some impressive acting and has a variety which makes it better entertainment than we are used to locally but had a competent psychiatrist wondered onto the stage early in Act One, I feel he would have made short work of the evening." A third critic wrote, "This play attempts the unusual in that the action is unbounded by ordinary limitations of time and situation." He ends by noting, "There is not enough genuine dramatic conflict to keep things moving, and the players are left to strut and fret in the Timeless Void in which they all too seldom come down to earth." After a week of struggling to stay alive, we gave our last performance on Saturday night. My first London play was a flop, thanks to the ineptitude of the author who never lived to write another dramatic mess, as far as I know.

While some of my offstage experiences tended towards bedroom farce, it was raw lust that next occupied me on stage. Phyll Payne called to say that Charles Killick, a well known London producer, was looking for a replacement for Captain Tim in his touring company of *Tobacco Road*, a book condemned to the flames by preachers everywhere. Killick wanted to see me at her suggestion. I went to see him and read for Robert Harrison who was the director and husband of Estelle Winwood, a famous English actress then nearing 70 years of age. She had just completed a starring role in a film with Truman Capote. Estelle Winwood was the oldest member of Equity, the English-speaking actors' union around the world. On her 100th birthday, she was asked how it felt to have lived so long. Her response was, "How rude of you to remind me!"

The spring of 1952 I spent touring England and Scotland with the Killick production of *Tobacco Road* which was adapted by Jack Kirkland from the novel by Erskine Caldwell. The book was a sexy shocker in its day but now wouldn't raise an eyebrow. In fact, almost everywhere we went by train, the railway stations in the towns where we played had a huge billboard on the platform facing us as we got off the train. It told of our arrival in big letters that read, "THE PLAY THAT SHOCKED THE NEWS OF THE WORLD," and underneath in equally large letters were the words, "TOBACCO ROAD." *The News of the World* newspaper has the reputation in England of being a weekly scandal sheet. We got a good sample of audience reaction in the cathedral of Salisbury, where we played to a matinee audience with a good scattering of vicars' wives at the famous Arts Theatre. They all sat in scandalized silence throughout the play and not a single clap was heard in the theatre when the curtain fell. We decided not to take a curtain call and we were right. The resounding silence was broken by the audience leaving its seats and the theatre. Suddenly we heard a voice cry out, "You're all no good and God will end your bloody lives."

Had *The News of the World* known of what happened to three of us in Darlington we would certainly have made the weekly paper with a headline such as, "Actors Spend a Night in Local Jail." However while true, the claim would be misleading. When we got to Darlington and tried to find somewhere to stay overnight, everything was booked up. The members of the company had great difficulty in finding digs as it was every man or woman for him or herself. Weary and footsore, Jane Howard, Richard Davies and I found ourselves in the main street with night falling about us and no place to sleep. Richard suggested we go to the nearby local police station and ask if they would tell us where we might get rooms and, if not, beds. The policeman on duty was most understanding of our plight, being himself a frustrated actor. He offered us the use of a three-bunk cell if and until it was needed for local miscreants. Fortunately it was a quiet night in the town and the three of us were able to sleep peacefully in jail until morning when we found a boarding house to take us in.

The entire action of *Tobacco Road* takes place at the farm of Jeeter Lester in the back country of Georgia. My role in the production was Captain Tim, owner of the estate on which the farm was located. The book's author, Caldwell, noted in the program for our presentation at the Arts Theatre, Salisbury, "Poverty, want, squalor, degeneracy, pitiful helplessness and grotesque, tragic lusts have stamped a lost out-paced people with the mark of inevitable end. Unequipped to face a changing economic program, bound up in tradition, ties and prejudices, they unknowingly face extinction. It is a passing scene, contemporary and fast fading, hurling the lie at nature's mercy and challenging a God who reputedly looks after his own."

One local newspaper, probably the *Salisbury Journal*, headlined its review, "*Tobacco Road* holds attention: is enjoyable." The drama critic went on to say, "*Tobacco Road*, which a touring company presented this week is a play set in Georgia, in the Depression. It is a squalid, embittered story of a family of poor-white, penniless cotton planters who cannot bear to leave the exhausted patch of soil their fathers farmed before them, even though they starve to death. The play holds the attention and its mixture of tragedy and comedy is even enjoyable but it is not entertainment in the normal sense of the word. One can imagine that it would have gone down well with a Left-Wing theatre club of a few years ago for it is of the 'slice of life' school and that is its excuse: it is a formidable record not so much of 'man's inhumanity to man' as to the brutality with which nature can retaliate and a way in which man will vainly but always hopefully resist nature. It is however a record and although it has been ably constructed to appear like a play there is no real development, and the play adds nothing to the situations. They are just placed before us, curiously static, yet vivid, and it is left for us to comment, or draw conclusions. There is little to shock one despite the advertisements. Such pawing and mauling as there is, admittedly is unnecessary but it remains as difficult to understand why *Tobacco Road* was banned for twelve years in this country as it always does in such cases. There's a striking performance by Peter Hunt as Jeeter Lester, the inbred half simple father of the family, which is fired with genuine feeling, and the remainder of the cast, on the whole, are up to the play's demands. Robert Henderson's production could perhaps have moved faster, but it certainly conveys the utter degradation of life in this 'dust bowl' better than one would think possible on a stage."

Another Salisbury critic wrote in the newspaper, "Peter Hunt gives an outstanding performance as Jeeter Lester in *Tobacco Road*, which Charles Killick is presenting at the Arts Theatre this week. Lester is the head of a poverty stricken North Georgia family, and it is in his broken-down shack that the drama of a set of people, unequipped to face a changing economic program, is played out. There is nothing nice about the story, but the sordidness of humanity, sunk to the lowest ebb, and almost animal-like in the struggle for material and physical satisfaction, is relieved by grim humour. That the play presents a true picture of the situation which arose when once-prosperous farmers found themselves with useless soil and equally useless minds and bodies, I have no doubt, but I found some of the stuff quite repulsive. The cast consists of Peter Hunt, Richard Davies, Christine Lander, Sheila Storri, Lois Shaw, Peter Jordan, Stella Maris, Jane Howard, Paul O'Neill and David Powell."

I believe the movie bit I most enjoyed doing was a scene in *The Gift Horse*, a film starring Richard Attenborough and the American pin-up favourite, Sonny Tufts, with Dora Bryan in a supporting role. The scene began with me and a female bit player entering a restaurant and sitting at a table. The waitress, played by Dora, paid us no heed for some moments. As we were about to shoot the scene, Compton Bennett, the director, called, "Silence...Action." The dialogue began with Dora asking, "What can I do for you, my love?" I did a double take and ordered, "Two *café au lait* please." Dora looked at me and asked, "With milk?" I answered somewhat puzzled, "Of course. What do you think *café au lait* means if not with milk." Dora shrugged and was about to stroll off behind the counter to get the coffees when the director called, "Cut." He had spied the assistant cameraman squirming on his knees beneath the camera trying to hold up the slate with information regarding the shot. Dora looked compassionately down at him and said, "Just talk to Billy Graham, love. He'll have you walking in a week." As the cameras began to roll again, the door to the café opened and in from the street came Sonny Tufts who walked up to Dora and said, "Where's Marge?" Dora looked him in the eye and said, "Annie doesn't live here anymore, leastwise Marge doesn't." There followed a brief conversation between the two and the scene ended with Sonny leaving. The scene was shot in a couple of minutes. It may sound impossible to those with no movie-making experience but the fact is our short scene had to be rehearsed a number of times before the director was pleased enough to do a final take. In spite of our scene having to be repeated for most of the morning, working on *The Gift Horse* with Dora Bryan lives on in my memory as a joyful day in my career. Another most unforgettable performer I worked with in England was Thora Hird, a truly wonderful person, and so like Captain Emily Ridley, a Salvation Army officer she played on British television in the *Hallelujah* series for three years in the '80s.

During the run of the Festival of Britain, a production of *Waters of The Moon* starring Sybil Thorndike, Edith Evans, Wendy Hiller and Kathleen Harrison, I had tea with royalty ... not political but theatrical. I had written Clare Tree Major in New York and told her that among the plays I was going to see in London was *Waters of The Moon* starring two Dames, Sybil Thorndike and Edith Evans. Mrs. Major wrote me back, "Do drop backstage and give my love to dear Sybil and Lewis." Sir Lewis Casson, Dame Sybil's husband, was also starring in the play. I then wrote Dame Sybil that I would be attending the performance on such and such an evening and was a former student of Clare Tree Major who asked me to give you her warmest regards. A telephone call came asking me if I would like to come to tea in the dressing room with Dame Sybil and Sir Lewis after the performance. A few nights later, I was quite thrilled to find myself backstage at Her Majesty's sipping tea with the legendary actress whose Saint Joan was the wonder of the age when she created the role of George Bernard Shaw's heroine. I found Dame Sybil straight as a whip and razor sharp but Sir Lewis was doddering. As soon as our tea was over their driver came in their car to take them home. I refused with thanks their offer of a lift.

I walked instead to the bus stop where I was amazed to see another of the stars of *Waters of The Moon*, Kathleen Harrison, also waiting for the No. 22 bus to Chelsea. I complimented her on her performance and she graciously signed my program. I rode beside her as far as Sloane Square where I got off. Before I got up to go I told her an actress of her magnitude would never be seen riding public transportation in New York. She smiled and said, "Well, ducks, I don't own a car." When she died at the age of 103, she was older than Estelle Winwood, but she had given up her acting career at the age of 87 while Estelle continued hers up to the age of 100.

In the autumn of 1952, my ever alert agent Phyllis Payne called to offer me a chance to do twice-nightly rep in Wales. Friends who had done twice-nightly rep advised me not to try it unless I was a very quick study, which I was not. Phyll told me the job was mine if I wanted it as the producer was a friend of hers and would accept her judgment of whatever actor she sent. The theatre wanted an actor with what was then called a "mid-Atlantic accent" as he would have to play both English and American parts. I was forced to turn down the offer because I had something else on the burner at the time. Simmering away there was a chance to audition for the Hilton Edwards – Micheál MacLiammóir Company at the Gate Theatre in Dublin.

I had written Hilton Edwards sending along my resumé. He wrote back that it would not be necessary to come to Ireland to audition as he was coming to England to hear some auditions there. An appointment was made for me to meet Mr. Edwards in his hotel room at the Savoy. Well prepared for a repeat of the Gilbert Harding episode, I went to do my audition. Hilton Edwards was nothing if not a gentleman. We talked and I read for him. He thanked me when I finished and showed me to the door. Weeks went by without hearing anything from Dublin.

Meanwhile, my father wrote that he was too ill to come to London with my mother, as all of us had been hoping, but he would now like me to come home for what turned out to be our last Christmas together. As an inducement he sent me a ticket for my passage on the Furness Line's *RMS Nova Scotia*, from Liverpool. The day before I was to sail, Florence, my landlady, answered the telephone at 16 Sloane Gardens and passed it to me saying it was a call from Dublin. Hilton Edwards was on the line offering me a winter season with his company at the Gate Theatre. I had a terrible decision to make and no time in which to make it. I did not want to disappoint my ailing father who had done so much for me. I thanked Hilton Edwards but had to refuse his offer because of family problems, saying, "Maybe next year." Had I realized there was never to be a next year anywhere in the professional theatre for me, the *RMS Nova Scotia* might have made that December voyage across the Atlantic without me.

Chapter 13

Ceaselessly Into The Past

After two years in England, which included several theatrical tours and a part on BBC-TV, as well as bit parts in several films, I went home on the *RMS Nova Scotia*, sister ship of the *RMS Newfoundland*, the vessel on which I had gone to England two years previously. I imagined I would only be gone for four or five weeks, but such was not to be the case. Dad did not enter St. Clare's hospital until early June. In the meantime, my presence had become rather indispensable to my mother so I abandoned all plans to audition at the Shakespeare Theatre in Stratford, Ontario, for that year. Instead, I hoped to return soon to England where my career had begun to take root but I was forced to drop all plans of moving on with my life until my father was well enough to leave in the hands of my mother.

In the spring of 1953, tired of sitting in St. John's with nothing to do while awaiting the outcome of my father's illness, I got myself a job at the CBC in the radio newsroom (there being no CBC TV in Newfoundland at the time). What I got was a temporary position which had been given to my lifelong friend, Tom Cahill, when he graduated from Memorial University that year but later surrendered by him on short notice in order to take a more lucrative job with the Canadian National Railway as a summer relief train porter. I went to see the CBC director for Newfoundland, William F. Galgay, who was rather upset by Tom's last minute resignation from the Corporation. He offered me the position he had given Tom in the newsroom. He said I would be there until September when the last of the news writers returned from being on holiday, but for one reason or another, the need for me in the newsroom stretched to Christmas.

Dr. Garrett Brownrigg, our family doctor for many years, finally operated on my dad after which he told my mother the operation was a great success. However, before my father was able to leave the hospital, his health began to decline rather rapidly. On 17 June, 1953 we got an urgent call to go to St. Clare's Hospital. When Mother and I got to his room he was already unconscious and died within a few hours, when, we were led to believe, the blood clot reached his brain. I had to call my brother with the sad news. John caught a flight from Boston and arrived home the following afternoon. I had already made plans for the funeral with Geoff Carnell, whose father, the founder of the funeral parlour, had been a friend of my grandfather.

When the funeral was over, John returned to Massachusetts where he graduated from Boston College several weeks later. I talked my mother into going down to the United States for the graduation ceremony. At first, she was reluctant to go so soon after one of the real tragedies of her life, but in the end told me she was glad to have done it as it got her away from all the activities in St. John's for a week of rest. The activities involved writing numerous letters to businessmen and friends of my father. They included everyone from the Governor to humble fishermen and their wives in the Bay de Verde area. It was amazing to me how his death affected so many people. Strange to say, he was admired and respected by numerous persons, unlike the robber-barron merchants Smallwood was always cozying up to while warning people against. In fact, I have no hesitation in saying my father was beloved by many in Bay de Verde.

I had spent all my savings and was living on borrowed money until I took a job at CBY, the CBC station in Corner Brook, where I replenished my financial resources. The studio was located in a house on Cobb Lane, an area where some of the swankiest homes in the west coast city were to be found. Cliff Hierlihy, the station manager, got me a boarding house a few minutes' drive from the studio. Sadly, I cannot remember the names of my hosts but I rather enjoyed staying with them. Mr. & Mrs. Hierlihy and their daughter lived on the second floor of the old mansion house in which CBY was located. Cliff had only to come downstairs on blustery cold winter mornings to be at work while the rest of us battled the elements travelling to and from the studio. CBY consisted of one studio room, that had been a dining room in the house, and the control room, which looked into the studio, was converted from a sitting room. After my time, a proper studio was built just above Western Memorial Hospital. I did a local show for hospital patients in Corner Brook every Saturday morning and a show about various west coast communities which Mr. G. (as we always called Galgay) complimented me on.

However, I was missing the theatre so much that I decided to join the Corner Brook Amateur Players, but when I went to see the woman who ran the company and told her I would like to join the group, she informed me I must audition for her as she couldn't accept just anyone. That put me off so I decided to form my own group and called a meeting at which the Playmakers Company was born. We immediately began rehearsals on our first production, *See How They Run*. *The Western Star* reported that the dress rehearsal performance at the West Coast Sanitarium "was put on for a delighted audience of patients and doctors…it's a fast moving, hilarious story, and the Playmakers made the play move with zip and dash. It's got an excellent cast who Friday night took advantage of timing and emphasis to set the audience into sustained peals of laughter." At the time of my leaving, the Playmakers had fifty members.

The call to return to the Newfoundland metropolis, St. John's, came within the year. In December, Mr. Galgay asked me to come to St. John's where I was informed he and Dr. G.A. Frecker, Newfoundland's deputy minister of education, had announced the inauguration of the province's first home-grown school broadcast series – three fifteen-minute programs per day for five days a week, produced in St. John's and geared to the Newfoundland curriculum. I was familiar with school broadcasts because every afternoon, from 2:15 to 2:45, we carried the Nova Scotia school broadcasts under the guise of Atlantic School Broadcasts, to which we contributed direct teaching programs two afternoons per week. They were now to be replaced by Newfoundland school broadcasts from 11:30 a.m. to noon, and in the afternoon to replay the half-hour of Nova Scotia school broadcasts we had moved to the afternoon from their morning slot. He told me he was looking for somebody to head up the Newfoundland school broadcasts and his eyes had fallen on me. I told him I had been arranging for an audition at the Shakespeare Theatre in Stratford, Ontario. However, after thinking over his offer, I decided experience in radio production could be of future value to me, so I agreed to take the position of school broadcasts producer with the intention of postponing my audition at Stratford until the following year.

Cloris Leachman and Paul, when they appeared together in S.N. Berman's play "The Second Man."

Paul and his fellow cast members in one of his many performances.

Paul O'Neill in the famous poker game scene from "A Streetcar Named Desire."

The Buckmasters Players dress rehearsal for "Reluctant Heroes."

Eddie Albert, Andrea Blayne and Paul O'Neill in "The Show-off."

Laraine Day and Paul OP'Neill in "Gaslight."

Victor Jory and Paul O'Neill in "The Spider."

Theatre Arts Club, "The Hasty Heart", Regional Winner.
Paul won best actor award.

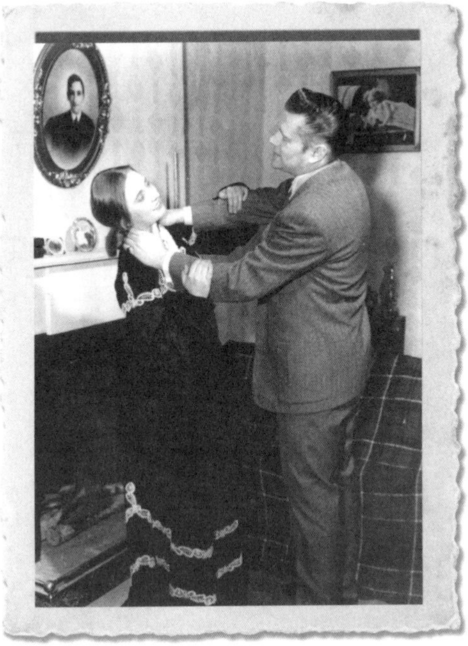

Paul O'Neill and Glenys Moore.
Theatre Arts Club, "The Late Emma Black" dress rehearsal.

Barbara Colbourne and Paul O'Neill in "Pochhontas" with Ted Stephens.

Opening night party at Norwich Summer Theatre, Conneticut.

Paul O'Neill

Afterword

Paul O'Neill never did go back to acting as a profession, although he was involved with amateur and professional theatre all his life. At the age of twenty-four, he established himself in a lifelong career with the Canadian Broadcasting Corporation in Newfoundland, first in radio and then in television. He headed up the drama department and then initiated Newfoundland School Broadcasts. He was responsible for popular programs such as "Reach for the Top," "Terra Nova Theatre," "Skipper and Company" and "Musicraft." He also wrote dozens of plays for broadcast, and commissioned works from then little-known writers such as Michael Cook and Helen Fogwill Porter before he retired from the CBC in 1986.

Although he had an enormous and beneficial impact on Newfoundland broadcasting, it was for his writing that Paul will be remembered. He published the first of two volumes of poetry, *Spindrift and Morning Light*, in 1968. His history of St. John's, published in two volumes in 1975 and 1976 as *The Oldest City* and *A Seaport Legacy*, won the Canadian Historical Association's Regional History Prize in 1979. His passion for history, particularly the history of St. John's, resulted in numerous pamphlets, articles and tour guides. He revised and republished his award-winning history in one volume almost thirty years after it initially appeared.

Although he had deep reservations about his association with the Roman Catholic Church, as is evident in this memoir, Paul maintained a steady and respectful interest in the history of the institution in Newfoundland and wrote several books about it. For six years, he wrote a monthly column in the provincial Catholic newspaper *The Monitor*.

In all, Paul O'Neill wrote more than a dozen books, edited others — including his father's diary of his tour of Europe, *No Need to Wear Rubbers* — and contributed poems, articles, stories and opinion pieces to newspapers and magazines across the country. He won nine Arts and Letters Awards in the provincial competition. His work is included in dozens of anthologies, both in Canada and Ireland.

Paul O'Neill served on the City of St. John's Heritage Advisory Committee, was founding president of the Newfoundland Writers' Guild, and was chairman of the Newfoundland and Labrador Arts Council, president of the St. John's Folk Arts Council, and president of the John Howard Society. He was an active and tireless member of the Newfoundland Historic Parks Association, the Theatre Arts Council, the Irish Newfoundland Association, ACTRA, and the Radio Producers Association of Canada.

In 1985 the Newfoundland Historical Society gave Paul its Heritage Award, and he received the National Radio Producers' Award for Lifetime Achievement in Broadcasting. He was awarded an honorary doctorate by Memorial University of Newfoundland in 1988, was named a member of the Order of Canada in 1990, was given the John Howard Society Humanitarian of the Year Award in 2001, and was elected to the Newfoundland and Labrador Arts Hall of Honour in the same year. He received the Order of Newfoundland and Labrador in 2008. The Historic Sites Association founded a university scholarship in his name in 2002, and he was given the Freedom of the City of St. John's in 2004.

Paul O'Neill never married and had no children, but he was a devoted uncle to his brother John's children, Sheila, James, Paul and Irene of Boston, Massachusetts. His concern for family and family history extended out to everyone who lived in Newfoundland and Labrador, as was evident in his record of service to his community. While his devotion to the arts was founded in his early reading and professional training, he sincerely believed in the dual purpose of artistic endeavour: to entertain and educate. His approach to life — to his own and others — was one of genuine curiosity and enjoyment, and no matter how painful life became, he was always prepared to laugh at himself. Behind the mask of the serious CBC executive producer was the face of Mr. Boser, the ever-youthful, fun-loving circus clown who entertained children all over America half a century ago.

Paul O'Neill died in August of 2013 at the age of 84, leaving behind an unfinished manuscript of his autobiography. The manuscript, which is considerably longer than the memoir published here, was written at various times and includes notes, anecdotes, fragments and a lengthy section on the history of the O'Neill clan in Ireland. The most complete section was that recalling his childhood in Bay de Verde and St. John's, followed by his training and experience as actor in America and England, before he returned to Newfoundland to begin his lifetime of work with the CBC. This is the section that was used to compile this book.

No substantive changes were made in the process of editing the text Paul left behind. Corrections were restricted to punctuation, spelling and modification, and the various sections were put in more-or-less chronological order. Repetitions were excised, but nothing was added. This is not the book Paul envisioned when he began writing it, but it is what we are left with — something of his life, not all of it. Restricted as it is to his formative years, it still says a great deal about the vital, generous, lively and gracious man Paul O'Neill was. May God be good to him.

"My Memories of Paul O'Neill"
by
Myra Colbourne

It was a privilege and an honour to have been asked to contribute to Paul O'Neill's autobiography, *Something of Me*, a title he had selected from the beginning stages of the writing process.

Initially when I was asked to work on this project, I was of the impression it was just to help with the technical aspect, as he was in desperate need of someone to type it for him.

Before we actually got down to work, Paul said he was far behind on all his correspondence and sure enough this was what we tackled for the first few months. Each morning I would go to his home on Rennie's Mill Road and sit with him at his computer as he dictated personal letters to old friends he grew up with in Bay de Verde who had moved away and to friends he had in Ireland, England, Australia and the United States. Next there would be emails to answer. He thoroughly enjoyed receiving emails from his nieces and nephews in Boston.

Paul was one of the most fascinating people I have ever met. He lived a life of fantasy, having acted on stages across the United States and England. I only learned about this after we got started on his autobiography. Each day's work on the book varied, sometimes I would spend the entire day typing and other days we would proof read and edit. He wanted things to be letter perfect! It wasn't long before he started to refer to me as his 'writing assistant' whenever he spoke of me to anyone.

Paul was so proud of his roots and was constantly searching to learn more about his ancestors. Meeting members of his extended family in Ireland was one of the highlights of his life. He told me his father made a trip to Europe years before he met his wife   Paul's mother   and he always wondered if there were still people over there who were related to him. Paul just wished that his father was still alive to see him make his own trips overseas, finding so many of his relatives and walking in the footsteps of his ancestors.

The town of Bay de Verde was a place he always referred to as "down home." Even though Paul was born in St. John's, his family lived in Bay de Verde at the time. He later told me that when the family moved to St. John's he and his brother John couldn't wait for summer vacation to begin so they could head back to Bay de Verde and be 'free' again, roaming the hills and playing with their friends. Whenever he talked to me about John it always brought a tear to his eye. He had such a soft spot for him. John died at an early age having gone to Boston to attend college. He later married and raised his family there. Unfortunately, John's wife Justine, also died young and Paul fell into the role of surrogate father and very proud uncle. He loved the visits those kids made and cherished the closeness he had with them. Even as they grew older and had children of their own, he still referred to them as "the kids" whenever he spoke of them to me, which was quite often.

I was very saddened to hear of Paul's death on August 12, 2013. My husband Art and I were traveling in central Newfoundland at the time and didn't get the message until a few days later. He was so well-respected in the city and his very large funeral at the Basilica attested to that. I feel so fortunate to have been a part of his life and still miss him dearly. My greatest wish would be that we could have finished his autobiography together before his death, but it was not to be.

Acknowledgements

My heart is full with amazing memories from my childhood of my Uncle Paul. His endless fascinating stories, fun-filled outings and numerous family vacations in Bay Bulls, Bay De Verde, St. Johns, Boston and beyond. These memories I shall always cherish. Paul O'Neill is many things to the readers of this chronicle of his early journey; a historian, author, producer, actor and friend. To me, he was so much more than that. He was my rock. He stood by me when I lost my mother and father, walked me down the aisle when I was married and was always there for me with sound, caring, wise and sometimes stern advice. I am truly blessed to have had him for so many years loving me, and always being there for me. After my uncle passed, and I learned that he had bequeathed me the copyright to his writings, I was truly humbled. I knew that publishing his memoirs, albeit unfinished, was something I was committed to do to honour his memory.

My heartfelt thanks to Myra Colburne for her unwavering dedication to my uncle, assisting him in the writing of this book. Without Myra this book would not have come to fruition. Myra became my uncle's tireless assistant and friend as his health began to fail and he was no longer able to type. I'd like to thank my cousin and godmother, Margaret Buckingham, for her wisdom, guidance, input, love and unwavering support through this process.

To Ed Roberts for agreeing to write the Foreword, I am honored you agreed and know my uncle would be as well.

To Donna Francis and her team at Creative who guided me through this, what was to me, a foreign process with ease, dedication, efficiency and knowledge, and at times much needed humour.

Thank you to my friend, and Attorney at Law John "Jay" Brooks of Boston who guided me through the contractual process with his knowledge, advice, patience, kindness and friendship.

Many thanks to Debbie Fleming who was instrumental in assisting the gathering, sorting and organizing of the many pictures, clippings and material that went into the book.

And finally to my Uncle Paul. Thank you for trusting me with your most prized possessions, your writings. I hope the book would make you proud. This has been an amazing learning experience for me, and I am forever grateful and humbled.

Rene O'Neil

"I will always have you in my heart, as you have deeply touched my life."

Paul O'Neill and niece Rene O'Neil, Order of Canada Ceremony, Government House.